A MILLION YEARS WITH YOU

Also by Elizabeth Marshall Thomas

THE HIDDEN LIFE OF DEER:
LESSONS FROM THE NATURAL WORLD

THE OLD WAY:
A STORY OF THE FIRST PEOPLE

THE SOCIAL LIVES OF DOGS:
THE GRACE OF CANINE COMPANY

CERTAIN POOR SHEPHERDS:
A CHRISTMAS TALE

THE TRIBE OF TIGER:
CATS AND THEIR CULTURE

THE HIDDEN LIFE OF DOGS

THE ANIMAL WIFE

REINDEER MOON

WARRIOR HERDSMEN

THE HARMLESS PEOPLE

A MILLION YEARS WITH YOU

A Memoir of Life Observed

ELIZABETH MARSHALL THOMAS

HOUGHTON MIFFLIN HARCOURT
Boston New York 2013

For information about permission to reproduce selections from this book,
write to Permissions, Houghton Mifflin Harcourt Publishing Company,
215 Park Avenue South, New York, New York 10003.

www.hmhbooks.com

Library of Congress Cataloging-in-Publication Data is available.
ISBN 978-0-547-76395-8

Book design by Melissa Lotfy

Printed in the United States of America
DOC 10 9 8 7 6 5 4 3 2 1

In loving memory of Pearl

CONTENTS

A MILLION YEARS
WITH YOU

PROLOGUE: GAIA

I LIKE TO LOOK at the stars, so far away, so steady on their paths through the sky. They've been credited to Gaia, the goddess whose name means Earth and who is best known for managing our planet, orbiting a little star among 4 billion others in our galaxy. Even so, however small, our planet is complex and took 4.5 billion years to reach the state in which we know it, thanks to measures which were also credited to Gaia. Imagine it: The crashing meteors! The chemical reactions! The climate changes! The ever-branching climb of evolution that turned bacteria into blue whales and giant sequoias, not to mention the millions of other life forms that we know today! If she could do all that, could she not have made the stars and written the laws of physics? According to the ancient Greeks she could. She made the earth, then made the universe to be its equal.

While wandering down the road of life, it helps to look for something more meaningful than oneself. Some find it in religion. Some find it in relationships. I find it by keeping my eyes open. I see the stars when I look up and the soil when I look down, where the microorganisms live that keep everything going. And as far as I'm concerned, this can be personified by Gaia.

One day my wonderful cousin, Tom Bryant, came to visit me and my husband, Steve, at our home in Peterborough, New Hampshire. Tom, an astronomer, was marvelously familiar with everything now known about the universe, and wishing to show us some of it, he brought a very large telescope. That night, after the moon set, a group of us went to the edge of a field where, in the northeastern sky, Tom pointed out what seemed to be a tiny, fuzzy star, just one among dozens of others, and not all of us were sure just which star we should be looking at. Tom then showed us the star through his telescope. This made it larger, about the size of a grass seed. It seemed to be a spiral and looked something like a snail seen from the rear.

It was part of Andromeda, Tom told us, a constellation of about four thousand stars, nine of which are known to have planets. But the tiny, snail-like thing we were looking at was not an individual star at all, and it wasn't a planet. It was a cluster of a trillion stars, collectively known as the Andromeda Galaxy, three times bigger than our Milky Way and closer to us than any other spiral galaxy. Its light had traveled for 2.5 million years before it reached us. When the light we saw that night left its galaxy, our *Homo habilis* ancestors were figuring out how to make stone tools. By the time that same light reached us, we were modern *Homo sapiens* with telescopes. Wow!

With my eyes on Andromeda that night, I remembered an experience I'd had during my freshman year in college, where I'd hoped to major in biology. My dad had given me a binocular microscope, through which I watched the little life forms in drops of water taken from a swamp. One day, as I was following what I took to be a paramecium moving carefully through the algae like a fox hunting mice in a field, an enormous creature suddenly loomed up and charged right at me, causing me to throw myself backward and tip over my chair. It took me a moment to realize that I was in my dormitory room and the terrifying creature was in the drop of water.

But what was it? I gathered my courage and looked again. It was not a protist, then called a protozoan. Instead, it was an animal—very small but an animal nevertheless. It had eight legs with claws, a face with a tiny snout, a mouth, and two eye spots, and a transparent body in which I could see its food as well as some oval shapes toward its hindquarters which I took to be eggs. Whatever it was, it seemed to be a female.

I consulted a textbook. She was a waterbear, a tardigrade, then believed to be a miniature relative of the mites. I was able to lift her up with the point of a sewing needle, and found, as I turned the needle from side to side, that she was just barely visible to my youthful naked eyes, and not visible at all if she was on the far side of the needle. She was that small. I put her in my jar of water so I could return her to the swamp.

Ever since then, I've been enthralled by waterbears. I later found what superscientist Lynn Margulis wrote about them[1] and learned what I'd already suspected, that they are among the most amazing creatures on the planet. Their many species live in all kinds of places, from the deep ocean to the Himalayas, from hot springs to the Arctic, because they can survive extreme temperatures. Some live in water that's 304° Fahrenheit, and others live at just three degrees above absolute zero, the point at which all thermal energy is gone. In other words, since few places on earth are that hot or that cold, waterbears can flourish almost anywhere.

In fact, there's almost nothing they can't cope with. If a waterbear is injured or starved, it forms itself into a cyst, a tiny roundish lump, in which it contracts its little body and repairs itself. Most waterbears live in swamps or in damp mosses and all of them eat liquid foods, but if the liquid disappears, they form themselves into "tuns," which look like tiny wine barrels. These tuns, like dust particles, ride the winds to faraway places which, with any luck, will be better than the places they left. And there's no special hurry to find a good place. In the form of a tun, a waterbear can live for about a hundred years.

And that's not all. Waterbears can survive 570,000 roentgens of radiation, when just 500 roentgens will sizzle one of us. It's hard to imagine how they evolved this astonishing ability or why they need it, as 570,000 roentgens might accompany a nuclear disaster but not much else. Waterbears had this ability before we invented the nuclear disaster. But when we did, they were prepared. They seemed to leave little to chance.

Perhaps for that reason, most waterbears are female. Without males, they lay eggs that hatch as females; thus just one she-waterbear could repopulate the planet if things went wrong. And evidently that's just what they've been doing. Creatures so tiny don't often leave fossils, but a few were found in amber from the Cretaceous era, and a few others from the mid-Cambrian era. Long before our ancestors came out of the trees, waterbears were here.

• • •

On the day I watched the waterbear, I was listening to a radio on the table with the microscope. The music was quite loud, and I wondered what the waterbear made of the sound. I didn't see that she had ears, so I believed she couldn't hear it, although she might have felt vibrations. But these would tell her nothing about the radio itself, nothing about the broadcasting station or the instruments that played the music or the species that composed it, nothing about electricity or power lines or even the electric cord from the radio to the plug in the wall. It's hard to imagine all the things about a radio that my waterbear was not equipped to understand.

Then it came to me that as the waterbear was to the radio, so are we to the universe. For all the characteristics by which we place ourselves above the other life forms of this planet—our language, tool use, and hind-leg walking (now more or less reduced to hind-leg walking, as language and tool use have been found in other species)—we're just another primate, and as such we have our limits. We think we're smart, way ahead of waterbears, but 15 billion years ago there was no universe, and whatever started it might very well be something that our simian brains are not equipped to understand.

We're part of it, though. If the first law of thermodynamics has anything to it, we're certainly part of it, made of atoms formed by forces that followed the Big Bang and have been here ever since. I like to think that some of my atoms once inhabited dinosaurs or even blue-green algae. We may never know more, but I like to think about it.

THE WOODS

M Y PARENTS TAUGHT ME to enjoy observation. They loved the sky and also the life of our planet. My dad, Laurence Marshall, would go out on the porch to see what the sky was doing, and if something exciting was going on he'd demand that the rest of us to come to see it too. He was clearly the head of our family and also our leader, and we always did what he said. So all of us—me, my brother, John, who was a year younger, our mom, her mother, and Dad's mother (both of whom lived with us)—would drop what we were doing and obediently troop out to the porch. Sometimes we saw cumulous clouds, sometimes falling stars, sometimes a spectacular sunset, and sometimes northern lights. Dad was a civil engineer with an awesome knowledge of math and physics, and northern lights enthralled him. They came from the sun, he said.

My mom, Lorna Marshall, was a caregiver to all life forms and a known animal lover to the point that she sometimes found cats in boxes on her doorstep, evidently delivered by someone who thought she'd take them in. She took them in. She never killed mice, although her cats did. And she never killed insects, not even flies. Instead, she'd put a glass over them, slide a piece of paper under the glass, and release them outside. To her, animals were on earth to be cared for. Her cats were so healthy that on one occasion a veterinarian did not believe her when she told him her cat was sixteen. The cat was in such good shape that he could only be eight or nine, said the veterinarian. But the vet was mistaken. The cat had been left on her doorstep as an adolescent, and she'd had him for sixteen years, so he was closer to seventeen. Just about everyone who knew my mother wanted to be reincarnated as her cat.

Everyone flourished who was in my mother's care. Her oldest houseplant was over thirty, and at the time of this writing, a climbing rose she planted is at least seventy-six and was an adult when she got it. My dad lived to ninety-one, his mother lived to a hundred and five, my mother herself lived to a hundred and four, and every dog or cat who came into her life lived well beyond the life expectancy of its species. Wild animals near her also flourished. She put seeds for birds and bread and peanuts for squirrels on the shed roof outside her kitchen window. The squirrels knew her. If she was late with the food, we'd notice a squirrel or two looking in the window to see if she remembered them. Of course she did.

Religion might have had something to do with this, because her mother, our gran, was a Christian Scientist. Our mom was not, due to a catastrophic event when she was six or seven and listening to Gran and some of Gran's friends discussing the power of faith. Fascinated, my mom asked if she could fly if she had faith. They said she could fly if she had enough faith. My mom was thrilled. Brimming with faith and prepared for a great experience, she climbed out a window to the roof of their house and jumped off. What happened next erased her religious inclinations permanently, but perhaps an aura still clung, because according to Gran, everything made by God was good. This, of course, included the flies whom my mother set free and the squirrels who looked in our window.

Gran's sense of global goodness was more extreme and included the famous hurricane of 1938, which she, age sixty-something, and I, age seven, went outside to experience. We were alone in the house at the time so no one was there to stop us. The wind lifted me off the ground and carried me about fifteen feet down a hill, so I got to fly even if my mother didn't. I found it thrilling, and agreed with my gran that a hurricane was good.

But I couldn't agree about gypsy moth caterpillars. The subject of their value arose during one of their population explosions, when these caterpillars seemed to coat the landscape. We could hear their dung pattering down outside our house and see the wide defoliation caused by their chewing.

My little brother was enthralled by such bounty. He brought hand-fuls of caterpillars indoors as pets, put them in a box, and gave them leaves to eat. Someone gave him a screen to cover the box, but as often as not he'd forget about the screen, so his caterpillars soon were every-where — in the dishes on the pantry shelf, in the clothes in our drawers, even in our beds under the covers. They scared me and I complained to Gran. But Gran insisted that even these caterpillars were good, or at least they weren't bad, because God made them.

Our dad's mother, Nana, was a born-again fundamentalist, and be-cause few animals are mentioned in the Bible, her religious views did not include them. But she was kind to them. Our cats liked to sit with her while she knitted or sewed and to sleep on her bed while she rested. It was good to see her lying down, covered with an afghan she had knitted, with a cat curled up beside her, purring.

However, Nana did not believe in dinosaurs. This caused profound distress to me and my brother, as we were enthralled by dinosaurs. Our dad read to us about them and gave us small, realistic models of them. We thought we knew the names of all dinosaurs (we knew five or six), and on the floor of my brother's bedroom we made a diorama for them with handmade trees meant to look like cycads. We made our own model dinosaurs too, using a clay called Plasticine, which we thought was pro-nounced "Pleistocene." In our imaginations we would live in the Jurassic age, watching our dinosaurs and escaping from them.

But dinosaurs never existed, said Nana. They're not in the Bible. "Then the Bible is wrong!" we'd shout. We'd tell her that our dad saw a dinosaur's footprints in some rocks in South Hadley, Massachusetts. And scientists had found dinosaur bones. If there were no dinosaurs, what made the footprints and bones?

Satan made them, Nana said. He buried the bones and made the foot-prints to turn scientists away from the word of God. My brother and I would yell that this was NOT TRUE, and Nana would cover her ears and pray for us aloud.

From our mom we learned not to tease animals, from Gran we learned that everything was good, and from Nana we learned that the Bible doesn't tell the whole story. But it was from our dad that we learned where our food came from, and to know the natural world. He had strong feelings about our leisure time and didn't want us spending the summers lying on a beach like the families of some of his colleagues. So when my brother was three and I was four, he bought the land in Peterborough, New Hampshire where, at the time of this writing, my husband and I live. Dad eventually owned roughly 2,500 acres of forest and farmland on and around the Wapack Range, most of which he gave to the Department of the Interior as a wildlife sanctuary. But on the road that passed through these acres — a dirt road — were two adjoining abandoned farms, and these Dad kept. Both are on hilltops but sheltered from the wind by higher hills, and both are free of frost much longer than those hills and the valleys. I suspect that before the old-time farmers chose these places, they found out where the deer stayed on cold nights, because deer know all that anyone needs to know about microclimates. To this day, on autumn nights, they sleep in our frost-free field.

My dad renovated one of the farms, then hired a farm manager and began raising Milking Shorthorn cattle. On the other he built a house for us, his family. The place had been known as the Leathers farm, half a mile through the woods from the other one, and had belonged to an elderly man named John Leathers. I believe this man's father was the John Leathers who — according to a commemorative plaque high on a hill on Grove Street in Peterborough — fought in the Civil War with the Peterborough battalion and died in Andersonville Prison. I think of that young soldier when I see the stone walls in our woods. Once, these walls were property lines and also the borders of pastures. Before enlisting in the Peterborough battalion, the young John Leathers would have helped to build them.

My dad found plenty of stones in our field which he used to build more stone walls, and my brother and I helped him, so we knew how hard it was to do this. Dad also made a pond by building a stone dam so perfect that even in the driest summer the lower spillway kept the stream flowing so the pond didn't stagnate, and even during the spring torrents the upper spillway contained all the water so it didn't flood the fields. It took the hurricane of 1938 to send water over the entire dam. How my dad did this I have no idea, as I can't even imagine what kinds of factors to start calculating. But then, I still count on my fingers, whereas my dad was a civil engineer.

When I look at the dam, now enhanced by beavers, I remember my dad and his work ethic. The beavers have it too, and have substantially increased the size of the pond. This was the work ethic that Dad expected from his children. No farm family would dream of driving their kids to soccer practice or to a friend's house as suburban families do today, and my parents wouldn't either. If we as children wanted to go somewhere, we walked. But we were expected to help with the farm work, and we liked that, so except for visiting the farm manager's children, Malan and Betty, whom we loved and who also were expected to work, we worked too. When I was seven, I helped my dad gather rocks for his projects by driving a tractor, inching it slowly forward as he hoisted rocks onto the sledge it was dragging. My brother and I also helped to make hay, clean the stalls, milk the cows, weed the garden, gather the eggs, or do any other chores that came our way, as did all other children on all New Hampshire farms. I can still milk a cow. And better yet, I learned to work hard and also to like it, which was useful in later life.

But Dad wanted us to know about more than farming. He wanted to us to know the natural world. Although we were learning on our own, roaming through the woods with Malan and Betty, our dad wanted us to understand what we were seeing when we explored. He read us books such as the works of Ernest Thompson Seton. But he did more than that. The Wapack Range was to our east, and young as we were, he'd take us there. We'd cross a series of forested ridges, then wide fields of blueberry and juniper bushes, up and up until we reached a summit, which was bare rock. At one time, our dad told us, the whole range except the summits was covered with trees. But the old-time farmers — among them, no doubt, the first John Leathers — cut down the trees to make pastures and marked their boundaries with the stone walls we found all over the mountains. It was these stone walls, still in their straight lines but overgrown with trees, that convinced me that things had been happening before I was born.

Later on, said Dad, the old farms and pastures were abandoned and bushes grew. That explained the blueberries and the juniper. But during our lifetimes if not his, he told us, the forest would grow back and the mountains would be as they were before the old-time farmers cleared them. At the time of this writing, my office window faces those mountains. The bushes are gone, and just as my dad predicted, mixed forest has replaced them.

The juniper is gone, but it lives in my mind because I remember pushing through it. It was hip-deep to Dad but face-level to me, my brother, and the dogs, and as soon as we got into it on our uphill journeys I'd ask every few minutes how far we were from the top. Dad's usual answer to a question about distance, whether we were on foot or in a car, was that we were halfway there. But one day he turned around, squatted down in front of me, looked me in the eyes, and told me to stop whining.

I was horrified to learn that I'd been whining. And if Dad mentioned it, it must have been pretty bad. Normally he was more than patient with us, waiting while we stopped to eat berries or pick up interesting pinecones or mushrooms or porcupine droppings to take home to our mother and grandmothers. But I knew that Dad wanted us to be strong and tough, to be of woodsman quality. I promised never to whine again, and I've tried to keep that promise. I thought he wouldn't take me with him if I didn't. And from that day on, I've tried to develop endurance. Once in a while, someone tells me that I'm tough. This makes me happy, and I thank my dad for the compliment.

My interest in wildlife was stronger than my little brother's. He preferred large machines — the first word he ever said was *truck*. Also he lacked my patience. So on a few rare occasions Dad took me alone with him to try to see wildlife. Once we went to the embankment of a certain wetland and sat there for hours, not moving, not even whispering, just watching. Sometimes we'd hear footsteps rustle the dry leaves on the forest floor behind us, but we didn't move our heads to see who walked there. On that particular day we saw only a towhee, a ground robin, who with both feet together was taking little hops through the underbrush. I had thought that all birds walked on alternating feet as we do, hence I learned something.

Inconsequential as this may seem, the experience was, for some rea-

son, so important to me that from the corner of my mind's eye I can still
see my dad beside me as we waited there. My mind's eye also sees the
towhee. That was the day I learned how to sit still for hours, waiting. I've
repeated this experience many times, most memorably some thirty years
later when, alone except for a few wolves, I spent a summer watching a
wolf den in the middle of Baffin Island. Even now I still watch animals
this way. A friend helped me make a platform up in a tree where I can sit
and watch what happens in our swamp. Most animals don't look up, or
not often; thus if I keep the most basic rules of observation — to be quiet,
patient, and motionless — those who live around our swamp behave as
if I weren't there. I'm grateful to my dad for the ability to watch wild
animals, as this has served me very well.

Normally we didn't see animals in the woods, even though our dad tried
to teach us how to walk quietly in dry leaves. But mostly my brother and
I would shuffle and talk and otherwise make noise, and usually the dogs
were with us. For miles around, the wildlife would hear us. However,
even if we seldom saw the animals themselves, we saw things made or
used by them, such as nests and holes in trees, or the den of a fox in an
embankment by a stream. Dad taught us how to recognize the scats of
rabbits, porcupines, and deer, although all these can be pellets with only
minor differences in shape. On rare occasions we'd find a small, dog-
style scat with hair in it. This, said Dad, was made by the fox.

It was from tracks in fresh snow that we learned the most. Sooner or
later, every creature who lived in the woods would leave a set of tracks,
and we could see what they'd been doing, where they'd been eating, and
in the case of deer where they'd been yarding. One winter day, in the
snow by our frozen swamp, we came upon fresh cat tracks that looked as
big as dinner plates. Now what was that? Bobcats and lynxes had been
exterminated by the old-time farmers and had yet to return to our forests.
Anyway, the tracks were too big for a bobcat or a lynx. We wondered if
it was a cougar, although cougars too had been exterminated. But at the
time something that people were calling a "black panther" had been seen
in our region, assumed to have escaped from a zoo.

As it happens, the eastern cougar who once inhabited New Hampshire
is said to have had a black or melanistic phase, just like certain leopards

and jaguars. The local weekly newspaper, the *Peterborough Transcript*, carried a sportsman's column written by the game warden, who reported sightings of the "black panther" whenever these occurred. Back then, I preferred that an adult read aloud to me, but I could also read on my own, and the one thing I never failed to read was the sportsman's column, in hopes of finding a report of the panther. One day a few months after we had seen the tracks, I read that this panther had been sighted in a town on the far side of the Wapack Range. Then I felt sure the tracks were made by the panther.

That was in 1938 or 1939, but I never forgot it. More recently I was looking out a window at that same swamp when a cougar came out of the woods. As it happened, I had spent the day writing about cougars I'd seen during a little cougar study I'd made in Idaho, Utah, and Colorado, so I thought I was hallucinating. But just to be sure I went outside with Pearl, my dog. She saw it too. She considered it her duty to keep the wildlife in the woods, and ordinarily she would run at any wild animal, barking. But this time she wisely decided to pass, and she just stood rigidly beside me staring at it. Then I knew I wasn't hallucinating, and the sight of those tracks came back to me. My mind's eye still sees them. In fact, I'm not sure I would have been as fascinated as I am by the sight of any tracks if I hadn't seen them.

The most important lesson, according to Dad, was not about tracks. It was about managing ourselves in the woods. There was only one thing to fear, he said, and it wasn't wild animals, not even the panther. The thing to fear was getting lost. To help prevent that, he taught us how to find the North Star. The North Pole was on the axis of the world, he said, and the North Star stayed right over it. But the North Star wasn't there in the daytime. How then to find direction? Moss supposedly grows on the north sides of trees, but it can grow on the other sides too and thus can be confusing. Instead, he showed us how to use a watch as a compass. Point the hour hand at the sun, he said. If your watch is set on standard time, halfway between there and twelve is south.

But when we were children we didn't have watches, so Dad gave us another helpful tool in finding direction — our shadows. During the middle of the day they were behind us if we were going south, to our left if we were going east, and so on. At the two ends of the day the sun itself would show us east or west and we wouldn't need the shadows. To this day when trying to find direction I still use the sun, not a compass. A compass can give a false reading, but the sun is unlikely to malfunction. And if it does, getting lost will be the least of my problems.

Yet finding south only helps if you're trying to find something long, like a river or a road. South isn't much help in finding an exact place, like your house. Sometimes our dad would let us try to find the way home, and often enough we couldn't. This shows that people can get lost, he said. Maybe they're in thick woods and can't see the sky. Or maybe the sky is cloudy. And people who are lost tend to walk in big circles, he told us. Thus if we thought we were lost we should just sit down and not wander around so that someone—most likely him—could find us.

He taught us never to go into the woods without string, a knife, and matches. He showed us how to make a fire even in blizzards or rainstorms using only things we would find in the woods, such as dead twigs and birch bark, which burns pretty well even when damp. He also insisted that we use only one match to light the fire, and not just a wooden, strike-anywhere match, but also a little cardboard book match. He made us try again and again until both of us could do it every time. Thus if we were lost in winter, we could keep ourselves from freezing. He read us the cautionary story by Jack London, "To Build a Fire," in which a man trying to survive a bitter winter night finally manages to build a fire but builds it under an evergreen tree. The fire warms the snow on the branches. The snow falls on the fire and puts it out. And the man didn't have another match. Even now, I would never make a fire directly under an evergreen tree, and I still need only one match.

The woods were the main part of my early education. I'd say I learned more from the woods than I learned in school, certainly for the first few years. I still find spelling and math elusive, while the things I learned in the woods stay with me.

That education took place in New Hampshire, but unfortunately we didn't live there year-round. My dad was the CEO of Raytheon, an electronics company which he had founded in 1922, four years before he married my mother and nine years before I was born. So we had to live in Cambridge, Massachusetts, to be near his factory. We were in New Hampshire every weekend, during all school vacations, and all summer, but the rest of the time we were stuck in the city. Thus it was animals in Cambridge who first opened for me a very important window of the natural world.

2

DOGS

OUR HOUSE WAS on a quiet street, two blocks east of Harvard's Museum of Comparative Zoology. My brother and I went to a private school. And because my mom did extensive community work and often wasn't home in the daytime, a Finnish couple named Tom and Kirsti Johnson kept house for us. Johnson is not a Finnish name, of course. Tom's real surname was Sammallahti. But when Tom's father came to Quincy, Massachusetts, via Ellis Island, the immigration official who processed him could neither spell nor pronounce Sammallahti and didn't want to try, so he simply changed it to Johnson. But nothing changed except the name. Tom and Kirsti were Finnish to the core.

They were like our second parents. Thanks to them, the adult/child ratio of our home was three to one. We adored them. Except for the work we all did together on the New Hampshire farm, we didn't know what our actual parents did because, of course, they didn't work at home. But we watched Tom and Kirsti constantly. I aspired to be like Kirsti, a cook in someone's household, an ambition that she crushed. She had come to America alone as a teenager, in hopes of getting a college education, but she had been unable to do so, and that must not happen to me. She told me I must not become a cook for any reason but instead must go to college.

Even so, she let me help her. My brother helped her too. We did such things as clean frosting from the stirring spoon with our tongues. We spent most of our time in the kitchen, where Tom and Kirsti spoke Finnish. Because of this, we also learned some Finnish. When I was older, perhaps fifteen or so, I could read the Finnish newspaper, *Raivaaja,* aloud to Tom's nearly blind mother. By then Tom, Kirsti, and Tom's mother had taken over the farm in Peterborough. My brother and I saw their house as our second home and spent as much time as we could with them. I didn't know all the words in *Raivaaja* by any means, but Tom's mother certainly did, and because Finnish is spelled as it is sounds, I could pronounce the words well enough so that Tom's mother understood what I was reading.

Tom told us stories from which we learned about life by leaps and bounds. We got an interesting picture of New York society, because before coming to live with us, Tom and Kirsti had worked as butler and cook for a rich family there. Our favorite story was about their employer, Henry, when he and his wife were giving a party and he got drunk. While Tom was passing yet another round of cocktails, Henry stood up from his chair and started to fuss with his pants. Tom took Henry's arm to help him to the bathroom. Henry shook him off and opened his fly. The guests were horrified. "Henry! Henry!" his poor wife cried. "Think of your dignity!" But Henry said, "To hell with my dignity! I'll piss right here." And he did.

Oh joy! Imagine a grownup doing that! There could not be a better story, and we couldn't hear it often enough. Tom obliged us. He'd tell other stories too, but at our urgent requests he'd always include a repeat of that one, and it was just as great the hundredth time as it had been the first. No wonder we loved to be in the kitchen.

Looking back, however, I wonder if my brother and I with our constant requests were inconvenient there. Tom and Kirsti were unfailingly good to us, but it's possible that we took too much of their time. The reason I think so is that one day our mom introduced us to a heavyset woman who, we were told, would be our nanny. The nanny would take care of us, she said.

Our mom then asked us to show the nanny around, so we showed her the dinosaur diorama. It was, after all, not a professionally made toy but just some sticks with green paper stuck on them and some little clay figures squeezed into shape by children. Our nanny gave a huff, as if she didn't like it, and because it made the room somewhat messy, she soon cleaned it up.

Even before this disaster, we knew we didn't like her. We had already noticed a difference between the bossy way she acted when alone with us and the sugary way she acted in the presence of our parents. Since the diorama had been in my brother's room, she must have thought it belonged only to him, because the next day, as if to compensate him, she gave him a toy Mickey Mouse. He didn't know what the Mickey Mouse was and didn't want it. Nor did he thank the nanny until she ordered him to do so. He dangled the toy as he grudgingly mumbled something. We started to make a new diorama, but she cleaned that up too, and we began to hate her.

A few days later, the nanny, my brother, and I were alone in the house. For some reason, the nanny went into a room to look out the window. My brother took the key from the inner side of the door, quietly shut the door, and locked it. I didn't see him do this, but when he strolled down the hall, I followed.

Soon the nanny was pounding on the door, demanding that we open it. I was a bit confused about why she was screaming. My brother didn't seem to know either, and anyway, by then he had lost the key, so nothing could be done. We wandered through the empty house listening to the noise made by the nanny.

She must have opened a window. We heard her shouting for help. She must have attracted the attention of a passerby, because suddenly a man was ringing the doorbell and pounding with the knocker. We weren't sure why. We only knew not to open the door to a stranger. So we sat on the stairs and listened. The man must have gone to a neighbor's house, and the neighbor must have made some phone calls. Much later both our parents rushed in together, all excited and angry, and demanded the key, but no one could find it.

So they called a locksmith. But the locksmith couldn't come right away, and by then the nanny needed food and water. Our dad got some clothesline, went outside, and threw it into the open window. The nanny then dangled it down, and our dad tied a basket of supplies to it. She pulled the basket up. Our dad had also brought a potty. She pulled that up too. Meanwhile, my brother and I were in our parents' study behind the window curtains, watching all that went on outside but not quite sure what we were seeing. At last the locksmith arrived and released the nanny. She burst through the door in a raging fury, which she took out on our humbly apologetic parents. Then she quit.

Our parents never hit us, rarely punished us, and seldom even spoke a discouraging word. But not that time. That time we were banished from the society of decent people. We had to stay alone in our rooms for months, it seemed, with nothing to play with, and eat our meals alone in the gloomy, closetlike back hall.

Our parents should have left us with our other nanny, the one whose orders we didn't challenge. We loved her dearly even though she was strict, but that's why we obeyed her. She wouldn't let us cross the street, for instance, although we knew that people could cross if no car was coming. But this nanny didn't care if no car was coming. If we started to cross, she'd push us back on the sidewalk. Her name was Mishka. She was every inch a grownup, and also a Newfoundland dog.

She was even stricter when, the summer before our dad built his house in New Hampshire, our parents rented a house by a bay on Cape Cod. That summer was blissful for the adults in the family. Every day they went swimming, boating, or fishing. But it was dreadful for me and my brother. The enticing ocean spread out before us, but Mishka wouldn't let us near it. The bay was so shallow we could have waded out for miles, but Mishka wouldn't even let us wet our feet. She didn't care that we only wanted to fill our pails with water to make sandcastles. If we went toward the water, she'd give a loud, commanding bark which meant *No!* If we kept going she'd grab our clothes with her teeth and drag us backward. Then we'd cry with frustration and yell at her, commanding her to sit, to stay, to lie down. She gladly did such things for the adults in the family, but when we gave her these orders, she'd look at us blandly. *You little things, who do you think you're talking to?* her manner said.

When Mishka and I faced each other, our eyes were level. I remember looking into hers and seeing that she meant business. Sometimes with angry tears I'd demand from her at least as much freedom as my parents gave me, but she paid no attention. She was in charge, and whether we liked it or not, we were forced to obey her. Yet she loved us and we knew it. Thus she felt like a mother. We felt like her children. We'd lie beside her on the floor and fall safely asleep, leaning against her soft fur. My favorite photo of that time shows her lying on the floor but with her head raised and me in a white dress behind her, ready to climb on her back. She knows what I'm about to do and she's going to let me.

So all in all, I felt about Mishka just as I felt about the adults in our family. She outranked me, but I knew I was young and I bowed to her authority. A bit later in life, it came as quite a shock to learn that some people think that dogs are their inferiors. How can that be, I wondered, when dogs are just like us?

The other dog in the family was smaller and younger than Mishka. His name was Taffy and he was a cocker spaniel. If Mishka was one of the grownups, Taffy was one of the children. He came to us on Christmas Eve, a gift from my dad's business partner, and his first act in our house was to grab a tinsel streamer on the Christmas tree and run with it so fast that the tree came crashing down in an explosion of lights and ornaments. My brother and I were shocked by the destruction, but also thrilled by his daring.

Unlike Mishka, who would lie on the porch and watch us while we played in the yard, Taffy would play with us. Our dad had made us a swing with a board seat that hung from the branch of a tree. Side by side, we would lie face-down on the board and swing out over Taffy. He'd bark as we sailed over him, then chase us as the swing went back the other way. He wasn't adamant about this, though, unless he had a bone. Wanting to be with us, he'd chew his bone near the swing. Then, when we'd sail over him, he'd get upset. He'd bristle and rush at us, barking furiously. We thought this was fun, and we'd keep it up until his bark was almost a scream and he was chasing us with blazing eyes and gnashing teeth. The adults of the family often told us not to tease him, but because he could always take his bone somewhere else if he didn't like what we were doing, we reasoned that we weren't really teasing. And it was fun. We didn't stop.

One day our dad heard Taffy roaring and came out to see what was going on. He walked up to the swing and Taffy, in his frenzy, bit him. Our dad yanked off his belt and lashed Taffy with it four times, which devastated Taffy. Nobody punished me and my brother, although the whole thing was our fault, and I felt terrible to see Taffy trembling and cringing and looking up at my father. That Taffy was beaten for our misdeed is one of my lifelong regrets.

Soon enough, though, Taffy and Dad forgave each other because of the deep bond between them. For all his willingness to play with us, Taffy at heart was a one-man dog, and that man was my father. Mishka developed arthritis in her hips and couldn't go walking with us, but little Taffy would follow our dad whenever he could, even through the juniper on the Wapack Range. He'd push right through it, never questioning or resting, just like Dad.

Dad and Taffy did favors for each other. Dad sneaked bites from his dinner plate to Taffy under the table, and Taffy took care of baby mice that we'd find in places like my mother's desk. My mom thought that Dad released them in the woods. Instead, he'd take them outdoors and secretly show them to Taffy, who ate them.

Mishka came to our family before I was born. She died when I was in my senior year in boarding school. Taffy came to us as a pup when I was four. He died when I was in my freshman year in college. On both occasions, my dad telephoned me with the terrible news, and both times as he described their deaths, his voice broke. For as long as I could remember, these dogs had been with us. Even now I miss them. No wonder we picture an afterworld where we can be with those we love. But even if there is no afterworld, those dogs live in my heart. As my mother's friend May Sarton famously put it: "The dead move through all of us still glowing."

3

CATS

F ROM MISHKA AND TAFFY I saw that dogs and people were alike,
just with different kinds of bodies, and never since then have I questioned the commonality of people and other animals. Yet it was from
our cats I learned that the lives of animals can be fascinating all on their
own, without involvement with people. Unlike Mishka, our cats took no
responsibility for me or my brother, and unlike Taffy, they never played
with us. Instead, as I was to discover, they had a world of their own, a
world of mystery and importance that had nothing to do with our family.

These cats were identical twins — two black-furred females named
Lilith and Eve. I could tell them apart, but only by their behavior, because Eve would sometimes let me pick her up. Another photo from the
past (one I'm not proud of) shows me lifting Eve with my hands around
her neck. In the photo, I'm burning with concentration, enthralled by
this cat. Eve's eyes are half shut, her tongue protrudes slightly, her tail
dangles, and her arms and legs are flung wide. She's enduring the experience as best she can.

Lilith, in contrast, allowed no such thing. She'd duck away if I approached, and if I managed to catch her by the tail and pick her up, she'd
fight back and scratch me. That's how I knew I had the wrong cat.

But both cats were devoted to my mother. When they were near her,
they purred. They also brought her gifts — dead mice mostly — and
would either place them in front of her or put them on the stairs where
she'd find them when she came down for breakfast. I was a little jealous
of the cats, as I could see they were trying to flatter my mother. They

never brought me any gifts, so I suspected that they wanted her to like them more than she liked me. I had no real cause to worry—my mom clearly showed that she cared about me—but I worried nevertheless.

Back then, most cats came and went freely, indoors and out, and most were not spayed or neutered. This, by the way, is why domestic short-hairs still resemble their ancestor, *Felis silvestris lybica,* the African wild-cat, and why cats live longer, healthier lives than dogs. Free to choose their own mates, female cats select for qualities such as strength, good health, and high status. Thus they do a better job than human breeders who select for pushed-in faces or flowing hair. Today such freedom is censured, so please don't send me e-mails or letters to tell me so, because I already know it. Here I'm only saying that at the time of which I am speaking, most cats could do as they pleased.

Our cats gained access to the outside world through little cat flaps in some of the regular doors—a cat could go from our back hall down the stairs to the basement and from there up another flight of stairs to the street. Other cats could come in from the street, but only as far as the basement. The dogs kept them off the upper floors. Thus the basement became a refugium for cats. From what went on there, I saw that cats in-volved themselves in dramas that were beyond my understanding. I only knew that whatever they were doing was significant to them, and soon enough, it was also significant to me.

Our house was heated by a coal furnace, and the heat came through large ducts to registers in the floors. Sometimes I'd hear a voice coming from a register, a long, forceful, meaningful call. I'd realize that right below my feet something strange and important was in progress, and I'd go down to look.

The basement was dark, with just a little daylight coming through a window. As I'd go down the stairs, the voice would stop. Then the si-lence would be awesome, as it is the woods when there's no wind and the wild things know that a person is near. I'd look around but wouldn't see anything. Then I'd look up. And there, on some of the hot-air ducts just under the ceiling, I'd see two or three pairs of shining eyes. Cats!

The eyes were a little scary. But after all, I was safe at home and the shining eyes were almost mesmerizing, so I'd sit on the floor and wait. Complete silence. Nothing moved, not even the shining eyes. But after a long time, perhaps feeling pressure from the issues that faced him, a cat would lift his voice in a drawn-out call that slowly got louder, held steady, and then faded, as if the cat ran out of breath. Again silence. The other cats would think things over. And then, after a moment, the first cat would repeat himself or one of the others would respond. To me, these eerie calls were also scary, all the more so at close quarters when I didn't know what was going on.

Sometimes I'd go back upstairs in a failure of courage, but often enough I'd stay where I was, wondering about our own two cats. Perhaps they also were a little scared. I'd look around for them and often didn't see them. But now and then I'd see them near the coal bin—an inconspicuous place but one from which they could see the cats who were calling. Imagining what my mother would have done had she been there, I once went to them and tried to lift Eve up to reassure her, but she got away, ran past me, and vanished. By then Lilith had also vanished. That was the last I saw of them that day. But for some reason I remember the event clearly, perhaps because it struck me that our cats weren't scared and didn't need help, and that they too were listening carefully to the eerie calls. It also struck me that however mysterious the calls might seem to me, our cats knew what they meant.

From then on, as long as we had cats, the basement remained a place of wonder. At the time I knew nothing about human reproduction, let alone feline reproduction, and not until later in life did I realize that the intruders were males who had come to inseminate our cats if our cats would have them. Thus the males were probably threatening each other, or at least were trying to show our cats that they had high status and power. But although I didn't understand the reason for the calls, I felt their suppressed emotion, their intensity, which is why I kept going to the basement. Perhaps the male cats clashed sometimes, but I don't remember any fighting. I remember only the strange, long-drawn-out calls and the two sisters crouched low, listening.

Now and then there would be kittens. The two sisters nursed each other's kittens. Sometimes they'd move the kittens to different places in the basement, carrying them by the back of the neck. When kittens were present, the males were unwelcome. Either they didn't come into the basement, or the two sisters drove them back up the stairs and out the cat flap.

There was so much to know, and no way to know it. All too soon the kittens would vanish. I'd get home from school and they'd be gone, evidently given away by my parents, who didn't tell me. But in time the threatening moans would rise anew through the hot-air registers, and the shadowy, fascinating life of cats would cycle again.

The awe I now feel for other species began in our basement. But at the time I didn't hope to understand what I was seeing. The urge to understand things came later in life. I was just looking at the cat world, experiencing it, identifying with it. I soon stopped thinking of our cats by their names, as I saw nothing about them that related to people. Names seemed alien to all cats. Unlike dogs, cats didn't take their names seriously, nor anything else we said or did — except to put cat food in a saucer. But they didn't even need our food. They were hunters. Our food was just a convenience. The world of these cats was complete, and entirely their own.

I wanted very much to join their world, so I tried to be a cat, to lap up milk from a saucer and walk on all fours. My mom had been a ballerina and enrolled me in a ballet school where we were instructed to invent a dance. So while the other little girls flitted around, pointing their toes and waving their arms, I crawled on my hands and knees because this was the closest I could come to shape-changing. At that age I didn't have the words to explain why acting like a cat was a good idea, but it wasn't ballet, and I soon was ejected from the class. Perhaps my desire shows why, in the abovementioned photo, I carried poor Eve by the neck. That's more or less how a cat would carry a kitten. Perhaps it was just another of my clumsy efforts at shape-changing.

When I was six or seven, Eve and Lilith vanished, and it was my fault. The pediatrician had told my parents that the bouts of bronchitis I'd been having were caused by an allergy to cats. I was devastated. I must have cried for weeks. I would gladly have endured bronchitis if we could have kept the cats, but no one asked me. Tom, who not only helped us manage the house but was also an accomplished artist, then painted a picture of a cat for me — not one of our cats but a beautiful, long-haired brown tabby. It wasn't as good as a real cat, but it helped. To this day it hangs on the wall by my desk.

I never learned what happened to our cats, except that, knowing my mother, I'm sure they went to good homes. What I do know is that I paid no attention to the pediatrician. When I grew up I adopted a cat, then another cat. I've had cats ever since — I have six at the time of this writing, all of them rescues — and the occasional wheeze or snuffle never bothers me. I attribute it to pollen.

Aware of my grief at the loss of our cats, Gran began to take me to the Museum of Comparative Zoology, which was near our house. I braved the filigreed metal stairs through which one could see from the top floor to the basement, and thus were scary. I thought I might fall through. But I'd screw up my courage and keep going because the reward at the top was great. There we'd see stuffed mammals, all kinds of them, ranging in size from a stuffed elephant and a stuffed camel to a stuffed mongoose and stuffed squirrels. I'd spend time in front of a lynx, but its neck was too thin, as it had been stuffed poorly, so it didn't seem lifelike and wasn't all that interesting. The cats I really went to see were the tigers, especially a Siberian tiger. To think that a cat could be so big! It was hundreds of times bigger than me, and true to the taxonomy of the time, it was mounted in attack mode with its jaws open, displaying its terrible teeth.

It was, in short, very scary. I was frightened but also enthralled. I wasn't sure it wouldn't come to life and kill us because we were standing too close. But if we moved away, we couldn't see it clearly because it was boxed in by other, less riveting exhibits, so we'd go back to face it again. Scared as I was, I was so entranced by that tiger that I had to see it at least once a week, and I'd stand in front of it until forced to leave, frozen in place with awe and fear like a bird hypnotized by a snake.

I began to have nightmares. When I was forced to go to bed (always, it seemed, in broad daylight), I'd imagine that once it got dark, a tiger, that tiger, would climb up the side of the house and come in the window.

Sometimes the wind would blow leaves against the house. The scratching sound, I knew, was the tiger's claws, climbing.

I'd call my mother. She'd sit beside my bed. I'd ask her over and over if anything would hurt me in the dark. She'd tell me over and over that nothing would hurt me. This went on for months, if I remember rightly, taking much of my mother's valuable time. Yet during those months I'm not sure she knew that the danger I envisioned was a tiger. Often enough people don't want to name the terrors that haunt them, and I think that happened to me, because Gran and I kept going to the museum, and with every visit my fears would be refreshed.

I remembered this clearly years later, when I had two small children of my own and they too had fears about a tiger. Having lost none of my fascination with the cat family, I had read to them about tigers. But I didn't have my mother's time or patience and wanted to erase their fears as quickly as I could. So when one of my kids would call to me that a tiger was under the bed, I'd go in and look at it. "Goodness me," I'd say. "That's a tiger, sure enough. Why don't I take him to the kitchen and see if he wants some milk?" Then with great effort I'd drag him out. "He's scared," I'd say to explain his reluctance. When he was out I'd pick him up, reassuring him as I did so. But he was really heavy. It took all my strength. My knees would buckle, and huffing and puffing, I'd stagger with him out of the room. My children thought all this was exceptionally funny. They'd laugh, and their fears would vanish.

My mother must have sat beside my bed hundreds of times, reassuring me about the danger in the dark. I only had to drag the tiger from under my children's beds two or three times, and after that he stopped coming. So I recommend the method.

The first book I wrote was called *Shege The Tiger*. I'm not sure when I wrote it because the date on the cover is "Tuesday." I signed it Miss E. Marshall, illustrated it myself, and bound its pages between cardboard covers held together with O rings. I do remember why I wrote it, though. At the time, I had no other way to obtain a book about an animal. Reading *Shege* wasn't as good as reading something by another author, but I had no choice. A disaster occurred that would have left me with nothing.

The scene is as fresh in my mind today as on the day it happened. On that black day, the school librarian told me I couldn't read any more books about animals. I'd read too many already, and there were more important subjects. She said I should read about people.

I was aghast. I already knew about people. I begged her. I said I'd just read a little and promised to read other things too. She said no. She would not let me take any more animal books from the library. The only books I would be allowed to read henceforth would be about people.

Her decree was like a death. With those terrible words, she cut me off from what I cared about the most. I stood speechless in front of her, suddenly aware of her power, knowing I couldn't change her mind, realizing how bleak my future would be.

For the rest of the day I was despondent. I had to do something. When I came home from school, I assembled some paper, a pencil, some crayons, and two pieces of cardboard that the laundry put inside Dad's clean shirts. Then I sat on the floor of my parents' bedroom and wrote *Shege*. The name, I think, derives from Shere Khan in Kipling's *Jungle Book*, and she's a Siberian tiger because, thanks to the Museum of Comparative Zoology, I knew these were the biggest kind of tiger. Therefore she lives in the "Siberian jungles," because from the *Jungle Book* I learned that tigers are jungle animals. If there was such a thing as a Siberian tiger, it followed that there was a Siberian jungle.

I couldn't spell, but I didn't know it — among other mistakes I wrote *nois* for noise, *frunt* for front, and *prytty* for pretty — but when a hydrophobic jackal enters the scene, I must have known I was out of my depth and got help in spelling *hydrophobia*.

Nor did I have much sense of drama. Here's the entire last chapter: *Chapler four. One day Shege told her children to stay in the den and they did. After a while they saw it was raining (cats do not like rain) harder and harder. Prytty soon it started to pour. rain. The End.*

My writing has improved since then, my accuracy too, but my spelling has remained uncertain, so much so that my first agent, Marie Rodell, said I was like a ship's captain venturing out on uncharted seas, trying my best to deal with each new difficulty that came at me. Maybe I was dyslexic or something, or school eluded me. I have yet to master spelling.

I kept *Shege* for a while, and when I got tired of it—after all, it wasn't particularly compelling—my mother kept it. When she was in her nineties and came to New Hampshire to live with me, I found it among her papers and realized that my career began on a Tuesday. Although practice doesn't always make perfect, practice certainly helps.

4

KALAHARI

WHAT I LEARNED from the woods, from dogs and cats, and from visits with Gran to the museum was enthralling. It set me on a lifelong journey. But it was something like reading the first page of a book without reading the rest, or even knowing that the rest existed. From the farm I knew about farm animals, and I was often taken to the zoo as well as to the museum, so I knew what wild animals looked like. I'd also seen how dogs and cats managed their lives, and had glimpses of how wild animals managed. But our human world was overwhelming. People had all the power and made all the decisions. With their indifference to anything nonhuman, the world was at their mercy. So as I saw it, there were two spheres of existence—the one I lived in, which was the sphere of people, and the one I barely knew, which was the sphere of everything else, from amoebas to blue whales, from duckweed to giant sequoias, from the floor of the Mariana Trench to the summit of Everest. Every living thing in that second sphere belonged to what I've come to call the Old Way, keeping the old rules that evolution set out for each species, the rules that helped us stay alive and move our genes into the future. The Old Way put us here, although we no longer respect that. But in the summer of 1951, when I was eighteen, I was extremely fortunate to learn something about the Old Way and that second sphere, the sphere of everything else. It isn't often that a person can point to a single decision and say, "This one made all the difference," but I know I would not be who I am had my dad not made this decision. He decided that we would go to Africa. I was a college freshman at the time. If metaphor can describe my learning experiences, college was a slowly dripping faucet and Africa was the thundering Victoria Falls.

During World War II, Raytheon made radar and other equipment for the navy, so the importance of Dad's work cannot be overstated. During the war years we saw very little of him, and it has often been said that he took his family to Africa because he wanted to reacquaint himself with his children. That notion is touching and often crops up when our family's African experience is mentioned. Even my mother refers to it in her first book, *The !Kung of Nyae Nyae.*

But it wasn't the whole story — not even close. Dad could have sat on his living room couch and chatted with us if he didn't think he knew us well enough. He didn't need to spend hundreds of thousands of dollars, commandeer years of everybody's life, and take us into one of the world's largest unexplored wild places, hundreds of miles from rescue if anything went wrong. Possibly my brother and I were marginally worth knowing, but nobody is that worth knowing, and who wants to know two teenagers anyway? Isn't it enough that they don't get pregnant or wreck the car? When I was fifteen, my mom told me I was so awful (she said "difficult") that she wished I were still fourteen. I'd guess there were times when our parents wished they'd never met us.

So no. I'm sure we didn't go merely so that Dad could know us better. We went because he liked wild places. Two thousand acres of New Hampshire forest were not enough for him. He wanted more.

At some point in my life, I began to wonder why this was so, and I think it came from his childhood. He was born in 1889 in Medford, Massachusetts, but grew up in Somerville, the only child of parents who were desperately poor. I've wondered if his father was abusive. I've also wondered if alcohol played some role in this. Most people's parents are not erased from living memory, but an abusive alcoholic might be, and that seemed to have happened to Dad's father. I had near-encyclopedic knowledge of my mother's father and her host of other relatives, but I knew nothing about my dad's because he and his mother, Nana, didn't talk about their past. Sometimes I'd question them, but they always changed the subject, and I soon learned not to ask. It was as if Dad's father had never been.

When Nana was in her nineties, although she was physically and mentally vital, when a census taker asked her his name, she couldn't remember.

Thus I have no idea where Dad's father was born, or when he died, or what he was like as a person. I only know that his name was George Marshall and he worked as a butcher's assistant in Boston's Faneuil Hall market. Nana washed floors in a nursing home owned by some relatives. Part of the mystery is that two jobs in the family weren't enough. On very rare occasions and without casting blame, Nana or my dad might let it slip that there was never any money, and they sometimes had no food to eat.

Dad's reticence about his early years had one important exception — he often spoke of his experiences in a place called "the north woods." At some point in his early life, he was befriended by a dentist named Doc Parker, who, I believe, was like a father to him. Every year Doc Parker would go to these north woods with Micmac guides and would take my dad with him. For weeks at a time they would hike through the forest and travel in canoes on lakes and rivers. This must have brightened my dad's life enormously. One summer he took all of us there — my mother, my brother, me, and Tom and Kirsti. We hiked in the woods, saw all kinds of wildlife, swam in the lakes despite the leeches, slept in an ancient log cabin overgrown with moss, fished in a stream for brook trout early in the mornings, then fried the fish with bacon and ate them for breakfast. Since several places are called "the north woods," I'm not sure where our north woods were, but I know what they were like, and thought I was in paradise.

I didn't put this experience together with my dad's abilities because I never questioned them. I never wondered how he came to know so much about the woods, or why he taught us how to say in Micmac, "The moose saw us first," or why, in Africa, he was such an absolute dead shot with a rifle. He'd see an antelope on the distant horizon, take aim, and fire a single bullet that dropped the antelope in its tracks. He didn't do this for fun, he did it for meat, but most people can't do it at all. To me, he was the wonderful father who could do anything, so I never asked how he came by these abilities. Even so, I'm sure he didn't get them as a poverty-stricken youngster in Somerville, Massachusetts.

My guess is that he learned them in the north woods from the Micmac guides and Doc Parker.

The north woods were as wild as they were beautiful, but the occasional visit to such a place was not enough for my dad. In the autumn of 1949, he retired from Raytheon and decided to experience wilderness on a much bigger scale. He consulted a map, looking for large, uncharted areas with no rivers or towns or other features noted — enormous unexplored places about which nothing was known. There is no such place on earth today except perhaps parts of the sea bottom. Even the moon has been explored, and also can be examined with a telescope.

Back then, however, there were at least three large unexplored places. One was Antarctica, another was southern Tasmania, and another was most of the western third of southern Africa, except for settled areas along the coast. Our dad chose the one in Africa, approximately 300,000 square miles of wild savannah covering much of what today is Namibia and Botswana. It also reached into southern Angola and the western edge of South Africa.

This was the Kalahari Basin. Around the edges, the maps indicated a few features, mostly small settlements and prehistoric riverbeds, but in the interior were 120,000 square miles where the maps showed nothing. On the map my dad used, there was a line for 20° east longitude and another line for 20° south latitude, and that's all. The first astronauts who set off for the moon had a better idea of what they would find than we did. Today such a place is impossible to imagine. It was known as the end of the earth.

Yet I'm wrong to call it unexplored. Bushmen[1] lived there, on the shores of seasonal lakes in encampments that archaeologists were later to discover had been occupied continuously for 35,000 years. The archaeol-

---

1. Bushmen are also called San. *Bushman* is to *San* what *Indian* is to *Native American*. *San* is a Nama word and is pejorative, yet despite its degrading implications (it applies to anyone who lives in the bush, has no livestock, and eats food off the ground), it was given to the Bushmen by well-meaning anthropologists who must have felt that *Bushman* was even more pejorative. But I'm in no hurry to follow their lead. According to Dr. Robert Gordon, a Namibian anthropologist, *Bushmen* is what the people call themselves, and so does everyone else in Namibia.

ogists stopped their work before reaching the lowest parts of the sites, but the sites were deeper, and Bushmen had been there longer. Recent DNA studies show that Bushmen were the first people, from whom the rest of us descended, and recent linguistic studies suggest that all languages may have come from theirs. This puts Bushmen on the "unexplored savannah" at about 150,000 BP, after a glacial period turned the world's water into ice and the forests into grasslands. None of this was known at the time except the age and action of the glaciers, but needless to say, that savannah had been thoroughly explored.

In the spring of 1950, my dad and brother made a survey trip. Why anyone would want to penetrate that waterless interior to live in camps, not in a house, was a mystery to many. One of my mother's friends said we would get dirty. My mother said, "The earth itself is not dirty." One witless anthropology professor published a paper in which he claimed that my dad was looking for a lost city. I'm glad I wasn't one of that professor's students — God knows what else he told them. The very last thing to be found in such a place was a city, and the very last thing my dad would want to find was a city. If he had wanted a city, there was a big one called Boston near his house.

Other people thought he was prospecting for diamonds. Rumor had it that diamonds were scattered all over the ground. There weren't any diamonds, at least none on the surface, but this theory had more credibility than the lost city, so more people believed it. Even so, it too was false. My dad went to the Kalahari in 1950 to learn what he'd need in 1951 if he wanted to travel for months through hundreds of miles of uncharted bushland. When he figured that out, he came home with my brother and prepared an expedition. In 1951, he and my brother went back there and my mother and I went too.

I've also been asked why I went. Not a few people have wondered why a teenager would want to leave college and all her friends to go somewhere with her parents. I find the question dumbfounding. I did know a boy whom I later married, but we were just friends at the time, and I was so excited to be going that I didn't realize how much I'd miss him.

I knew I wouldn't miss college. My parents had forced me to major in English, so why would I want to listen to some professor droning on about *Pilgrim's Progress* when I could listen to lions roaring in the African night? The slowly dripping faucet did not compare to the thundering Victoria Falls.

I've written many articles and two books about my time in the Kalahari. One of the books, *The Harmless People*, I wrote soon after my last long-term visit there, and the other, *The Old Way: A Story of the First People*, I wrote about fifty years later to review what I'd seen in the light of some of the scientific knowledge that has been gathered since. But one way or another, the Kalahari is in all the books I've written. To put it differently, I always seem to write the same book. Whether I'm writing about dogs, cats, deer, people, or anything else, the lens through which I see them is the Kalahari. With the exception of some jobs I've had — teaching in various universities, teaching in a maximum security prison, and working as an academic adviser for the Embassy of the State of Kuwait — all of which required at least a college degree if not an MA, I could have skipped college altogether.

My dad wanted the time and energy we'd spend in the Kalahari to amount to something, so after his first visit, he discussed his projected return with his anthropologist friends at Harvard's Peabody Museum, next door to the museum that housed the stuffed tiger. Bushmen were known to live in the interior, but little was known about them, and much of what was said about them was not true. They'd kill us, some white South Africans had told my dad. But we'd never see them. They'd hunt us down and shoot us from ambush with poisoned arrows and we'd never know they were there. That was the state of knowledge of the Bushmen at the time — they were mysterious, invisible devils.

Dad was not impressed by these claims. When he met with his friends from the Peabody, he asked if an anthropologist would come with us to study the Bushmen. He offered to pay that person's salary and all expenses. But at the time, the world of anthropology was focused in other directions. Not one anthropologist could be found with any interest in people who seemed to lack complex societies. The Bushmen were wrongly believed to be refugees who, it was said, had been driven into the backcountry by white farmers and Bantu pastoralists. I thought this was true when I wrote *The Harmless People,* and for years the concept clung. One anthropologist was later to say that the Bushmen in the interior were a "devolved" people who had once been farmers with cattle but then lost the cattle and resorted to eating wild foods for lack of anything else. Any further knowledge of such uninteresting people we would have to get for ourselves.

Fortunately, my dad arranged for his expedition to be sponsored by the Smithsonian Institution and also by Harvard's Peabody Museum, and by the time we boarded a freighter bound for Walvis Bay on the coast of South West Africa (now Namibia) he had acquired a Dodge Power Wagon, two six-by-six army trucks, and an army jeep, all but the Power Wagon being World War II surplus that I believe he had obtained with the help of the Smithsonian. We also had camping equipment, camera equipment, recording equipment, a thirty-thirty rifle, and books about anthropology.

While crossing the Atlantic, we read the books, or my mom did. My brother hung around with the first mate, who told fascinating stories about his maritime adventures, and my dad visited with the captain — both had served in World War I, the captain on a warship as a naval officer, my dad in France as a second lieutenant in the field artillery — or he spent time in the hold, checking on our equipment.

As for me, I watched the sea, looking for whales and porpoises. One day I saw two huge fins going in the same direction and took them to be those of two big sharks, one following the other. But, oh my God, these were the tail and dorsal fins of a single shark, a supershark, a shark as big as the freighter! I wouldn't have seen that if I had stayed in college.

One night, near the equator, we saw the Southern Cross. The first mate pointed it out. I found it unimpressive compared to the Big Dipper and the North Star. Dad said it was all we'd have at night to know which way was south, so we'd better remember how to find it. And also, he reminded us, from then on the sun would be in the north, and we'd better remember that too, because where we were going, there would be little else to help us find our way if we got separated.

The freighter was bigger than the town of Walvis Bay, or so it seemed. At least it was longer. When viewing the scene from afar, I saw the town's little buildings in a cluster with the bow and stern of the docked freighter sticking out on both sides. The crane that successfully if scarily unloaded our vehicles stood up above the rooftops.

We packed our equipment into the trucks and drove to Windhoek, which, although a small town at the time, was the capital of South West Africa. There we gathered our supplies, including empty fifty-gallon barrels for gasoline and water, and began the task of finding a camp manager, three mechanics, and interpreters who spoke English and !Kung,[2] the language of the Bushmen we hoped to visit. We had to settle for two interpreters, one who spoke !Kung and Afrikaans and another who spoke Afrikaans and English. We knew our conversations would be something like the game called Telephone, wherein a whispered message is passed around a circle, getting mangled as it goes. Better that we should speak !Kung ourselves, an effort that we began immediately.

When we were ready we set off to the north, where Dad had met a German farmer named Fritz Metzger. Fritz spoke some !Kung. He had agreed to join us for a while, and with him he brought two Bushman men who were laborers on his farm. These men, Fritz told us, had heard of a source of water in the interior. We were grateful to have them.

The Kalahari is called a desert, but only because the annual rainfall can be as little as three or four inches. The land slopes gently up and down so that from its higher contours one can see literally for miles, and what one sees is a mosaic of open grasslands with long stretches of sand dunes covered with heavy thornbush or groves of different kinds of trees — most of them thorny, most of them acacias — and now and then a seasonal lake that fills with water during the rains but for the rest of the year is a salt flat.

The Kalahari is not a true desert. But at the time we didn't fully understand it, with its open, sweeping landscape, with its sunlight and long grass. We didn't know, for instance, that the antelopes who lived there didn't need to drink water. I was later to learn that they don't sweat or pant to cool themselves, because their body temperatures can rise with the heat of the day, which would kill us but does them no harm. We saw

---

2. There are five Bushman languages, all of which have clicks. The ! in !Kung is such a click. The others are /, //, and ≠.

them often, usually resting in bushes or under a tree. Their bodies store heat, but they can't overdo it, so by day they seek the shade.

We didn't know the names of most of the plants, and we didn't wonder why most of them had thorns. I later learned that thorns are little water-savers, as were the thick, shiny leaves on most of the bushes. My task was to drive one of the six-by-six army trucks, and I remember the strength of those bushes, because I'd have to put the truck in its lowest gear to push through them. How old would a bush have to be to become so strong? I later learned that the roots of these bushes were very deep, going down to places where they found residual moisture.

What we were seeing was a timeless ecosystem complete with flora and fauna that had evolved to fit it, an ecosystem that had been in existence for over a million years. We drove right over it. But we had to. We were not like the plants and the antelopes. We had to keep looking for water.

We soon found ourselves in some very rough, very wild country. Our vehicles had blade springs, and often enough we'd break them. Worse yet, now and then we'd break an axle. Dad had foreseen this, so we had more springs and axles. But when such problems occurred we'd need to camp for as long as it took to fix them. So travel was slow. A Bushman on foot would have gone faster.

In the dunes the trucks got stuck. We had a winch and would winch them out if we could, but as often as not we'd have to dig them out with shovels, laying brush under the tires for traction, then getting behind the truck and pushing while the driver roared the motor and spun the wheels. In places the thornbush itself was very thick, and I well remember thorns showering through the open window of my truck. It was too hot to shut the window. I just put up with the thorns.

Looking back, I regret the ecological damage, but ecology drew less attention then, and anyway, there were 120,000 square miles minus the width of our track that we didn't damage. I console myself with that thought.

I also loved every minute of it. The following is from my journal. (All italicized passages henceforth are from the same, unless otherwise noted.)

It was very cold last night. The south wind blew from the Antarctic all night long, sweeping the haze out of the sky, leaving the brilliant, hard, white moon. We moved on shortly after dawn, through this gorgeous dry rolling veldt, by little forests, over outcrops of rock. We went through valleys and burned areas, and over plains so long you could see the trees in the haze miles away, like a distant shore, until we came to a dry pan where we hoped to find people. We found no people's footprints on the edge of the pan. A little way into the veldt, which here is yellow pinkish grass like old bloodstains, we found high spring-bushes with karu vines on them. We then walked all around the pan and found high ant heaps all grown over in a tangle with bushes. We climbed the ant heaps and looked around. And we found a tree full of weaverbirds' nests swinging in the wind but all empty, and we found a shoulder blade, all white, bleached, and dry, of some large antelope. We even saw a little round mouse nest, also empty, hanging from the branch of a thornbush. We walked farther but found no signs of people, so we got back in the vehicles and drove for the rest of the day down a series of vast, long, narrow plains. There we saw the smoke of a veldt fire on the horizon which might have been lit by people, so we left the plain and drove toward it, through heavy, low thornbush, until we reached the fire. We found a way through the wall of flames and found our way to the source, where we looked for a sign of what set the fire, but the burned area is very large and it is hard to be sure. The fire has run on and on and is now far away against the evening sun like the smoke from a train traveling far away. It is very quiet and lonely here. We called for people but there is no answer. We have searched through about 100 square miles of veldt and tomorrow we will search some more.

We slept all night under the frosty moon. We got up from time to time to feed the fire, and when it got light we cooked the remainder of last night's meat. When we woke we could see our breath, but when the sun came, it suddenly got warmer. We are on a rise of ground and you can literally see for miles. A range of mountains, which are about 13 in number, are far away on one side, and on the other, towards the south, the land falls away and away and away, down and down, much farther than anything I have ever seen before, until all the trees are obscured, on and on, until the horizon looks like the ocean seen from miles away, just a blue line a little darker and hazier than the sky.

When we'd camp in the evenings we'd take care of the vehicles, brushing grass seeds out of the radiator screens, topping off the radiators with our precious water, filling the fuel tanks with our precious gasoline, and checking the springs and axles. We'd also pull up grass to make a large, snake-free clearing and on it we'd build our fires.

Then it would be dark, and the world of the night would open. The night sky looked as it did when *Homo erectus* saw it. There were millions of stars, many more than I've ever seen since. Under the trees the darkness was complete until, far away, the moon would lift from the horizon, erase the stars, and fill the world with its pale light. We'd listen for sounds such as a rock striking something as someone cracks a nut for the nutmeat or a bone for the marrow—a sound which in that silent world travels for miles—but we heard no sounds made by people. Instead, we'd hear guinea fowls calling as they flew, one by one, to their roosts in the trees. We'd also hear the predators calling—basically the only animals who vocalize at night. From the enormous, darkened veldt we'd hear a faraway jackal calling, or we'd hear far-apart lions roaring to tell each other where they were, or we'd hear spotted hyenas making the *hahahaha* calls that were known as laughter but really are signals of agitation, usually because the hyenas are upset with each other. I didn't know that at the time, though. I just listened to their calls with excitement and wonder.

After many days of travel, we heard only insects and the wind in the long grass. Unlike the Kalahari antelopes, the predators had to drink. The silence meant that we were far from water.

We hoped to find a place that the two Bushman men called /Gam. It wasn't on a map and we had no idea how far we would have to travel to find it. But it was the only possible source of water that we'd heard of. If this was so, and since it was the dry season, we hoped to find not only water but also Bushmen.

After we had traveled about two hundred miles—which is a very long way through heavy bushland—the Bushmen with us thought that /Gam was near. They probably would have found it more easily had they been on foot, because sensing the landscape from inside a truck can be confusing.

By then we had used almost half of our water. My dad's plan was to travel until we used half of our supply, at which point we would follow our tracks back to the nearest settlements, refill our fifty-gallon drums, and try again. The time was coming when we might need to do this. But one day the guides saw smoke and realized from its appearance that it wasn't a wildfire but a campfire. We went in that direction and found /Gam.

We had hoped to find a Bushman encampment. But as we came near we saw several cattle, then several small, round Tswana-style dwellings made of poles with grass thatches. Two Tswana[3] men wearing shorts, shirts, and broad-brimmed hats came to meet us. We were to learn that they were the relatives of a cattle-rich man who lived about a hundred miles away in the Bechuanaland Protectorate. Tswana people divided their large herds into smaller herds and distributed them among different relatives to take to better pasture. This was why these cattle were at /Gam. They had come there about eighteen months earlier, or so we were told, during the rainy season.

But how did their owner know of /Gam? He had learned about it from Bushmen. That certainly told us something. We had learned about /Gam from Bushmen two hundred miles to the west. The rich man had learned about /Gam from Bushmen a hundred miles to the east. It would seem that the Bushman community, sparse though it was, reached right across the interior.

One of the men who came to meet us was clearly in charge, so we asked his permission to camp nearby and take some water. He graciously welcomed us and granted us permission. We set up our camp and filled three of our fifty-gallon drums. That was a hundred and fifty gallons of water, but the water level in the water hole hardly went down. Where, in that dry country, did it come from, with only a few inches of rain a year? I wish I could answer that question, but all I know is that it wasn't fossil water from one of the prehistoric lakes that are found at great depths in

---

3. I use the name Tswana throughout, which seems fairly customary, although in reference to people, Batswana is the plural and Motswana is the singular. Setswana is the language, and Botswana, of course, is the name of what was known as the Bechuanaland Protectorate at the time of our visit. I mean no disrespect by Anglicizing Setswana.

places like the Kalahari, because the water hole itself was dug by hand and wasn't deep enough for that. Perhaps the water hole was in some kind of basin that collected water from the rock ledges above it. We were later to take three hundred gallons and more at a time without worrying anyone, because overnight the water in the hole would return to its normal level.

We were also to learn that the water at /Gam was the most plentiful of all the Bushmen's sources. So /Gam was unique. But /Gam no longer belonged to Bushmen. Thus the Bushmen at /Gam were something like the two Bushmen who came with Fritz Metzger. Their people had lost their land to Fritz's father. They didn't "use" it, according to the occupying farmers, and they didn't have a deed. Nor could they resist the farmers. Their groups were too small. They became farm laborers.

The same thing was starting at /Gam. The Bushmen performed some services for the Tswanas, such as collecting firewood and herding some of the livestock. They also hunted and gathered to feed themselves, and were free to leave /Gam if they didn't like it, because all of them had relatives at other water sources, so they lived in the Old Way, to be sure. But they were tasting their future.

As we set up our camp, the headman's young wife came to see us, carrying a baby. Our camp manager, Philip Hameva, told me that she was Herero, not Tswana, and that her name was Kavasitjue, which means "submission to the will of God." Kavasitjue wore a headscarf and a long dress, and, as I was thrilled to learn, she spoke a little Afrikaans.

I did too. Soon we were chatting as best we could, each of us glad to meet a female age-mate whom she could at least try to talk with. I'd been a bit lonely, as by then I was missing my boyfriend. Kavasitjue was lonely too, as she was a six-day walk from her family. We both saw an opportunity for friendship. But where to start?

The baby seemed so young that I wondered if he was born at /Gam. In my limited Afrikaans I tried to ask. Like me, Kavasitjue didn't have enough Afrikaans to express herself clearly, but I believe she said he was born on the way to /Gam. That must have been fun, I thought but couldn't say, bearing your first child in the back of beyond with no woman to help you.

We then tried to talk about earrings. Hers were made of small beads. Mine were safety pins which I used to keep the pierced holes in my ears from closing. In my stumbling Afrikaans I tried to explain the safety pins, which wasn't easy, but Kavasitjue understood. She knew about ear holes closing.

Over the next few days our friendship blossomed. We had many a confusing conversation. She let me hold the baby. He was a joyous little guy — we laughed with him and with each other. I believe that thirty years later he became one of the owners of /Gam when, after Namibian independence, the vast Bushman lands were split up among white farmers, Bantu pastoralists, and World Wildlife, which took a large section for a tourist hotel and game reserve. /Gam was given to the Hereros. Herero people trace their lineage through their mothers, so because Kavasitjue was Herero, her son was also Herero, and thus may have been a good candidate for ownership. If any non-Bushman was to have /Gam, I hope he got it.

After we had been at /Gam for a while, I was given the name Kothonjoro. Such names often describe a personal characteristic, and I think mine means "one who laughs." I believe that Kavasitjue gave me the name, but it was Philip who explained it to me. The reason I laughed — hence the reason for the name — was to hide that my heart was sad.

I was astonished. Kavasitjue had seen right through me. Without my boyfriend I was often plagued by sorrow, which I tried to hide by doing my best as a comic. The very last thing I'd expected to find in this unending wilderness was insight into my psyche from a brief acquaintance with a woman from a different culture whose mother tongue was Otjiherero. But it has since become my impression that many Bantu people, and also many other African people, are substantially more sensitive, perceptive, and intuitive than Western people, and thus are our superiors in almost every social exercise. So I treasured the name Kothonjoro, and kept it in my much happier heart.

The Bushmen at /Gam were Ju/wasi, one of the five groups of Bushmen in southern Africa, each of which speaks a somewhat different language. In !Kung, the language of the Ju/wasi, *ju* means person, *si* makes it plu-

ral, and /wa (sometimes spelled *h/oan,* but it sounds like /wa) means
pure, as water is pure if nothing bad is in it. By this concept, a person is
pure if he isn't carrying a weapon. For the first book I wrote, I translated
/wa as *harmless* and used it in the title, *The Harmless People.*

White people did not meet that description, so everyone was wary
of them with good reason, and the Ju/wasi at /Gam were wary of us.
Even so, they were willing to talk with us, and from them we learned
that /Gam had been their place, which is called a *n!ore.*[4] A *n!ore* is where
a person has the right to live. We had been told (but didn't believe) that
Bushmen were nomads, wandering here and there in search of food. We
knew this was sure to be wrong, but we were later to learn how very
wrong, as almost every Ju/wa person we came to know had a *n!ore* and
virtually every *n!ore* was a source of water. Its owners spent the dry season there, just as the Ju/wasi at /Gam were doing.

In the area we were soon to study, an area of some six thousand square
miles called Nyae Nyae, there were seven permanent and eight semiper-
manent water sources, each of which was the *n!ore* of a group of people.
/Gam was the most important.

We stayed there for while, interviewing the Ju/wasi about various subjects, including places where we could find people living in the Old Way
without interruption. Because any wilderness environment, particularly
one as specialized as the Kalahari, is altered by domestic animals and
plants, human life that is closely tied to the environment can be altered
along with it. This could make a difference to hunter-gatherer activity.
But how would we know? My dad decided that we must go deeper into
the interior to look for people still living completely in the Old Way, a
way that did not include domestic plants and animals, and we asked the
Ju/wasi at /Gam to help us find them.

Perhaps two thousand such people lived in that vast interior, most of
whom we came to know as our work there developed, but we might have
met none of them had not a man named /Kwi and his wife, //Kushe,
walked into our camp in single file one evening, /Kwi leading. They
were barefoot and were dressed in purely Bushman clothing — /Kwi

---

4. Omitting the click, this word is pronounced "nor-ay."

with a leather loincloth, //Kushe with a leather front apron, a leather back apron, a long string of beads made of ostrich eggshell, and a leather cape with the corners tied across her chest and a sinew string tied around her waist. This formed a pouch at her back where her baby could ride, but that day he was riding on his father's shoulders. He was a little boy named /Gao. As a necklace he wore a long sinew string, on which hung a single bead.

/Kwi and //Kushe sat on their heels by our fire. Through our interpreters, /Kwi told us that his wife no longer wanted to live at /Gam. She wanted to return to her *n!ore*, the place she came from, and if we wanted to go there, they would show us the way.

We accepted the offer. The next day we took down our camp, topped off the water in our fifty-gallon drums thanks to the generosity of the Tswanas, and made our grateful farewells. I was sad to leave Kavasitjue, and gave her two gifts, which, as I recall, were a scarf and a blanket. She started to thank me, then folded the gifts in her arms and said, "Too much thanks is like a curse. I sit here with my delights." Then we got in the trucks and headed for that next place, //Kushe's place, which, we were later to learn, was Gautscha.

The trip wasn't easy, certainly not for /Kwi or //Kushe, who until we came had never seen a vehicle, let alone ridden in one. The trucks lurched and bounced as usual, and thornbushes crashed against their sides. //Kushe wanted to get out and walk, but our Bushman guides persuaded her not to. As I remember that journey, I think this was when the leading truck went over an aardvark's burrow of which there was no outward sign. The driver couldn't see it and the truck fell through. The crash broke a spring. I was concerned about the aardvark, but luckily for him, he wasn't in his burrow. We had to replace the broken spring, so we camped, and drove for most of the next day until /Kwi told us we were there.

5

THE JU/WASI

G AUTSCHA WAS AN ENORMOUS clay pan of perhaps three hundred acres — a white, seasonal lake from which the rainwater had evaporated. On its eastern side were three baobab trees in full leaf, the biggest of them a hundred feet tall, thirty feet in diameter, and easily two thousand years old. On the northern and western sides of the pan, bushes and long, pale grass stretched to the horizon. We arrived at the southern side of the pan, and right in front of us was green grass, conspicuous among the miles of yellow grass. The grass was green because it grew beside the water hole.

/Kwi and //Kushe got out of the trucks and walked off into the bush. The two Bushman guides from Fritz Metzger's farm looked around uneasily. They were not Ju/wasi but belonged to another group entirely, and they were not sure how people so deep in the interior, so mindful of all the old customs, would receive them. The reason for this was demonstrated years later by an anthropologist named Polly Wiessner, who showed arrows made by one group of Bushmen to Bushmen of another group. They were not at all pleased by the sight, and said they'd be upset if they found such arrows on their land, as it would show that people of another group had been intruding. In those days, Bushmen were of necessity territorial, and the Bushmen from the farm were not sure of their welcome.

Nor were we, especially when no one seemed to be there. Some unseasonal rain had fallen, so we wondered if the people were off in the veldt, finding water in hollow trees. We waited for several hours, and thought of moving on to look for people elsewhere. But then two men came walking toward us. We told them our names and they told us theirs, which were /Gao and ≠Toma. We explained our presence, saying that we came in peace and wanted only to meet them. They listened. We asked their permission to camp and drink the water. They gave us permission. Then they showed us their encampment—a group of small, dome-shaped shelters made of branches thatched with grass, back in the bush in a grove of trees about two hundred feet from the water hole. We pitched our camp nearby. As we did this, the people came out of the bush a few at a time and went to their encampment.

That night, when we were at our fire and the Ju/wasi were at theirs, we heard them talking about us in soft voices. As we learned later, a young boy was telling the other people that our trucks sounded like lions roaring, but not ordinary lions. This had frightened him, he said. The moon rose out of the grass on the horizon and the people with us went to sleep. But beyond us, by their evening fires, the Ju/wasi kept on talking.

I try to imagine the courage of /Gao and ≠Toma at that first meeting. The Ju/wasi had no chiefs or headmen, but if we had been gorillas, these men would have been the silverbacks. About twenty-five people lived at Gautscha at the time, and all but these two men had hidden in the bush when they heard our vehicles. The two men must have been unsure, yet when they came to meet us, they left their weapons behind. Those people didn't call themselves Ju/wasi for nothing, and it was considered bad manners, and inflammatory too, to meet newcomers while carrying weapons. Most of the people encamped there had never seen white people or vehicles, but they certainly had heard about us, and what they had heard was both accurate and frightening, so it must have taken courage to approach us unarmed.

I was later to learn that Bushman men did not consider themselves to be courageous. Or, to put it differently, what seems courageous to us seemed normal to them. They did such things as hunt Cape buffalo weighing 1,500 pounds, using a small bow with a twenty-five-pound pull that shot a six-inch poisoned arrow. Cape buffalo are the world's most dangerous game, and are not at all compromised by a Bushman arrow, or not right away, as the poison takes several days to work. Hunting Cape buffalo with little poisoned arrows is not safe, but Bushmen did it anyway. A westerner hunts Cape buffalo with at least a .458-caliber rifle (the bullet is about four inches long) and considers himself to be the utmost in machismo and valor.

Bushman men didn't consider themselves brave or macho even when they drove off prowling lions, which they did without weapons, just by talking to them respectfully and showing them burning branches. And when white strangers appeared in roaring trucks, which these people had never seen or heard before, their men came out to deal with us too, appearing to be calm even though they might reasonably have thought we were dangerous. It was very much the Old Way.

Gautscha means "place of buffalo." But buffalo didn't live there and probably hadn't for about eight thousand years. True, they sometimes came during the rainy season, at which time the Ju/wa men hunted them, but Cape buffalo are not like the Kalahari antelopes and must live where they can find surface water and plenty of grazing. Gautscha had not met that description since a long-ago wet period when several huge prehistoric rivers—leaving riverbeds known as omarambas—drained into the Okavango River. These omarambas were perhaps forty miles west of Gautscha and had been dry for thousands of years.

So I believe that the name Gautscha was as prehistoric as the omarambas. We have places like that too, if not as ancient. Every town named Newton, for example, is now an old town, but the name will remain as long as people live there, which probably will not be as long as people had lived at Gautscha.

So if Gautscha is an ancient name, it's no wonder. As has been said, archaeologists were later to find encampments by seasonal lakes that had been occupied continuously since the Paleolithic. My family was to make many expeditions to Nyae Nyae, three of which I accompanied, always visiting Gautscha and the people we knew best, and at one point a young archaeologist came with us and found small stone tools scattered around the edge of the dry lakebed. He identified these tools as from the Wilton culture, which meant they had been lying there for perhaps six thousand years. The Ju/wasi knew about the stone tools but did not know who made them. Unfortunately the archaeologist stopped his investigation at the surface, so no one knows what might be underground. Other archaeologists investigated other long-occupied encampments, but not the one at Gautscha.

The Ju/wasi used a few stone tools but by then were making their arrow points of bone, which is more easily worked. However, after the Bantu migration from West Africa about five hundred years ago, when Bantu people settled around the edges of the Kalahari Basin (but, because of lack of water, not in the area of 250,000 square miles that attracted my father), the Ju/wasi and other Bushman groups began to trade items such as jackal skins for metal, then passed the metal around among themselves. They cold-hammered wire into arrowheads and sharpened small pieces of metal to make knives.

It might take a year for a piece of wire to travel from the early Bantu settlements into Gautscha, as we later learned. During our first expedition, my mom gave every woman enough cowrie shells to make a necklace. Before that, cowrie shells were unknown in the interior, but when we returned about eight months later, they were spread all over Nyae Nyae, the six-thousand-square-mile area we were investigating, owing to the fact that the Bushmen exchanged gifts. The population density of Nyae Nyae could be described as sparse—one person for every ten square miles—but even so, those shells had traveled.

Except for the wire and small bits of flat metal, the Gautscha people were living entirely in the Old Way, as our species had lived for thousands of years. They made their shelters from the branches of bushes stuck in the ground and woven together, then thatched with grass, creating little half-domes which are reminiscent of the nests made by the great apes. If you cup your hand and turn it sideways, it looks like the shelters of the Bushmen. If you cup your hand and turn it palm up, it looks like the nests of the great apes, and it's made in the same way, by weaving branches together and stuffing them with leaves.

This suggests that the concept of the Bushman shelters may be older than our species. When a glacial period trapped much of the world's water and turned the forests into grasslands, the trees withered out from under us. We adapted to the savannah just like the water-independent antelopes. But like everything else that lives in the Old Way, we didn't change anything unless we had to. Surely we kept on weaving branches together and stuffing them, by then not with rainforest leaves but with savannah grasses, because such nests or shelters protect their occupants from predators. After we lost our rainforests, we lost the safety of the trees, but we seem to have kept the nests, and wisely so, because lions and leopards — especially leopards, the most important predators of large primates — attack from behind when they're hunting. In the Ju/wa encampments, the shelters faced in all directions so that anything approaching someone from behind could be seen by someone else.

Why would people keep the same custom for hundreds of thousands of years? Because nothing that lives in the Old Way makes unnecessary changes. Because the shelters did what they were supposed to do. Because the shelters were easy to make, the materials were always available, nothing about them had to be transported, and they offered excellent protection. It would have been madness to make a different kind of shelter, especially a permanent shelter. And nobody did, because the nestlike shelters were perfect.

As for the antiquity of Ju/wa culture, I think of their religion. They had two gods, both of whom lived on the horizon, one in the east and one in the west. I found this very interesting, as the horizons are areas of transition, day to night, night to day, when the diurnal and nocturnal populations of the savannah change places. The god in the west was involved with the /gauasi, the spirits of the dead. His name was /Gaua (/gauasi is the plural of /Gaua) and he had to do with death. Evidently he had been around longer than the other god, probably from a time when our ancestral hunter-gatherers had only one language and one culture. Over the centuries the Bushmen divided into five groups, each with a different language and with varying views of the supernatural. But all of them knew /Gaua, which means he was with them before they separated, and may have been the first god in the world. Clearly, he is the oldest god now known.

I admired the Ju/wa religion. The two gods were not moral policemen, and took little interest in people except to send them good or bad luck for no better reason than that they felt like it. For instance, a god might take the form of a gemsbok, and if a hunter in all innocence shot him, the god would wait for him to eat the meat and then, once inside him, would kill him. Frankly, I thought that was a more realistic view of how life works than the views offered by the more modern worldwide religions.

I wonder about the anthropologist who claimed that Bushmen were a devolved people who lost their livestock and were forced to live on wild foods. If that were true, Bushmen were the fastest learners in human history, because within a very few years their entire population would have learned everything there was to know about their environment, down to the last detail, none of which had anything to do with pastoralism. In later years, professors from universities such as Harvard came to investigate Bushman knowledge, and despite their PhDs, the professors didn't have enough information to know what questions to ask. For example, no one asked about a weaverbird's nest, which, according to the Bushmen, had a compartment for a snake. Obviously superstition, of course, or so it seemed until an ornithologist learned that when a snake climbed the baglike nest, its weight opened the snake compartment while closing a higher compartment in which were the eggs or fledglings. The snake would find nothing and leave.

If you don't know that, you have no way to ask about it. So the best the professors could do was to see if what the western world knew — the various plant and animal species, for instance — compared to Bushman knowledge, and of course it did, because those who live in the Old Way must be accurate. Their survival did not allow for mistakes. I was wowed by a Bushman man named Ukwane who dissected an antelope for us, naming all of its parts — heart, stomach, kidney, testicles, and the like — and accurately describing their functions. When I was in college I dissected a dead cat in a biology class, learning only about half as much as Ukwane knew, but at least I learned enough to appreciate his knowledge. But no professor with a PhD had taught Ukwane.

To me the most stupefying piece of Bushman knowledge involved their arrow poison. It comes only from the pupae of two species of beetles and their parasites, all of which live on certain kinds of trees. But not on all of those trees, only on some of them. The adult beetles can be seen on the trees, but the adults play no role in human life and supposedly aren't poisonous. The adults lay their eggs on the leaves of the trees; the larvae climb down the tree under the bark and go out through the roots to pupate, making casings for themselves from the lumpy sand around them. It is in this state that they are poisonous. I often watched Bushman men digging for the pupae casings, but I couldn't distinguish them from the rest of the sand. The men could, though.

The trees are something like black walnuts in that nothing much grows around them, thus there's no special reason to dig there. Only a people who knew every detail of their environment could find, among the thousands of species of beetles, those who have poison, and at that, only in the pupae, which are encased in bits of the sand that surrounds them. If that's not enough, in one kind of beetle the poison gland is under the grub's arm so the arm must be pulled off to get it.

Yet the Bushmen learned of this poison long ago and have been using it on their little arrows ever since. It's one of the deadliest poisons on earth. It must enter the bloodstream, where it disintegrates the hemoglobin. One drop of it will kill a person in a day and will kill a large antelope in two to four days. Needless to say, the hunters must then track the antelope until she dies, so this brought out another astonishing skill of the Ju/wasi — their knowledge of tracks, which was phenomenal. They could read tracks as we read written words. My introduction to their ability involved a snake.

Near our camp, Ukwane found the hole of a great mamba. From its track, /Gai could tell that it was a black mamba twenty feet long and thicker than your arm, a monster. It lived in a "deserted" spring-hare burrow. Ukwane believed that the mamba has left for the veldt because so many people are present. We burned the hole with gasoline but nothing was in there. But I saw its track with my own eyes, so big my heart sank and my hairs stood on end or my knees turned to water — a terrifying sight, and we thought at the time, I remember, that there we were, talking, while just under our feet in the cool ground coiled in great coil after coil lay the black mamba, more deadly than a land mine, as my brother said, and ticking like a bomb. /Gai spent hours explaining the difference between the tracks of various snakes until at last he said, "We have lived a long time among the snakes and we just know when we see it whether it is a mamba or a puff adder or a python!" I learned that a puff adder track winds back on itself, a mamba track is more straight and larger than a cobra's, and a python's track is larger still and smooth (from the marks of scales) but not as smooth as a mamba's. Then there is the track of the tail—up the middle, a groove in the basinlike body of the track. A python's track shows the marks of his two tiny feet by his anus.

Before one of our expeditions, someone asked me to get the Ju/wa children to draw pictures. So I provided some kids with paper and crayons, neither of which they had ever seen before. Nor did the Bushmen we knew make any kind of visual representations. The girls refused to draw, but the boys were willing, and not surprisingly, they drew tracks. Of course they did. They were asked to produce a visual image, and the only visual representation of something that wasn't actually present would be its tracks. As each boy carefully drew a set of tracks, his friends would identify the animal who made them, meanwhile making the hand sign for the animal in question—the first and second finger up and straight to represent a gemsbok's horns, up and curved for a kudu's horns, thumb and little finger up and curved for a wildebeest's horns, and so on. These were the signs that hunters made when they saw something and wanted to tell their companions, but didn't want to spook whatever it was by talking. All the tracks the boys drew were those of antelopes, as these were the animals of greatest interest. Wherever people went—men, women, or children—they unfailingly observed and reported such tracks if they saw them.

One winter day I was off in the veldt with one of the boys who had drawn tracks. We came across the tracks of a hyena. The boy, who was nine or ten years old, showed me that over one of the hyena's footprints were tiny little pinpoints, which were the tracks of a beetle. He named the beetle. He also knew that those beetles don't move about until the air is warm enough, which on that day would have been shortly after sunrise. That meant that the hyena had passed by before sunrise, but not long before. The boy pointed out that the tracks were fresh, with no tiny crust around the edges made by drying dew.

That's a lot of knowledge from one kid about one footprint. If you multiply that by the 6,000 square miles of Nyae Nyae and the 35,000 years (at least) that people had lived there, you get a sense of Ju/wa information.

Something I treasure from my time at Gautscha is the name I was given. All of us received names, as the Ju/wasi based their relationships on kinship. Not to have kinship was to be an outsider, in which case the people would have difficulty relating to you. But to be a blood relative was unnecessary—their complex kinship system had arranged for all that. Your place in the system can depend on whom you're named for, and I was named Di!ai for a woman with whom I went gathering. I was honored to have her name, and I felt I belonged.

About thirty years later I returned to Nyae Nyae, not at first to Gautscha but to a government post called Tsumkwe that had developed in the interim. I was traveling alone in a rented pickup and knew of a gas station at Tsumkwe. But when I arrived, it was lunchtime and the gas station was closed. So I sat on the front bumper and waited.

Far in the distance, I noticed a Bushman man raking the lawn of one of the white people who worked at Tsumkwe—a missionary or a government employee. The man stopped raking and looked at me for a little while. Then he dropped his rake and started walking toward me, not by way of the footpath that led across the lawn he'd been raking or by way of the road that led to the gas station, as a western person might have done. Instead, in the manner of the Old Way, he walked straight across the white people's yards, as if the path and the road meant nothing to him.

I watched him coming, wondering if I knew him. As he got nearer, I saw that I didn't, but still he came. He walked right up to me, stopped in front of me, looked me in the eyes, and said, "You're Di!ai."

Good God! I was Di!ai! But who was he? And how did he know me? No one knew I was coming—no one was expecting me. I asked his name. He told me, but still I didn't know him. Apologetically, I asked for the names of his parents. And when he told me that, I understood who I was looking at—a man who had been five or six years old the last time he had seen me. But that's the Old Way for you—if you don't write things down, you need memory. And you need to know what you're looking at too—he recognized me after thirty years from forty or fifty yards away.

What I saw that day was just another mind-bending, jaw-dropping ability of the Bushmen.

For the rest of my life I've thought about the Bushmen. I've thought of the way they lived, the things they did, their social culture, and their material culture. Everything they owned except for a few beads and some pieces of wire for their arrowheads was made from things of the veldt — not many things, to be sure, but as many as anyone needs to live in reasonable comfort. No one really needs beads, for instance, but it's nice to have them, although not everyone did. So one day, as I began to write about these people for this book, I decided to compare their material culture with ours. I started with Di!ai, the woman I was named for, and remembered that she owned her front and back aprons, also her leather cape and the sinew string which served as a belt, also her digging stick, two or three empty ostrich eggshells in which the people carried water, the grass stoppers for those ostrich eggshells, her necklace of ostrich eggshell beads, perhaps four or five hair ornaments (actually, Di!ai gave her ornaments to someone else, but let's say she still had them), also a pair of leather sandals, and a tortoise shell in which she carried a sweet-smelling powder. If you count the sandals as one item, her possessions added up to nineteen items. This was entirely typical, as any woman might have a similar number of objects. Another woman did not have a tortoise shell but had a special string to tie around her waist. As I noted in my journal, *the string was to wind around her waist when she was very hungry to ward off the hunger or to kind of anesthetize it.*

As for a man, he would own his leather loincloth, a leather bag, perhaps a leather cape for warmth, perhaps a pair of sandals, also a quiver, perhaps eight or nine arrows, a knife, a spear, perhaps a digging stick, and a pair of fire sticks. He might also own a necklace or some other ornament, although many men did not. But let's say he did. That's also nineteen items, or twenty if you count the fire sticks separately. One man who happened not to have a necklace had an unusual object: *a thing which I have never seen before or since, like a fungus or a honeycomb, which he used, he said, when he was hunting. If birds saw him and made a noise he would bite off a piece which he would chew but not swallow, and would spit it at the birds to silence them.* All in all, you could almost hold the worldly goods of one of these people in your two hands.

Interestingly, although I own plenty of clothes, I wear about the same number as would a Ju/wa women — underpants, bra, jeans, shirt, sandals, belt, wristwatch, glasses. It's the rest of the stuff that's different. At the time of this writing I have nineteen items just on my desk, including a computer, a monitor, a printer, a keyboard, a mousepad, a rectangular plastic box which I turn upside down to cover my keyboard so my cats don't walk on the keys, also a telephone, a telephone book, a lamp, an empty cat food can that serves as an ashtray, a pen, an ordinary pencil, a red pencil, a pencil sharpener, a letter opener, a notepad, a box of Kleenex, a thesaurus, and a dictionary. The extension of my desk — just the surface — has one hundred and fifty-four items, not counting all the pens and pencils, just counting their containers, but counting a file holder and twenty-three files. The rest of my office has twenty-one pieces of furniture or other large objects, such as a wood stove, a fire extinguisher, a cat tower, and six filing cabinets (never mind the files inside). My office also has twenty-four bookshelves, each one filled with books. On just one of those shelves there are ninety-two books and three pamphlets. So far I've mentioned three hundred and ten items, but with the rest of the books, the contents of the filing cabinets, the contents of the desk drawers as well as two deer antlers, one moose antler, three mobiles, an empty birdcage, and a cat-sized radio collar which I sometimes use to follow the doings of my cats, I have literally hundreds more.

And that's just my office. To list everything in the house, garden shed, and toolshed is beyond my powers, to say nothing of the garage with two cars and all that's inside them. In my sewing basket alone there are thirty-nine items — spools of thread, scissors, sewing needles, a tape measure, a small, sharp gizmo with which to open a seam, and a rotating gizmo with which to cut a big piece of cloth laid flat. That sewing basket has twice as many items as the average Ju/wa of the Old Way. No doubt my house, or for that matter anybody's house, has more items than all of those owned by the entire Ju/wa population of the 1950s in the six thousand square miles of Nyae Nyae. Interestingly, we can name every single one of those items, and most of them we don't need.

What the Ju/wasi needed, and had in large quantities, was accurate knowledge—not just general knowledge but thousands if not millions of specific facts. So here's another contrast—the contrast between our knowledge of the natural world around us and the Bushmen's knowledge of the natural world around them. In our case, that would be the trees and bushes that we see from our windows and whatever else is alive out there, most of which we can't name and don't understand. We might say that a certain tree is an oak, but that's not the same as saying that the microwave is an Amana Touchmatic Radarange or the car is a 2001 Subaru Forester with 186,000 miles on it. We know our possessions much better. But for every natural feature we could name, the Bushmen could have named fifty.

One night I was watching a television program when the host of the show (maybe Jay Leno) asked a woman which was bigger, the moon or an elephant. Yes, she said the elephant, but if you think that's bad, try asking a few college students where the sun rises. Many of them won't know even that. The Bushmen, in contrast, could name hundreds of plants and tell you their properties and who ate them. They also knew every amphibian, reptile, bird, or mammal they encountered, also most of the arachnids, insects, and other invertebrates, knowing not only the animals themselves but also their tracks and their habits. To this day, I can't help but compare the ten- and twelve-year-old Bushmen children to my adult self in my own woods, where perhaps I know the mammals well enough, but certainly not all the insects, fungi, and plants. And I think of myself as some kind of naturalist. So rather than listing all the things in the environment that the Bushmen knew, it's easier to say that there was virtually nothing that they didn't know.

None of us would be on earth today if our Bushman ancestors did not have that kind of knowledge, and I think I had a glimpse of how they got it.

Today I noticed the attention to the tiny paid by the Bushmen. One woman was given a handful of tobacco which she seemed to reckon by the grain rather than by the handful or pipe full, and when two shreds of tobacco dropped into the sand she picked them out and lifted the sand grains away from them and put them in a tiny bag with the rest of the tobacco, then picked all the tiny shreds and grains that clung to her palm and put them in the bag too.

Other people tend to pay attention to the big things, and might see the tobacco as one handful rather than as a collection of grains. But it's the sum of all the tiny things that informs you, and the Bushmen knew that. How else would they have found their arrow poison?

Such knowledge is essential for all who live in the Old Way. Chimpanzees, for instance, have been called excellent botanists by the primatologists. According to a bear biologist, bears are excellent botanists too. Bears not only recognize a plant when the edible berries are on it, but also when it's sprouting (the bear comes back for the berries later) or when it's dry and brown in the fall. The fact is, we have very little concept of the knowledge of those who live in the Old Way, especially the nonhumans, and we tend to attribute such knowledge to "instinct," as if they didn't learn. We also belittle this kind of knowledge because, as my friend Sy Montgomery has pointed out, it's for animals and "primitive" people, and we, the advanced, modern people, have outsourced our knowledge to our electronic devices and the Internet. But if our ancestors hadn't had trustworthy knowledge in their heads we wouldn't be alive today to scoff at them.

I'd say that virtually everything the Bushmen did, including their social stability, was geared for survival. Their kinship system, which is unlike any other but which my mother managed to fathom, is vastly more complex than our rather simple kinship system (which at the time was called the Copper Eskimo system). Many westerners don't understand this. In later years, for example, a western visitor to Nyae Nyae asked the anthropologist Megan Biesele how the Bushmen managed to avoid incest. I don't think I've ever heard a more stupid question. The answer is simple. They don't fuck their relatives. But Megan is too classy to have said that. In fact, the incest taboos of the Ju/wasi are stricter than ours and probably always have been. DNA studies show more genetic diversity among these former hunter-gatherers than in any other human population. This fact alone would have aided their survival.

In addition to the unification arising from kinship and marriage, the

Ju/wasi were further unified by a system called *xaro,* for which I'd say there's no translation. As the anthropologist Polly Wiessner discovered, it's the practice of giving gifts. Almost everybody had one or more gift partners whom they would visit, sometimes traveling great distances to do so. That's how the cowrie shells—my mother's gift to the Gautscha women—spread through the length and breadth of Nyae Nyae in just one year. People gave them to other people, who in turn passed them along. And why was gift-giving so important? Nyae Nyae provided a good example, because it had only eight permanent water sources. If, in the dry season, people were living at a water source that failed, they would need to travel to another, which would already be occupied by other people. Whoever needed to go there would want to be welcomed, and the strong ties of kinship and of gift partnerships helped to assure a welcome.

Survival of the individual mattered enormously, of course, but so did the survival of the group. Without the group, our species would have vanished long ago. In the interests of group cohesion, all important foods were shared. Women were equal to men, although there was a division of labor in that women did most of the gathering but didn't hunt. Important decisions were always made by consensus arising from discussions in which every adult who wanted to took part. To keep survival as a goal wasn't always easy—the tracking part of a hunt could take many days during which the hunters might go without food or water—and a woman giving birth to a second child too soon after the birth of her first child might have to dispose of the newborn, as her milk would support only one child and her choice would be to lose both infants or just one. This happened extremely rarely, but it could and did happen, and it wasn't any easier for the Bushman women than it would be for us.

For a sense of what survival meant, I remember a note I made about the hot season:

The women go gathering just as soon as it is light enough to see, and they come back by 9:00 AM and bury themselves [in the sand] and stay until 4 or 5 when it's cooler, and thus do they survive the waterless, scorching drought.

The people at Gautscha had water. They drank from the water hole by day and filled their ostrich eggshells in case they got thirsty at night, because a pride of about twenty lionesses and a lion lived nearby and at night would drink from the same water hole. So did a leopard and three or four brown hyenas. Sometimes at night I would drive the Dodge Power Wagon down to the water hole and watch to see who came there, as I was fascinated by the wildlife. Most of the predators had an equal interest in us, especially the lions, who sometimes would come to our encampments to see what we were doing. I remember being in my tent, falling asleep, when I heard the loud voices of the Ju/wa men speaking strongly. The people didn't use that tone with one another, so I went out of the tent to see what was going on.

Four lionesses were standing on tiptoes at the edge of the Ju/wa en-campment, looking over the tops of the shelters at the men. The men spoke respectfully to the lionesses, but told them that they had to leave. One man reached behind himself to grasp a burning branch that some-one was handing him, then flourished the branch over his head. Sparks flew. Perhaps the lionesses knew about burns, because they seemed to be thinking things over. They turned their heads, then soon turned sideways and walked off quietly into the night.

This was, we were to learn, characteristic of the Nyae Nyae lions. They did not hunt people, and nobody really knows why. If those lions had meant to hunt, not just to observe, they probably would have suc-ceeded.

Once when we were traveling, we were very tired when night came so we didn't make a camp. We just put our sleeping bags on the ground. In the morning we found the tracks of lions all around us. They had even looked down into our faces. I was glad not to have opened my eyes to look up into the nostrils of a lion. But this, we were to learn, was normal lion behavior. The Ju/wasi didn't hunt them, of course, which seemed to have something to do with the situation. As one Ju/wa man told us, if people hunted lions, as did the pastoralists who lived at the edges of the Kalahari, the lions would hunt people, but if people left them alone, they wouldn't.

As for me, I've come to think of the arrangement as a truce. The people and the lions both lived in groups, using the same water and hunting the same game, so there was a similarity, but the people went about in the daytime and the lions went about at night. Surely they had coexisted for thousands of years, which, I think, could have been due to these similarities, especially because these two groups of high-end predators needed to use the same water. The people who owned the water could have gone to live with relatives if the lions had raided them, but they'd live there as guests, not as owners. And the lions would have had nowhere else to go. In that pristine, Paleolithic wilderness, every source of water would be owned by a different pride of lions. Either the refugee lions would drive off the resident lions or they would be driven off themselves, to the tune of much injury, which would compromise their survival. Without the human-lion truce, both populations would have been at risk. Better that the people and the lions used the area at different times of day. That way, they could hunt the same animals and drink the same water without risking injury or death by making problems for each other. People from agricultural or industrial cultures would feel the need to kill the lions, but that wasn't the Old Way.

The truce did not apply to leopards or hyenas. Not that people hunted them, but they hunted people. However, it was easier to discourage them than it would be to discourage lions. One night a hyena put his head into the open door of my tent. Hyenas sometimes took bites out of sleeping people, so perhaps he wanted to learn if I was sleeping. I wasn't. Our noses almost touched. We looked into each other's eyes. I asked, "What is it?" The hyena turned his head and withdrew politely.

Such restraint didn't always work, however, as several people had been killed by hyenas. In the instance I knew most about, this happened when people were traveling and the man who was killed was unable to keep up with the group. His was an unusual situation, as by the time this happened he had no relatives, no one tied to him, no one who cared about him. He was the only person we knew who had never married — this was because he had never successfully hunted, which was a prerequisite for marriage — thus he had no in-laws. His elderly sister had looked after him, but she had died. They had been living with her husband's people, and when those people decided to travel to another place, he followed them. But when night came, he had dropped behind, and the others didn't go back to find him. The event was exceedingly rare, and was one of the many reasons that the Ju/wasi took such care to be cohesive.

Strangely enough, a tent, like a Ju/wa shelter, was good protection, not that a predator couldn't tear through the fabric. But for some reason they didn't. Perhaps by watching from afar how people went in and out, my hyena used the front flap and thus exposed himself to view.

I loved my tent — a little one-man tent made for a backpacker. Not only did it protect me from the prowling hyena, but to be inside it was beautiful.

I was thinking that after you have lived in a tent and slept in a tent for night after night, a house seems as solid and dark as a cavern, part of another world. A tent is loose and waves about you, sifting in to you through pale green fabric the light of the sun and the moon. A tent is many things in one — a shelter from the cold night wind and from the rain which when it falls you can see the drops through the fabric, letting in shining light like drops of liquid on ground glass. A tent is a shade from the sun or a place that catches the early morning sunlight and warms the air inside like an oven. In a tent you can rig up the door-piece so that it forms a little porch for you, a shade for your door. When you wake up in the morning you see the sunlight shining in the tree roots right under your nose because you sleep on the ground, or you look up at the sky through the doorway and see the stars, or the sun rising right behind the sliver of the waning moon, and smell the first wind that lifts before dawn, which blows right over you. A house has its own individual smells and sighs and noises, like a creature, and is a world within a world, stubbornly standing up to the sun and the rain with its outside walls like a barricade so that inside the climate is always the same, the ideal of the owners. But a tent is hot at noon and cold at night, bright by sunlight and pale in the moonlight, wet when the rain falls and sighing, blowing, moving backwards and forwards with the wind.

Because you sleep on the ground you can hear things that walk past in the nighttime. The grass moves and if the creature is big enough you hear the footfalls like those of the lions who came the other night. This you never get in a thick, walled house. I've slept in a Bushman grass shelter and a Herero rondavel and they're pretty good too, but I'll take a tent any time.

My tent is only a disheveled, dilapidated old thing, worn thin by wind and sun and rain, but such is the sensation of living in it.

As I remember the Kalahari, I believe I loved every moment of my sojourn there. This can't be true, of course, but it's a pleasant trick of memory. I saw things I'd never seen before and did things I'd never done before, many of which I recorded. For instance:

We went down on the flats to inspect the damage of the wildfire. Our camp is in a grove that didn't happen to burn but the land below is in utter deso-lation, only the orange sand and black ashes still in the shape of the grass that made them, with here and there the black ashes of leaves fallen off the bushes, or still on their vines, just in the shape of the leaves that made them but black and disintegrating into a pinch of dust when you touch them. And all around are the smoldering great carcasses of fallen trees, burned around the base but the leaves at the tops are still green and the air is filled with the smell of wood burning, and the ground is warm to walk on. And all the little succulents and all the vines that show the water-roots and all the tsama melons are burned, and no snake or lizard is here, all have been burned or gone. We saw two greater kori bustards [large, grassland birds] walking, white against the blackened ground. As you walk, black powder rises. My legs are dusted with black up to the knee. But Ukwane, walking along, saw a nest of edible ants — small heaps, brown, exposed because the grass has burned — and he ate some. As he did, the soldier ants swarmed all over him and bit him but he brushed them off.

I ate one too — a bite from the abdomen. You can only eat the large-headed soldier ants. The workers, I am told, are tasteless. But the soldiers taste sour and very watery, very like a blackberry a little on the green side, almost refreshing. Mine opened his jaws wide to fight my thumb before I ate him.

Perhaps my favorite memory is of a trance dance. These dances took place at night, and their purpose was usually to exorcise something called "star sickness," which would often manifest itself as jealousy and other emotions that cause divisions among people, thus compromising every-one's survival. The songs that people danced to were given to them in dreams, and were meant not to influence any natural feature but to use its power. The rain dance, for example, was meant not to bring rain but to use the power of rain when people could feel it coming. Thus it was the powers of the natural world—the powers of giraffes, elands, rain, the sun, and other features—that united the people, bringing them together by dissolving emotional complexities that threatened to divide them. The strongest power, I believe, was that of the sun. A dance was supposed to start soon after dark and last until sunrise. When the sun's first flames appeared, the people would use its power and dance the sun dance. Then they'd stop, seemingly relieved and quite happy, and would go back to their shelters to rest for a while.

A dance almost always took place on the night of a full moon. If the people felt they needed to dance, the men would ask the women to start a dance fire. The women would lay a fire at a distance from the encampment, and when night came, they would light the fire, sit in a circle around it, and begin to sing. The men would join them, to dance in line around the fire, and soon enough some of the men would fall into a trance. In that trance they encountered the spirits of the dead, who were drawn to a dance fire, and also lions (perhaps also drawn to a dance fire, at least to see what was going on), as both kinds of creatures are dangerous. The trancing men would run out into the dark, cursing the spirits and the lions and demanding that they go away. The trancing men would also pull star sickness from the women and from one another and would scream it up to the sky, sending it back to the spirits who brought it. I included the following description in the second book I wrote about the Bushmen, *The Old Way*.

I remember the first dance that took place after we came, and how I sat in the circle of women at their invitation, not knowing the wordless song, which was complex and had nothing in common with music I knew, and I remember how I was able to keep time by clapping one line of the rhythm, trying to copy the woman next to me. I still remember how it felt when one of the trancing men, with a touch as light as a bird's wing, put his trembling hands on my chest and shoulder, and with his head beside mine pulled in his breath with long, slow groans, then suddenly leaped back and shrieked at the sky, then, almost staggering, moved on to the next woman. He had taken something out of me and thrown it into the night. At the time, such trance dancing was not known to the Western world, and I had no idea what he was doing or what I should do. So I did what the women on either side of me were doing, and continued clapping. By then, other trancing men were leaning over other women in the circle, over the children squeezed in beside their mothers, over the little babies in their mothers' capes, pulling something out of us, screaming it up to the sky.

In time, I came to understand what had been happening, what most of it meant, and I would later sit in the circle of women at many other dances, but I will never forget that first one — the dancers between the fire and the moon, the voice of the healer in my ear, the heat of his face against mine with strange, loud singing all around us. To have been part of that, that's something to remember now that I am among the last of those people to be left alive, after everything has changed.[1]

My parents and brother returned many times to Gautscha, and my brother devoted his life to the people there. I accompanied three of their expeditions, once staying for a year. To be in the Kalahari was surely the most important experience of my life—but it wasn't perfect. My wonderful parents, however loving, however understanding, were products of their time and culture when it came to gender issues. They believed that men were meant to do the important things and women were meant to help them. Women should involve themselves with home and children. Thus I doubt that my unassuming mom saw her own work as being of great magnitude.

This wasn't true—her findings proved to be very important—but as she saw it, it was the Ju/wasi who had great magnitude, not her. So she saw her work as useful. She was simply doing her absolute best to produce a complete and accurate record, which was what my dad had wanted her to do. His role, in contrast, was to get us in to that vast wilderness, to keep us safe while we stayed, and to get us out of there without getting lost, with enough to eat, and with enough water, gasoline, and auto parts to accomplish the mission. When he wasn't attending to these necessities, he mapped the area and took still photographs of just about everything the Ju/wasi had or did.

My brother made films. Our dad had provided him with all kinds of cameras, film, and recording equipment. In contrast, he provided me with nothing. This was not because he preferred my brother, but simply because I was female. My brother went hunting with the men and saw all kinds of wildlife in which he had no interest except as game. I couldn't go hunting. Women could have nothing to do with hunting. They couldn't even touch the bows and arrows. I could accept that, because the last thing I wanted to do was to render a hunt unsuccessful.

What I really wanted to do was to observe the wildlife. But inquiry into wildlife was unknown in the world of anthropology. At the time, any work I might have done involving wildlife would have been seen as an irrelevant aside. So the tasks assigned to me were to help the camp manager, Philip, with camp problems, and also to assist my brother in making his films by helping with such things as the sound recordings. The entire last part of the journal I've been quoting consists of notes on what was happening when photographs were being taken, and my entries are numbered according to what action the camera had captured. For instance:

Black and white stills. Films and notes on child behavior. (1) Dabe Ma (Di!ai's baby) urinates in Di!ai's cape. She hands him to his grandmother and wipes out her cape with straw. (2) Dabe Ma sits with his grandmother. (3) Dabe Ma walks back to Di!ai by himself. (4) In a few minutes he sits on her lap and nurses. (5) Dabe Ma gives Gao Lame [the baby's teenage uncle] a piece of food which Gao pretends to eat then gives it back.

But even these small interactions could prove fascinating. For example, I learned how hyenas copulate because some of the Ju/wa boys performed a reenactment. The event went into my journal as a photo entry because my brother happened to be filming when the boys did this. Here's the entry:

≠Wi/abe was playing the giraffe and the hyena songs for sound sync [playing the songs on the string of a hunting bow, tapping the string with a stick, changing the note by pressing the string with a finger — no doubt the origin of the guitar and violin] *and in the middle of it he stopped, and he and /Giamakwe pretended to be two hyenas copulat-*

ing — a majestic imitation with snarls and growls, sniffing the female's behind, and so on. One boy started as the male and the other as the female, then they swapped, shivering with ecstasy, then more growls, until the male fell away, exhausted, and curled up on his side, whereupon the female attacked him. The play lasted for hours, it seemed. The boys seemed so literal that they probably imitated the copulation process exactly, taking the same amount of time to do it. Both boys were deadpan; neither was excited or laughing, although the boy who was the male pretended to use his penis. They did this again and again and with growls and all, and it sounded exactly like 2 hyenas who were heard copulating outside of camp a few nights ago — and that went on for hours. A curious thing — when the kids acted it out, the female bucked the male off by raising her hindquarters and letting the male slip down over her head.

Being a girl, I was also assigned to learn as much as I could about the women and children — this being a suitable female province — which I did by going on gathering trips with the women and helping out by sometimes carrying the children whom the women brought along. My mom meticulously recorded the names of all the plants the women gathered. She produced quantities of notes such as the following, which I have chosen at random from her lengthy list.

> 23. **tshũ** *Wallerina nutans* Kirk. A small plant with grasslike leaves has a firm round storage organ about the size of a golf ball which grows near the surface of the ground; gathered by Band 1 in the direction of Gura and in the vicinity of Nama Pan.
> 24. **/dobi** **unidentified. A climbing vine; a fibrous watery underground storage organ, resembles a large turnip in size and shape, has rough-looking but thin brown skin; grows elbow-deep and deeper. The tubers become woody and bitter when old and are thrown away; cooked like n≠wara (#21), split on top of coals. An important food during the dry season in the Gautscha vicinity.[2]

A more comprehensive account of plants used by the Ju/wasi has never been made. And while my mom was doing this, I was out in the veldt experiencing how these plants were collected.

I'm glad I went. There's more to the cultural implications of gender than one might think. In some cultures, women with their menstruation and sexual allure pollute the world of men and are suppressed for that reason. Not so in Ju/wa culture, where women were the equals of men in every way that mattered—substantially more so than in our culture. But they were barred from hunting, also from contact with men right before a hunt, and also while menstruating or giving birth. I have come to think that this was not because of a polluting factor or a weakness, but because of female power. Hunting was by far the most significant male activity, requiring not only great skill but also training, experience, and voluminous knowledge. Yet a woman—with no instruction, no relevant skill or training, no former experience of any kind—can make another human being. Thus female power was the antithesis of male power, and because it was so prevalent and so strong, it could overwhelm a hunt. Best to keep the two powers separate. Best to go on gathering trips. Best not to interfere with male power.

The gathering trips that I accompanied were neither easy nor exciting—at least I hoped they wouldn't be exciting, as excitement could mean encountering a cobra or even a lion—but they were fully as interesting as hunting, or so I soon discovered.

Perhaps five women, or six counting me, would go together on a gathering trip. I usually went with two sisters—Di!ai, the woman I was named for, and her younger sister, !U. They almost always went gathering together. With them went their children—Di!ai's two little boys and her ten-year-old daughter from an earlier marriage, and !U's five-year-old son and nursing baby. Her ten-year-old son, old enough to get along without his mom, stayed home. With the two sisters came their first cousins—//Kushe, the woman who brought us to Gautscha, and her older, widowed sister, !Ungka. //Kushe would bring her little boy.

Speaking of female power, these four women and their much younger brother were the owners of Gautscha. Their parents were a brother and sister who had owned Gautscha earlier—a lineage that may have reached far back in time. The husbands of these women lived there at their pleasure.

On a gathering trip, each woman would take an ostrich eggshell full of water. I didn't have an ostrich eggshell and was seldom foresighted enough to take a jar of water, so I often went thirsty. Each woman would take her digging stick, made from a straight hardwood branch about three feet long and pointed at the tip. I once took a shovel to help with the digging, but the shovel was heavy and awkward and I never took it again. Instead, I'd borrow a digging stick and take turns with its owner, usually Di!ai, who had a sore shoulder and welcomed the rest.

We would leave the encampment at midmorning. Why so late? Because by then the predators would have finished their night's hunting and would be sleeping in the shade. Night was for the predators. People used the day. So we'd wait until the day was warm enough to make the predators sleepy, then we'd walk for several miles, passing berry bushes on the way. We would chase off the birds who were eating the berries and pick them ourselves. We would also come upon vines with tsama melons — the little green African melons that are the ancestors of all squashes and melons (and to which all squashes and melons revert if left to pollinate themselves) — and we would pick them too. If I picked berries or melons I'd give them to someone else because our group had our own food — we didn't want to compete for the people's resources. I'd eat a few berries only if someone gave them to me. Then we'd keep walking.

The anthropologist Richard Lee, who in later years also studied the Bushmen, reported that a Ju/wa woman walked about 1,500 miles a year. I'm sure that's true, but I didn't know it at the time. I only knew that we spent lots of time walking, usually most of the morning. Then we'd come to a place where certain kinds of tubers grew, and the women would sit on their heels and start to dig.

So much for wandering aimlessly over the veldt in search of food, as the Bushmen were assumed to do. Those women knew precisely where those tubers were growing. They knew the place because they'd been there before, or perhaps because earlier in the year some of them had seen the stalks or vines of the tubers in passing and knew just what they'd find when they went back later. They shared the information, of course — the Ju/wasi shared everything — but no one would dig the tubers without permission from the people who found them. What would those people think if they came later only to find the food gone? To dig the roots without permission would be theft, and at the time the Ju/wasi didn't even have a word for theft. (How different from us, with our lexicon that runs from *pilfer* and *swipe* to *armed robbery* and *grand larceny*.)

At first I had no idea how the women knew where to dig, because I'd see nothing that showed the presence of anything below the surface. But Di!ai took it upon her generous self to teach me, and if I asked, she'd show me a little pinch of withered vine mixed with all kinds of other little stalks and grass blades — something I would not have noticed. It was, of course, the remnant of the vine put up by the root she had been looking for. To appreciate what kind of observation was required to notice from a distance a tiny shred of plant material down in mixed, dry grass, I'd say you had to be there.

Di!ai would then dig for a while, scooping up the loose dirt with her hand, until she'd gone down about eighteen inches. I wouldn't see anything in the hole except dirt. Di!ai would rest for a moment, and then go on digging. When she had dug down about two feet, removing an astonishing amount of dirt, we might see something brown, perhaps a little darker than the dirt, which would be the top of the tuber. She might chop out a small piece of the tuber and taste it to see if it was too old and bitter to eat (see my mother's note on 24. /*dobi*) and therefore not worth doing the work to remove it. If it was bitter and too old, she'd spit out the bite, sigh, stand up, and move on to another place to start digging again. But if the root seemed good, she'd expose it, pull it up, brush off the dirt, and put it in the pouch of her cape. Then she'd go on to another tuber.

By midafternoon the women would be far apart. Now and then they'd call to each other. A pure, high woman's voice breaking the otherwise perfect silence was a surprising sound. A little later, when the sun was looking down at the western horizon, they'd think about going home. They would collect their children. They'd put the tubers in the pouches of their capes. They'd fish out their ostrich eggshells and drink a little water. Then they'd start walking, all in single file, almost never talking, often stopping along the way to gather firewood, which increased the weight of their loads until their knees were all but bending. It was at this time that I could be helpful. I could carry a child or a load of firewood.

Perhaps digging tubers or picking berries wasn't as exciting as hunting, and perhaps I was a bit disappointed with my role at first. But looking back, I'm content to have done what I did. I learned a great deal about edible plants, thanks to Di!ai, her sister, and their cousins. I also learned about the single most significant aspect of living in the Old Way for our species, because for millions of years, vegetable foods were the mainstay of our primate diet, with a tasty ant or the odd dead animal as an occasional treat. To know this was compelling. I came to the conclusion that the Neolithic was a really bad idea. If I were Gaia, I'd go back in time to find the *Homo erectus* people and make them get back in the trees. As a species, we did best as hunter-gatherers.

After my third and last long-term stay with the Ju/wasi, I wrote *The Harmless People,* a travel book which, however naive, was my first significant literary effort as a full-fledged grownup. But before that, I got married.

6

STEVE

HIS NAME WAS STEVE. He was a friend of my brother. He was also the boyfriend who had earned me the name of Kothonjoro. At the time of this writing, we've been married for over fifty years. We met during our sophomore year in college, after my family's first trip to the Kalahari, when I was at Smith and Steve and my brother were at Harvard. But after that we were together because my parents wanted me to take courses in anthropology and Smith didn't offer any, so for my junior year I transferred to Radcliffe. By then, though, Radcliffe was a college in name only, and all courses were offered at Harvard. I had loved Smith, so I transferred with some regret. But by then I also loved Steve.

I was smitten the first time I saw him. This took place one September evening in my parents' house in Cambridge, in the study where, years earlier, my brother and I had hidden behind the curtains watching the rescue of our imprisoned nanny.

Steve was there to visit my brother. I came down the front stairs wearing a red plaid dress with a full skirt that fell way below the knees, and a wide, shiny leather belt. For those too young to remember, this was called the New Look (by now a Dreary Old Look), but all of it except perhaps the plaid was stylish in the fifties. Normally I wore jeans, and I no longer remember why that day I was wearing a dress. I'm glad I did, though. Steve has never forgotten my descent of the stairs.

He was wearing jeans and a navy sweater. I was enormously attracted to him. This was unusual for me, as I had never before experienced love at first sight. I was even more attracted when I learned that he owned a motorcycle and also was a climber.

The latter resonated strongly with me, because up until that evening one of my most memorable experiences, the summer after I graduated from boarding school, had been climbing the Needle of M in the Alps with the help of a French guide. I'd gone to France with my mom for the chaperoned, precollege travel experience that back then was mandatory in my parents' socioeconomic circles. The Kalahari would have served the purpose, but not until a year later, and at the time we weren't sure that we were going.

So perhaps I was too hasty in saying that falling in love with Steve was my first such experience, because while clinging to the cliff that rose to the summit of the Needle, I looked down and saw an eagle flying far below. It was a large European eagle, I think a golden eagle, but from that distance it looked smaller than a wasp. At that moment I fell in love with everything — with the eagle, with the Alps, with the guide, with France, with climbing. Then I came off the cliff, dropped about thirty feet through thin air, and stopped with a jerk. I was roped, and the guide had caught me. I dangled below him, looking up. His eyes met mine, and his were critical — a fiery blue stare. I had not been paying attention, and if he had been equally careless he would have lost a client and damaged his reputation. I apologized. But I wasn't scared or even grateful. I was too happy.

Steve would know about things like that. In fact, on the very day we met, he had climbed the famous tower of Harvard's Memorial Hall. It may not have been a first ascent, as others had also tried it, but Steve's intention was to summit, which he did. The tower has since burned and was not rebuilt, so his triumph will never be repeated.

The campus police nabbed Steve when he came down and there was some trouble about it, but he didn't get expelled. On the contrary, he was invited to join the Harvard Mountaineering Club and some of its prestigious members for an ascent of Mount McKinley (now Denali). Steve felt honored. He joined the club but did not accept the Mount McKinley invitation, as his climbing experience had been limited to buildings and to such places as Cathedral Ledge in North Conway, New Hampshire, and the Shawangunks in New York State. This was serious climbing, to be sure, but it was rock climbing, not mountaineering. Neither he nor the people who invited him had coped with a whiteout blizzard, or detected a crevasse, or rescued someone who had fallen into a crevasse, or predicted an avalanche, or escaped a falling rock or serac—all of which could be expected on Denali.

Years later our son became an International Mountain Guide, the first American guide to work legally in France. He lived in Les Houches in the Chamonix Valley and worked mostly in the Alps, but he also climbed and guided in the Andes, the Rockies, the Himalayas, and other formidable mountains, including Denali. He could navigate in whiteout blizzards, predict avalanches, avoid crevasses, and rescue people who fell into them. When he learned that Steve had declined the invitation to join the Denali expedition, he commended his father's discretion very strongly.

At first my romance with Steve seemed star-crossed. One day I asked how old he was. He said he was eighteen. Gosh. I'd thought he was older. But after all, I was also eighteen—my nineteenth birthday was still a few weeks away—so it was hard to find fault with him for being the same age. But then I asked the date of his birthday, unaware of the disaster that would follow. He said he was born in July. Horrors! He was nine months younger than me. And we had been getting along so perfectly! But back then it wasn't possible to date a younger man. Sophisticated college women like myself did not acknowledge their existence. A relationship with Steve would be out of the question. But there I was, stuck with a powerful attraction to him.

Steve and I spent much time together, which was lucky for me as he was an exceptionally good student and he also knew which courses were easy—not that he took them. He just told me which ones they were and I took them. I found this helpful because, having so recently transferred to Radcliffe, I knew nothing about the Harvard courses. Nor was I in Steve's league as a student. So Steve served as my adviser. Perhaps I also had a faculty adviser, but no one told me, and I didn't know to ask, so I never met that person.

I learned that Steve led a fascinating life when not in college. He worked in the summers, at first on an oil rig in Texas, later laying the Transco gas pipeline, and later still constructing I-95. A veteran hitchhiker, he would hitch to the job site, work all summer, and hitch home in the fall with so much money that his father could no longer claim him as a dependent. This was in marked contrast to my other boyfriends, most of whom spent their summers at play on Martha's Vineyard or Nantucket — just what my dad had wanted me and my brother to avoid, and part of the reason he bought the land in New Hampshire.

Steve's experiences were enthralling — the enormous machines he had handled, the men he had met, the adventures! While laying the pipeline, for instance, angry men with shotguns stood nearby to be sure no worker set foot on their property. One of his tasks while laying the pipeline was to assist an Italian stonemason in rebuilding the stone walls that had been the property boundaries of the angry men and had been taken apart so the pipe could be put in the ground. The stonemason was so skilled that he had only to look at the pile of rocks to know which rock would fit, and he'd point to it. Steve would carry it to him; he would place the rock, then scan the pile again and point to another rock. The stone walls were rebuilt to perfection in no time at all, and the skill and artistry of this man is one of Steve's favorite memories.

My favorite of his memories was of his work on the oil rig. Steve worked the night shift, and by day slept in a still-warm bed vacated by a man who worked the day shift. The rig was near a river on a prairie that sloped gradually upward to the crest of a hill, but the noise of the rig was so loud that Steve would lose all sense of his surroundings, working as if in a cavern of noise. Sometimes the machine would stop suddenly and there'd be silence. Steve would need a moment to remember where he was. Then he'd see the prairie drenched in moonlight. One morning the rig stopped just as the first dawn light appeared. A group of pronghorn antelopes came up from the river and went over the crest of the hill.

That story was enough for me. I wanted to go with him. Girls couldn't do things like that back then, for fear that their adventures would compromise their virginal reputations, so I planned to cut off my hair and dress as a boy. I never got to do this, which is one of my regrets. But I did ride with Steve on the motorcycle he purchased with his summer earnings, on which we went everywhere, the noise in our ears, the wind in our faces. That made me very happy.

Steve also was funny. I fancied myself as the queen of comedy, but he was twice as funny. His humor had a brainy quality that I couldn't resist. Once some of us were playing "I want to be an animal" and coming up with such choices as horse and panda. Steve said he'd be a sessile benthic organism. And what might that be? It might be a tubeworm stuck to a rock at the bottom of the sea, far away from silly games and ill-equipped to play them.

And then there was the first time he asked me for a date. Dressed not in his usual jeans and sweater but in a necktie and an ill-fitting, second-hand tan suit which he might have obtained from the Salvation Army just for the occasion, he came to our house and rang the doorbell. When we opened the door, he seemed unsure, and as if to escape a suddenly daunting situation, he shinnied up a post that supported the porch roof. He wanted us to know that he was respectful and would take nothing for granted. My mother thought his behavior was strange, but I was enchanted. Even though he was nine months too young, I thought he was wonderful.

Not so my parents. They had liked him well enough as a friend of my brother, but they didn't like him as a friend of mine. They had no notion of his star-studded academic record, and everything they did know about him, such as his motorcycle and his scofflaw attitude regarding the Memorial Hall tower, went against their grain. They didn't think anyone should climb cliffs and mountains, at least not without a responsible, professional guide, and as for the tower, they didn't want to believe that anyone, not even he, would do anything so pointless. He did it, of course, for the same reason that Hillary climbed Mount Everest—because it was there—but to my parents this was not a good reason. They kept pushing me toward some of my other suitors, all nice young men who planned to be businessmen or other professionals and who never did things that seemed unusual. I liked these young men too, but Steve wowed me. My parents sensed this. Once when Steve came to our house to get me, my dad shut the door in his face.

Steve's parents didn't like me either. They lived in New Canaan, Connecticut. Steve's father was an executive of a pharmaceutical company and he commuted by train to New York. Steve's mother, every inch a lady, was a homemaker and a deaconess at the Congregational church. She traced her ancestry to Priscilla Alden on the *Mayflower* (yes, Priscilla Alden, not John Alden, perhaps as a rebellious stab at feminism), and she embraced the social values of country-club Connecticut. She was horrified that Steve was interested in someone like me — someone who cursed freely, wore jeans, never went to church, and scoffed at the debutantes she kept trailing in front of him, hoping he'd choose one of them instead of me.

The subculture of my parents and Cambridge did not include debutantes or "coming out," which in those days had nothing to do with sexual preference but was a party given by a girl's parents to announce her entrance into adult society and her readiness for marriage. My parents would have nothing to do with such a thing. To them, I think, a coming-out party was nothing but an upscale form of pimping. I didn't like the idea either. Why would I want to parade myself around so that strangers would know I was marriageable? How disgusting. Steve knew I was marriageable, and that was all that mattered.

Steve's mother once described in roseate terms the party of a girl who came out and asked if I had done the same. She knew perfectly well that I hadn't, but she didn't know why, and she hoped to force me to admit my failure, proving that I was of less value than the girl she had described. She all but sneered, anticipating her triumph.

I would rather have lost an arm than be a debutante, and loftily told her that while that girl was prancing around at her party, I was driving an army six-by-six through the Okavango Swamp. To me, a debutante was a moron in a prom dress. To my future mother-in-law, a swamp was unclean mud, especially if it was in Africa, and I was nothing but a tomboy in an army truck. We turned up our noses at each other.

Many years later, when she was a widow in her eighties, she told me how much she had hated me. By then I was older and wiser and wondered if she had more in mind than just the jeans and bad language. I wondered if her hatred had to do with the difference between her early choices and those that I seemed to be making. She was extremely intelligent — her IQ, which Steve inherited, was astronomical — and although many women of her generation did not go to college, she went to Smith and majored in geology. There she achieved such high academic standing that at the end of her senior year she was invited to join the Smith faculty immediately, to teach geology.

She didn't accept. Why not is unclear, except that brilliance and scientific excellence were not much valued in women back then except by other brilliant, scientific women such as those who taught at Smith. Believe it or not, to marry a successful man and keep house for him was generally seen as a higher calling, certainly in top-drawer Connecticut. So instead of having a career, Steve's mother did what was expected of women of her upbringing. She got married, wore a mink coat, drove a Cadillac, belonged to an exclusive country club, and had a maid and a manservant. These people were African Americans. I don't know what she told them to call her, but she told them to call Steve "Master Steve." Perhaps they did when she was present. They didn't when she wasn't, though. Instead, they befriended Steve, and the man taught him how to throw a knife.

Steve's mother was a product of her time and culture, with no outlet for her intelligence and high standards except her house. Every stick of her furniture sparkled with polish; every closet, drawer, and cupboard was organized to perfection. But the perfection didn't make her happy. I was not nearly as intelligent, but my opportunities were different, hence my choices were too, as I unfailingly pointed out when visiting her. I didn't know what I'd do with my life, but I knew I'd do more than get married. Thus, to my way of thinking, I would be a better match for her truly brilliant son than some of those airhead debutantes she kept talking about. I even scoffed at her ambitions for Steve — she wanted him to be a stockbroker. How horrifying her picture of me as a stockbroker's wife must have been: smoking cigarettes, stomping around in boots and jeans, telling his clients to fuck off. How could she not hate me?

When she pointed that out, we were in my car, on our way from a retirement community in New Jersey where, as a widow, she had been alone and unhappy, to an apartment in a retirement home very near our house in New Hampshire, where she would live from then on. I had been driving to New Jersey once a week to visit her, and knew that she was lonely and that her alleged caretakers not only were neglecting her but also were stealing her things. In her new apartment, she would have better care and we could be together. At that point in her life she was very fragile and her voice was weak. In the car, I could barely hear her. It took me a moment to realize she was asking why I was doing all this for her, considering her former negative feelings about me. I said it was because we loved her and she was Steve's mother. Whatever she might have felt long ago didn't matter, and anyway, I hadn't known what she thought because she had hidden her feelings.

But that last part wasn't true. She didn't even try to hide her feelings. And that was why, when Steve and I decided to get married, we kept it to ourselves.

We graduated on the same day but didn't attend the ceremony because we thought it would be boring. Before graduation, we both were called upon by the deans of our respective colleges to discuss our futures. Steve had excelled in all his courses, and had been urged by the professor of Anglo-Saxon studies to apply to the Harvard graduate school in that field. But the Korean War was in progress, and Steve was about to be drafted. He couldn't accept the offer, nor would he have done in peacetime. Somehow, in addition to Anglo-Saxon, he had managed to learn French, German, and Russian. His real interest was in the history of Russia and Central Europe, even though, because of the Cold War and the Iron Curtain, he had little chance of working there. His future remained unclear.

Mine did too. Rather than following my inclinations and majoring in biology, I had reluctantly majored in English, which in those days meant English literature, because my parents wanted me to. I never asked myself where it might lead, except that it would make my parents happy. And why was that? Even in Cambridge in those days, a woman was expected to prepare herself to be a perfect wife, able to talk winningly at cocktail parties about poetry, music, and art and thus enhance her husband. She would not enhance him if she talked about snakes, rodents, and bacteria. So I did what my parents wanted of me. After all, they had my best interests at heart. But the lure of biology was hard to shake. I spent class time looking out the window at the squirrels in Harvard Yard, and on the day the professor discussed the umpteenth verse of Spenser's *The Fairie*

Queene, a poem of 15,000 words in over 200 verses, very few of which I'd read, I realized I could recognize most of the squirrels as individuals. That would have been a huge advantage had I been studying squirrel behavior, but it didn't help on the exam, although I somehow managed to pass, and anyway, unknown to my parents, I was going to marry Steve, who didn't need enhancing.

The squirrel-watching didn't help my grades, of course, so I was merely an average student, never expecting an A, glad enough for a B or a C. But thanks to majoring in English, I could take writing courses for credit. I was pretty good at writing and was accepted into the prestigious courses, and the grades I got in them raised my cumulative average to a respectable level. In my junior year, a writing teacher suggested that I enter a fiction contest sponsored by the now defunct girls' magazine *Mademoiselle.* So I did, with a story about a Herero woman in Angola. Exotic subject matter always helps. That year, two of us won the contest, me and Sylvia Plath. Good things came from this, not the least of which was my career. But I had no idea what that might be until I met the dean of Radcliffe for the obligatory senior interview.

My mom came with me, I'm not sure why. Maybe she wanted to protect me from the dean, or maybe she also wanted to know my plans. Maybe she hoped I had some. Alas, I did not. I felt that my biology dreams would never come true, and I lacked enthusiasm for a substitute. It was only when the dean asked what I would do after college that I suddenly realized I was expected to know. So with only one real skill at my disposal, I made a quick decision and said, "I guess I'll be a writer."

The dean was infuriated. "You *guess* you'll be writer?" she cried. "Have you any *idea,* any *notion at all,* of what it *takes* to be a writer?" She must have seen my grades. But then came one of the best moments of my life.

"Well," I said, "last year I was cowinner of the *Mademoiselle* College Fiction contest, the story was published in *Best American Short Stories,* and I have a book contract with Knopf. My agent thinks I could be a writer."

The dean almost exploded. I believe it was the word *agent* that did it. This underachieving student in front of her, this nobody wearing jeans and sneakers without socks, had an agent! My mom, who already knew all this, of course, never changed her congenial expression, but the dean turned bright red. "Why didn't anyone tell me?" she shouted.

Ordinarily, I would have felt guilty. I didn't know I was supposed to tell her. But I didn't feel guilty. In fact, my sense of triumph at that moment was so great that it became another memory to cherish. So, rather than abandoning my dreams, I joined the American Society of Mammalogists, did a little reading, did a little fieldwork, made some observations, and wrote about animals. I wrote about people too, but only about those of different cultures who were involved with the natural world. You could say I devoted my professional life to the Old Way—partly as a rebellion against people like my dean. But I think it may have been my calling ever since my father took me for walks in the woods.

7

MARRIAGE

I MARRIED STEVE when he was in the 525th Military Intelligence Unit at Fort Bragg near Fayetteville, North Carolina—home of the 82nd Airborne and also the Green Berets. In Fayetteville we rented an apartment upstairs from some very southern southerners, one of whom was still fighting the Civil War but had become despondent. "You in the North have the A-bomb now," he told Steve bitterly. I was astonished. To me, the Civil War amounted to a few boring dates I was forced to learn in high school and forgot right after the test. Now here was a man who was living it. That was my first hint that life in the South would be a little different.

Steve's pay was low, so we had almost no money. We would listen to the radio for a food sale, figure out how much we'd spend on gas to drive there, count the pennies we had in the jar in the kitchen, and then go or not go to the sale, depending on the cost. I remember one disastrous decision that took us many miles out of town to buy meat advertised at ten cents a pound. The meat was a ground-up gray substance that I could hardly look at and didn't want to touch, let alone eat. And the trip had used half a gallon of gas.

I tried to get a job, but the best pay I was offered was $25 a week. For years I had earned that much by babysitting, and despite our current poverty, I came from a well-off family who would spend that much on a pair of gloves. I wouldn't look out the window for $25, let alone work for a week in the hardware store that made the offer. So I got a job as assistant to the principal of a school for disabled African American children, who were not, of course, admitted to the school for disabled white children. I loved my employer, Edna Fuller, and offered myself as a volunteer — if I was going to work for nothing, I wouldn't do it for that hardware store — but the congregation of her church insisted on paying me.

It wasn't long before I got a feeling for Caucasian Fayetteville. It soon seemed that race loomed even larger there than in apartheid South West Africa, strange as that may seem. But I think it can be explained by population numbers. In South West Africa, as grim as the white people were, there weren't many of them, and unless they were actually present they did not have to be dealt with. Black people outnumbered them by at least twenty to one, probably more, because nobody counted the people in outlying areas such as the Ju/wasi. Except in the specifically white communities, everybody was a black person. One could spend months or even years without encountering a white person. Also, the African people retained their cultures. Their customs and their social systems were their own, as were their religious practices. The names of some of their leaders, such as Tchaka, Mosilikatsi (it means Path of Blood), and Dingaan the Vulture, were widely known in many different countries to many thousands of people. To be sure, these men were known for the carnage they caused, but also for their military genius. They are usually described as evil, as are some other successful military leaders, such as Genghis Khan, but those who described them were usually from populations that had been threatened by them. People in Europe wrote about Genghis Khan, and white people wrote about the Zulu warriors.

On the lands assigned to the African people, their own laws were in effect. To assign a piece of land to people who had already been there for hundreds of years and force them to stay on it was certainly the heart and soul of apartheid, and was instantly canceled as soon as apartheid South West Africa became independent Namibia, but at least while on these lands the people didn't have to deal with whites every day. In short, much of life could go on even under apartheid, with the whites mostly looming as a negative force, hostile and dangerous but often remote. I came to compare the South West African whites to New Hampshire hurricanes. We have hurricanes, but not all the time, and unpleasant as they are, when we've cleaned up after one of them we can forget them for a while.

Not so the racial situation in Fayetteville. Not counting the army—
which by then was integrated, or was supposed to be—the whites outnumbered the blacks by five to one and also controlled the world as they
knew it. They wrote all the laws, controlled all the elections, and put
WHITES ONLY signs on just about everything. It seemed to me that a
day could not pass without a black person having a bad experience with
a white person or at least with white culture. For all the time I'd spent
in South West Africa, for all the cultural differences I'd seen, by far the
greatest culture shock I ever felt was in my own country, from Cambridge, Massachusetts, to Fayetteville, North Carolina—a journey I
would not want to repeat.

One day when I was crossing a street, a white man deliberately tried
to run over me. Of course he did; I worked for a black person. I had un-
wittingly broken the racial rules. Had my attacker succeeded, the judge
would undoubtedly have seen the event as my fault and would have ex-
onerated my attacker.

Why would I have such an antisouthern notion? Because of what happened while I was there. One day the white authorities castrated a little
boy who was a student at our school. Some white girls had made a pet of
this boy, and because his disability was cognitive, he would run to them
when they called. He was their little dog, it seemed. That was fine as long
as this boy was young, the white community believed, but he would grow
up, and the sexual fears of the white community were boundless. For a
cognitively disabled black man to be accustomed to the company of white
girls was asking for rape. The medical authorities castrated the child as a
preventive measure.

The day that Steve was discharged from the army, we got in our rattling VW bug and drove straight to New York, where Steve had been
admitted to a graduate program at Columbia. The GI Bill would pay his
tuition. My only regret—a big one—was parting with Mrs. Fuller and
the children at the school. We lived in New York for several years, during which Steve went to his classes and I, to put food on the table, got a
job as secretary-receptionist for a life insurance company. Jobs like that
are not inspiring—one of my duties was to put green coloring on the
leaves of the only houseplant. The sun could have done that at no cost

to the insurance company, but the plant was kept in an interior office on somebody's desk.

At one point I gave birth to our daughter. A few months later I became pregnant with our son. And all along, in what little spare time was left to me, I was trying to finish that first book of mine, *The Harmless People*. It was published the day our son was born.

What took me so long to finish a book? Many years later I gave the reason in a speech at the fiftieth reunion of my Harvard class, when graduates from the various professions were asked to talk about their work. I was invited to join my former classmates Edward M. Hoagland and John Updike to make a presentation about writing. Since John and Ted were the writers whom I most admired — I'd read everything they'd written and had taken classes with both of them, and to this day can quote passages from the brilliant class work they submitted[1] — I couldn't say enough about them in my talk. But then, toward the end of my speech, I also mentioned that although all of us were writing our first books while still in the classroom, their books were published soon after graduation but mine wasn't published for five years. And why was that? Because of our circumstances. John and Ted had wives and I had a husband.

The two literary giants looked a little guilty, bless them. But many women in the audience related strongly to that thought, and spoke to me about their own experiences afterward.

I'm sure that the leaders of the women's movement were already astir, challenging what the social system was doing to women, and thank God for them. But I knew nothing about all that. I just struggled along with what I'd been handed. The man's work came first — an edict I had never questioned, not even in the Kalahari, where I'd helped my brother with his filming projects when I could have been out looking for lions — and

---

1. A circus tiger is trying to mate with a tigress but she doesn't want him. "She let him lick her tail, though. She let him kiss her ass." Hoagland. This later appeared in *Cat Man*, Ted's first novel. A mother gives her baby a bath in a tub but the baby drowns. The mother realizes that "the worst thing that could happen to anyone had happened to her." Updike. This later appeared in *Rabbit, Run*, John's first novel, and caused me to bathe my infants in a special baby tub, not in the bathtub.

the wife supported him, often by getting a job, as I did, but always by keeping house and doing all the incidental work, such as making sure the car got inspected, taking the dog to the vet, balancing the checkbook, shopping for everybody's Christmas present. And all that time we were expected to have our hair done and wear makeup, high heels, and dresses. Much against my will, I had to do this for my job with the insurance company. I was no longer Liz Marshall, wild and free, but the indentured Mrs. Stephen Thomas. None of this was Steve's fault, or my parents' fault, or even my fault. It was the culture of the time and not a good culture for women.

I might never have finished that first book if not for my mother, at which point I learned that if men won't help you, women will. My mom came to New York and took care of our infant daughter while I wrote without stopping. My book had been partly written, of course, as I started it while in the Kalahari and scratched away at it afterward when I had moments to myself, but thanks to my mom, I wrote the rest in a few weeks. I thank her very deeply for that, and also for the name I signed it by, Elizabeth Marshall Thomas, which came about because of a cultural complication pertaining to women that my mom foresaw at my birth.

The issue now seems pointless, but back then a woman's maiden name was dropped after marriage unless she had no middle name, so that Jane Iphigenia Jones became Jane Iphigenia Smith unless she was just Jane Jones to start with. If so, when she got married, she'd be Jane Jones Smith. My mom knew this, and purposely did not give me a middle name.

I didn't stay with Elizabeth Marshall, although I could have and maybe should have, as my prizewinning short story was published under that name. But I wanted a name that joined me with my husband and children. I might also have been Elizabeth Thomas, but another writer was already using Elizabeth Thomas. So I went with the eight syllables, and from then on, it seemed too late to change. The name is much too long. It takes forever to say it and on beyond forever to scribble those twenty-three letters at a book signing. I've come to envy Amy Tan. I should have used Di!ai or Kothonjoro.

. . .

But even with an impossible name, I finished *The Harmless People*. Then what? The book got good reviews and was nominated for the National Book Award, and William Shawn, then the editor of *The New Yorker*, took note of it. He asked my agent why she hadn't shown my book to him. He would have published it in its entirety, he said. She told him she had submitted it, but whoever read it had turned it down. He wondered if I would write something else for *The New Yorker*.

Do bears live in the woods? I'd do it for free. But write about what? People, not animals, were believed to be a suitable subject, as I had already learned from the school librarian so many years before. And I'd done pretty well with *The Harmless People*.

I was even called an anthropologist, which surprised me because *The Harmless People* is a travel book and was published as such. If I remember rightly, I took only two courses in anthropology, both of them as an undergraduate and one of which I walked out of because the professor was so mean. One day, for instance, he suddenly stopped his lecture in midsentence to declare that knitting was a form of masturbation. Most of us were shocked, because at the time masturbation was not generally acknowledged. But the student who was knitting in the front row and to whom his comment was directed was not at all disturbed. "When I knit, I knit, and when I masturbate, I masturbate," she told him calmly, pulling more yarn from the skein in her pocket and starting the next row.

I lacked her serenity and sophistication, so another day when the professor said something equally offensive about people without graduate degrees who do fieldwork in anthropology — meaning, I realized, my parents, whom he not only knew but who lived three blocks from where he was standing — I just got up and left. At any rate, I didn't become an anthropologist.

But evidently, all you need to do to be called one is to write about unfamiliar people, and as long as I seemed to be in that arena, and since I had just written about hunter-gatherers, I thought I should write about another kind of culture. Pastoralists, maybe. At least they had cattle.

I had been to a lecture by Neville Dyson-Hudson, a real anthropologist who with his anthropologist wife, Rada, had studied pastoralists in Uganda and Kenya. In anthropological circles, the people they studied were known as Central Nilo-Hamites. Neville's account of them was fascinating. They were warlike, had big herds of cattle, and were contemptuous of anything western. All that seemed good to me. Shawn thought that Central Nilo-Hamites would be just fine, and gave me lots of money. I was also fortunate enough to get a grant from the Guggenheim Foundation. With the money I bought equipment and plane tickets, and the next thing I knew, I was living among the Dodoth in northern Uganda.

8

❧

UGANDA

Tom and Kirsti offered to come with me. By then they were raising perennial plants instead of chickens and the plants didn't need their constant attention, so they could travel. I could not have been happier, as the reason for their offer was to help me take care of my children — Stephanie, age four, and John, age two — when I was out in the field. Steve came too, but only for a few weeks because he was still in graduate school. The photographer Tim Asch also came with us and took hundreds of photographs, many of which appeared in *Warrior Herdsmen*, the book I eventually wrote about the Dodoth. On his own, he also made a splendid film called *Dodoth Morning*. We took tents and other equipment with us, and I bought a Land Rover when we got to Kampala.

At the time, Edward Frederick Mutesa II was kabaka, king of the Baganda people, and while in Kampala we visited the Basi Kabaka's tomb, built for three of King Mutesa's predecessors, including his father. We were awed by the large traditional building made of thatched poles, very dark in its wide interior, where, when our eyes adjusted, we saw a stuffed leopard and long curtains of bark cloth concealing something unknown to us but obviously important. Sitting next to the far wall was a group of elderly women, the widows of King Mutesa's father. Their role was to care for the tomb.

They were kindly women who welcomed us as we went in, then held out their hands to my children. I was focused on the leopard, as leopards had cultural importance throughout the forested parts of Africa. The anthropologist Colin Turnbull had once described to me a leopard society that flourished in West Africa from Sierra Leone through Liberia and into Côte d'Ivoire, but especially in Liberia. Colin almost turned into a leopard himself as he told how members of that society would become leopards, hiding near a water source as leopards do and killing the first person who came along, no matter who that person was. A real leopard would do nothing less. Colin's fingers seemed to turn into claws, and his teeth, which appeared through his slowly widening smile, seemed to sharpen. Although we were at a party in his Manhattan apartment at the time, his reenactment scared me half to death. I don't believe the society extended into Uganda, but the power of a leopard is almost beyond description, and I wasn't surprised that the Baganda kings were associated with them.

I was therefore having anthropological thoughts — *Gosh, among the Ju/wasi it was lions, here it's leopards* — so I wasn't paying much attention to my children. Then I looked around to see my four-year-old daughter walking quietly and politely toward the women's outstretched hands.

But my two-year-old son stood open-mouthed, looking at everything. Then he bowed low, put his hands on the floor, and walked on hands and feet toward the women. The kabaka's widows seemed puzzled for a moment, then suddenly they understood his motive — he was in awe of the tomb. They were impressed, and watched with wonder the little foreign white guy coming so reverently toward them. And then, for a long time, they praised him. What would have happened if he had done the same thing for the same reason in an American church? He'd have been tossed out on the sidewalk. But that's the African people for you, with their insight and perception.

The next day we went north. Our journey began in farmlands where, in small fields, people were raising bananas and other crops, but by the time we reached Moroto, a government post some two hundred miles to the north, the road had become a track and the farmlands had given way to forest and savannah.

I had an attack of doubt. I was the so-called leader of this project but had no idea where to go or how to begin, except to find a Central Nilo-Hamite who'd be willing to talk to me. That meant I had to be able to ask questions. We had a letter of introduction to some British people in Moroto, who very kindly put us up for the night and in the morning introduced me to a tall, lanky youngster named David bin Lotuke. He graciously held out his hand and greeted me in perfect English. *Good God*, I thought, *this kid speaks English better than I do*. I asked how old he was. He said he was eighteen. That wasn't true. He was fifteen. But I believed him at the time. I asked who his people were, and he said they were Karamojong. That was good, because the Dodoth language is more or less a dialect of the Karamojong language, so I hired him on the spot. He went back to the boarding school he'd been attending and got his things, a little bundle, then got in the Land Rover with us and again we went north.

Perhaps it's hard to believe that hiring a teenager as the key to successful research was a good idea, but as time would prove, I've never made a better or more fortunate decision. And it wasn't long before I found that out.

We drove about fifty miles toward the Sudan border. The road was a bumpy dirt track that led to a tiny settlement known as Kaabong in the heart of Dodoth country. As we came to Kaabong we saw two men wearing nothing, not even sandals or earrings, but carrying nine-foot spears. This was more or less the national dress of all the so-called Central Nilo-Hamites who didn't live in towns. One of the men glanced at us, but neither of them reacted to our presence. Nor, once they reached the road, did they turn and follow it. This, I learned, was characteristic of the Dodoth, for whom western people and their roads held little interest. I was later to learn that lions used the road more often than the Dodoth, although the lions used it at night. So I took the men's indifference as a good sign. *Okay, we're here*, I thought. *Now what?*

In Kaabong was a store owned by a man from India named Mr. Patel. We went in and bought some crackers. I asked him where the Dodoth lived, and he told me we'd find their settlements as we went north—large, round, stockade-like structures in which were small, round, thatched houses and, in a fenced-off section, cattle. So we got back in the Land Rover to look for these structures.

Half an hour later David told us to stop. He had noticed something on a nearby hillside. We looked where he pointed and saw in the distance a little cluster of Dodoth people sitting around a big, tall man standing over a smaller man who seemed humble and was crouching. The tall man was making a speech.

For a while David listened to the man's faint voice, then told us that the crouching man was a thief and the tall man was judging him. We got out of the Land Rover, and in respectful tones David called out to the tall man. I don't know what he said, but it assured our future in Uganda, because the tall man invited us to join him. Through David, the tall man told us that the thief had stolen pumpkins from the garden of one of his wives and he had planned to give the thief a beating. But, he said, he had decided to show mercy, and rather than beating the thief half to death, he would make him eat a raw pumpkin. The audience laughed loudly and the thief looked relieved and even happy.

The tall man seemed to be an interesting person. His name, we learned, was Locul Lomurri.[1] He told us the names of two of his wives who were sitting nearby, also the name of one of his adult sons who was present, and also the names of some of his neighbors who were there to watch him try the thief. Here before us was the real thing, a group of Central Nilo-Hamites.

I was impressed by Lomurri. He was a man of substance, as I saw from his dwelling at the bottom of the hill. He had wives and children, he was on good terms with his neighbors, and although his cattle were away for the day, I assumed from the size of the cattle section of his distant stockade that he had plenty of them. From the demeanor of the people around him, I assumed that he had power, and I also saw that he had a sense of humor, or so it seemed. At that point in my Uganda sojourn, I didn't see why forcing someone to eat a raw pumpkin was funny, but the people around him found it hilarious, so I bowed to their more informed judgment.

Who better to visit than someone like Lomurri? I asked if we could camp nearby and talk with him. He said we could. We made our camp in a grove of trees from which we could see for miles around and also could see his dwelling. The beautiful hill on which we camped was not on the map, but its name, he said, was Morukore.

. . .

That evening Lomurri's second-oldest son, the herd boy, brought home his father's cattle. Lions and leopards lived in Dodoth country, the leopards more or less in forests and the lions more or less on grasslands, as one would expect. Thus cattle were threatened in both environments and could not spend a night without protection. The cattle seemed to know this, and all on their own, without being herded, they went into the cattle portion of the stockade, where, as if voluntarily, they would spend the night without food or water. They did the same thing the next night too, and again the following night. I saw they had a social order, because every evening the same cattle went in first and the others stood by, awaiting their turns. I mentioned this to Lomurri's senior wife, who was standing beside me as I watched, and she smiled brightly because I'd noticed. She liked that. It struck me that I was in the right place with the right people.

And so began our life in Uganda. We ate sparingly so that our food supply would last, we got up early to observe the cattle going to the forest in the morning, we went to bed long after dark, and we got up fairly often during the night because we were concerned about a leopard who seemed to be studying our camp. At Tom's suggestion, we made a high, wide thornbush fence with the thorns sticking out to discourage him.

We were also concerned about thieves. We weren't there for long before a thief came at night and robbed us of some tools, so Tom made a gate for the fence and at night, by means of a wire, attached the gate to the horn and headlights of the Land Rover. That night, when the thief opened the gate, the headlights went on and the horn blew. We rushed out of our tents, but the thief had vanished, and he never came back. The leopard didn't use the gate and could probably jump over the fence if he tried, so he was of greater concern.

Lobi and Lomurri were delighted with our solution to the thieves. They knew about the leopard too, but didn't worry about him because if he jumped over the stockade into their cattle pens, the bulls would deal with him, or the men would spear him, and the leopard probably realized this. Then too, because grown cattle are too big for most leopards, he was probably looking for calves, and at the time there weren't any.

Why then did he visit my camp? I thought he might be considering my children. After dark I kept them close beside me and didn't tell them why.

At first Lomurri would visit me at our camp to talk with me, as would his friends, but soon enough I began to join these men at Lomurri's *etem*, the lookout post where a man would spend the day. Many of his neighbors would be there, and I soon learned that they were watching for Turkana raiders who came up from the Rift Valley.

Raiding had gone on since the beginning of time, according to Lomurri, but until recently there had been a truce. But perhaps four months earlier, a group of Dodoth men had raided the Turkanas and broken the truce. The men at Lomurri's *etem* agreed that this was unfortunate, but also seemed to understand the motive for doing it — the men who made the raid were young, and because a man couldn't marry until he had enough cattle to give to his bride's family, these men needed cattle for their marriages. However, the Dodoth had only their spears to fight with, and the Turkanas had rifles.

The spears were dangerous weapons, to be sure. Once, to show me how dangerous, Lomurri threw his into the trunk of a tree about fifty feet away, then yanked it out and touched up the edge of the blade until it felt as sharp as a razor. Most men carried two spears, one to throw and the other for close fighting. In battle, they also picked up and threw the spears of fallen enemy warriors. But a thirty-thirty bullet can travel five miles. The Dodoth were at a disadvantage.

Even with spears, the Turkanas were excellent fighters. They didn't use heavy leather shields, like some of the other pastoralists. Instead they used the little stools that all male pastoralists in that part of the world carved for themselves to sit on. If a Turkana saw a spear coming at him, he'd deflect it with the stool. "You can't kill a Turkana when he's looking at you," said Lomurri.

Cattle and raiding were the realm of men. Men were more important than women, just as bulls and oxen were more important than cows. But I was fortunate. Unlike the Ju/wasi, the Dodoth overlooked my gender. The role of Dodoth women was to tend to their gardens and defer to their husbands, and thus, at least in spirit, wasn't much different from the role of American women at the time. Lomurri's four concurrent marriages, I noticed, were pretty much like mine in that his wives were expected to do the women's work and be his helpers. But if I had been a woman to the Ju/wasi, I didn't seem so to the Dodoth—I was someone strange from somewhere else, with no Dodoth-style femininity about me. As for Lomurri, if he saw me as anything but a foreigner, he saw me as a daughter. He once told me that.

After I had been there a while, a man offered me two hundred head of cattle plus some sheep and goats for my four-year-old daughter's hand in marriage. The offer was generous, as David told me, but I declined, of course. However, it may have been the first time that anyone made such an offer to a girl's mother. Always it was made to the father. Steve had gone home by then, or probably the offer would have been made to him. But if anything showed how unwomanly I was, it was that offer.

This also was good. I was able to meet virtually all the men Lomurri knew, and if at first some of them were reluctant to talk with me, he'd prod them until they did. He had no reason to do this except that he seemed to enjoy my company as much as I enjoyed his, and he wanted to help me. Looking back, I'd say he understood why I was there and planned a way for me to achieve my goals. Thanks to him, I was able to talk with two of the most important people in northern Uganda. At first I had no idea who they were or why they were important, but I had only to be with them for a very short time before I found out.

The first was a man named Lokorimoe. It wasn't his birth name, which was Lokiding, but an honorary name to show he had killed an enemy. He had eight wives and many children, ranging in age from toddlers to young adults, and he lived in a large stockade dwelling about two miles from our camp. His cattle pen was enormous, and every night was filled. Lokorimoe had other herds too, distributed in various places; thus he was one of the richest men in Dodoth. Although many people, men and women, came on their own to visit me in my camp, and although Lomurri brought many others, Lokorimoe was too important to visit anyone. People went to him. Lomurri told me I should meet Lokorimoe, and one day he took me and David to Lokorimoe's impressive stockade.

Lokorimoe was elderly and overweight. He walked with a cane. His arms and shoulders were covered with faint scars to show that he'd killed other men in battles. He greeted us with great courtesy and told one of his wives to bring us beer. It was tasty and also healthy, made from millet. His wives had brewed it.

After that, he and Lomurri did all the talking, and I didn't know what was being said because young David had too much respect for the two men to translate words that were not spoken to me. But perhaps Lomurri said good things about me, because after that, Lokorimoe allowed me to visit him often, although he made sure I knew he was doing me a favor. One day he asked if I had cattle. I said I didn't. He asked if I had killed a person. I said I hadn't. "Then you are a woman," he said scornfully. I smiled to show him I knew that already, so he rephrased his message. "Then you are nothing," he said.

Even so, the respectful way to address a woman was by the name of her youngest son, so he always addressed me as Mother of John, and he didn't seem to mind my visits because he liked to talk about himself and I liked to listen. He told me he had raided the Turkanas many times, not only for cattle but also for little girls. At first I assumed he had captured the girls for sexual purposes, and I began to dislike him, but one should never assume anything about people of another culture, and I soon learned that he captured girls not because he wanted sex but because he wanted cattle.

He raised the girls as his daughters and their marriages substantially increased his herds. I later learned that this was an acceptable practice not only for the Dodoth but also for other, related pastoralists, and that a warrior's relationship with his captive girls was fatherly. By the time I began my visits, all of Lokorimoe's captured daughters were married and lived far away with their husbands, but at one point two of them walked sixty miles just to visit him. I happened to be there when they came, and saw that his relationship with them was easy and friendly. He had other such daughters too, but he wouldn't say how many, because the Dodoth refused to number people just as they refused to number cattle. He told me some of their names, though—he named the two I met and three others, and he mentioned one more whose name he couldn't recall. So I did the counting for myself. He had six such daughters.

• • •

Another elderly man was one of the most important people in Uganda. His name was Lochobarri and he was a prophet, famous not only in Uganda but also in Kenya and the southern Sudan. People came from these places to see him. Like Lokorimoe, he was too important to visit people, so Lomurri took me to visit him.

Lochobarri's family lived a few miles northeast of our camp, not in a stockade like most people but in dark, thatched rondavels with only the smallest stockade for cattle. I'm sure he had more cattle, a possibility he would not discuss, but if he did, he kept them elsewhere, as he was on the front line of Turkana raiding. The Dodoth who lived between him and the Kenya border had moved away. But Lochobarri was fearless. I was told that on several occasions when raiders came, he took his spear, elderly as he was, and went after them. I have wondered about this since then. He may have been elderly, but with his enormous, supernatural power—a power that was internationally acknowledged—the raiders may have known who was on their trail and taken care not to encounter him.

On our first visit, Lomurri and I, with David, went to his rondavel and stood outside, waiting for him to come out. At last he did and greeted Lomurri. Lomurri introduced us. David was just a boy and not a Dodoth, and I was about as much of a foreigner as it was possible to be, also a woman, and much younger than Lochobarri—he was probably in his late sixties or early seventies. I therefore was nothing and David was next to nothing, so at first, understandably, Lochobarri didn't even look at me, although he nodded to David. Then we all sat down in front of the rondavel and he and Lomurri talked while David and I listened. I tried to ask a few questions, but Lochobarri wasn't interested in answering them. Soon enough, we said our farewells and went home. On our second visit, at Lomurri's suggestion, I gave Lochobarri a shirt. He still didn't seem to want to talk with me. On our third visit he was wearing the shirt. Again I tried to get him to talk with me and again he didn't, so Lomurri said bluntly, "This woman wants to know something for that shirt." After that he talked freely.

The protectorate government seemed unaware of Lochobarri's existence—as were all other nonindigenous people, as far as I know. But then, we were the only outsiders who lived in the countryside or took an interest in what went on there. Thus Lochobarri's fame was not on the surface. Nor, I'm sure, did he want it to be. Not only could he see the future, but I believe he influenced it. He seemed to know when Turkana raids were coming, and he also could predict when Dodoth raids would succeed. People would ask his advice and then do as he said. Thus to a certain degree he shaped what went on.

But he was not, as I was to learn, a very realistic person. I felt that he saw deeply into things while ignoring the practical implications, and thus he may have had something to do with the raid on the Turkanas that ended the long truce. Perhaps he saw the need for cattle but not the value of the truce. I know he had something to do with other raids because after I got to know him, I realized that he would tell me where and when they would happen, and he'd predict the results. Raiding was forbidden by the government, not that the police or soldiers did much about it. But they would if they knew of impending raids, so Lochobarri had no reason to trust me with this information except that I knew Lomurri.

That worried me somewhat. The protectorate government, via the police or the army, would expect me to share such information. I didn't. However, if I thought I was about to hear sensitive information, I'd tell Lochobarri I shouldn't know about it. Lochobarri had no fear of any-thing — not the protectorate police and not the army — so as often as not he'd tell me anyway. In that case, I kept it to myself. Perhaps I wasn't an anthropologist, but I knew that when anthropologists work in other cultures, they give themselves to the people they're with and never compromise them. I would not have dreamed of doing differently.

Lochobarri also gave advice about witches. He knew who they were and what they'd done, and could advise their victims about how to counter them. All this was valuable information, and I think more people went to him for advice about witches than for advice about raiding. As for me, I was glad to hear about witchcraft. Witches were associated with hyenas, he told me. That came as no surprise, because the Dodoth didn't bury all their dead. They buried important elders in the cattle pen, but most other dead people were left in the bush for the hyenas to eat. I'd seen several such corpses myself, one of them the corpse of a robber not thirty feet away from the stockade he'd been robbing. A few days later the corpse was gone. Hyenas had disposed of it.

Witches, said Lochobarri, would ride on the backs of hyenas to people's dwellings and there would cast their spells. The people in the dwelling would sicken. They would come to Lochobarri for advice and he would help to heal them and also identify the witches. I knew one of the men he identified, and the man didn't deny it. That he belonged to a witch family was well known. He mixed often and freely with everyone else, but one day at my camp when people were talking in his presence about his witch association, he asked why they were saying this in front of me. "You don't need to warn her. She's not going to marry into our family," he told them.

All this made me very interested in witches, but perhaps too interested. Lochobarri answered my questions willingly enough, but I came to wonder what he thought of me. Why was I so interested in hyenas? After the raiding had displaced many of the Dodoth families north of us, we'd see women and children walking south, on their way to places where they hoped to find food and safety.

One day a woman I didn't know came to our camp. With her were two children, a daughter who was about ten and a son who was about five. Evidently the woman didn't know whose camp it was, and she seemed surprised to see me.

The little boy was so thin that his ribs showed, and so weak that he staggered. I wanted very much to help these people, especially when I learned that the woman was Lochobarri's daughter and was on her way to a place about forty miles south. I welcomed them warmly and offered them food and a ride to their destination. The children beseeched their mother to accept, but to my amazement, she refused. To my further amazement, I learned from David that she believed I was a witch. Who might have given her that impression?

I doubted that the little boy, thin and sick as he was, would survive the journey. The daughter also feared for him, and again she begged her mother to let me drive them. David and I also begged her. I drove the Land Rover up beside them and opened its doors. But no. The woman said something bitter to me — I don't know what because David didn't want to translate it — then led her children away in the opposite direction. They seemed crushed with disappointment and looked back at me with yearning. I don't know what happened to them.

By then the Turkana raids were near us, although the men I knew were not involved, because the Dodoth didn't see themselves as an organized unit. The men of each neighborhood defended themselves, keeping watch for raiders from their lookouts. Nor was anything visible to us about the raiding. We didn't see Turkana warriors or know they'd been raiding until their victims told us. We didn't hear them either. Not all Turkanas had guns, and anyway, the best way to conduct a raid was to find someone's herd of grazing cattle, round them up, and drive them to Turkanaland, scaring off the herd boy or spearing him if necessary. Spears don't make any noise. Time would pass before the owners of the cattle knew they had been raided. Before they could mobilize and do anything about it, the herd would be far away. The only battle likely to result would be if the owners caught up to the raiders.

When it became clear that the Turkanas had taken many of the herds north of us and might soon be raiding our area, I worried about the Dodoth but not about us, because we had no cattle. We would be less important than flies to the Turkana, because flies are associated with cattle. Stray bullets didn't worry me either, because I assumed that vehicles were bulletproof and if the raiders came, we'd be safe inside the Land Rover. I'm not sure where I got this impression.

Lomurri and others were concerned, however, and decided to sacrifice an ox, the most significant creature in Dodoth culture. Every teenage boy was given a young bull, who then became his "name ox." From then on the young man would be known as the ox's father. In English, the word *ox* refers to a bull who has been castrated, but a name ox might or might not be castrated, because *ox* seemed to be the anthropologists' translation of the word for these important companion animals. The Dodoth word for "bull" would refer to a herd animal. (This was complicated, however, because some name oxen were bulls and some castrated male cattle were herd animals.) The young man would compose songs about his ox and call his name in battle. The sacrifice of such an important animal would cast a spiritual net of protection, and would take place under a sacred tree beside a river.

When Lomurri set off to attend the sacrifice, I asked if I could go with him. He frowned. The sacrifices were strictly for men. He thought this over for a while—perhaps considering my gender, perhaps deciding that I wasn't particularly female—then he said I could, and taking his spear, he set off for the river. With David, I followed. When we arrived, about seventy men were gathered by the sacred tree, waiting for the ox. I sat at a distance, not wanting to intrude in case some of the men would disapprove, but no one seemed bothered by my presence.

At last someone brought the ox. A long discussion followed, as the owner of a sacrificed ox was supposed to be reimbursed with a heifer. The owner of this ox wanted his reimbursement quickly. At last an agreement was reached, and a few men drove the ox to the right place, where another man killed him with a spear. The men drank his blood, cooked his tongue and ate it, then opened his belly so that certain men with a talent for prophecy could read the future in his intestines. Raiders were coming from the northeast, the intestines told them. Several men, Lomurri among them, then made speeches. Lomurri walked back and forth, exhorting the other men to be ready to fight, not to stay at home when the raiders came but to support their neighbors and stick together. The next speaker said, "The Turkanas marry with Dodoth cattle." His voice rose. "Why do we let them? The Turkanas have blood too! If they come now, let us fight them! They will meet a spear!"

A middle-aged man made an impassioned speech about herds guarded only by boys coming together all at the same time to drink from the same place at the river. That would be the perfect place for raiders to capture cattle, the speaker said. Then an elder called out, "My people are here!"

"They are," roared the crowd in the forest of spears, and before the sound died, the elder shouted, "Our cattle will drink in peace!"

"They will!" answered the crowd.

"The disease of cattle will go!"

"It will!"

"The disease that weakens the legs will go!"

"It will!"

"It will!"

"It will!"

"And all bad things will be destroyed!"

"They will!"

The elder commanded the young men to gather. Perhaps thirty of them did, and stood together with their spears, facing the older men. They sang an almost tuneless hymn, "The Bellowing of Calves," then raised their spears and charged the crowd. This was, of course, a demonstration, not an attack, but even so, it's alarming to see thirty warriors with spears running at you. I thought of the Zulu kings Tschaka and Mosilikatze, whose warriors used a similar technique in battle.

The elder told the young men to go to a certain pass between hills through which, as the sacrificed ox had shown them, the Turkanas would come. The young men sang another song, "A Man Is a Man in Cattle," then left in a body for the pass. Dodoth men walk faster than many of us can run, and the young men were out of sight in minutes. The older men then cooked the meat of the ox, all of which had to be eaten before the ceremony could end. The ceremony appeared to have been effective. Raiders may have come, but not to the neighborhood of Morukore.

Another sacrifice was held perhaps a week later. Again rumors of a raid were circling, and again all the men went to the ceremonial grounds beside the river. The ox was killed, the intestines were examined, speeches were made, and prayers were offered, but just as the ceremony was ending, we heard the alarm call. In the distance, some people were shouting *lulululu* at the top of their lungs. The men looked at each other, and those who had spears grabbed them. Lomurri hadn't brought his spear. He looked at me and shouted, "Run!"

I felt a bit uncertain, as I didn't know which way to go. David seemed equally unsure. Lomurri grabbed a big stick and flourished it as if to clobber both of us. So we ran away from him, presumably going in the direction he intended. But that was Lomurri for you, a caring guy, albeit macho and impulsive. He chased us all the way back to our camp and then ran past us. His son and his cattle were in the forest. One of his wives held out his spear and his leather shield. He grabbed them and ran into the forest. Later he and his son came back, together with the cattle. On the way home, they heard that the alarm had been a false one. People had seen a group of armed men leaving the ceremony and had assumed they were raiders.

No raids came to Lomurri's neighborhood while we were there, although raids took place all around us. Our camp may have had something to do with that. Because the protectorate government was opposed to the raiding, police were supposed to stop it (not that they did), so our camp could have seemed like some kind of government entity. Perhaps we didn't look like the police or the army, but we obviously weren't locals.

The Dodoth and the Turkanas used the same spies, a people called the Ik or, as others called them, the Teutho. They lived in the hills between Kenya and Uganda and had no cattle, so they were poor. The Dodoth were contemptuous of them and called them "bush" and "dog," which reminded me of what non-Bushmen called the Ju/wasi. Even so, the Ik spied for both sides in exchange for food or favors, and one of them, a nice young man named Toperiperi, would sometimes visit our camp. Who knows what he said about us to the Turkanas?

One day he came because someone had cut his throat. He wanted medical help from me, but his wound went from ear to ear and was so deep and terrible that I knew it was far beyond my powers, so I put him in the Land Rover and drove him to a dispensary in Moroto. Many Dodoth men came with us, perhaps to question him, perhaps to mock him. I don't know why his throat was cut, but I suspect it had something to do with spying. Perhaps he gave false information, or someone thought he did. He didn't know about the dispensary, although David and I tried to tell him, and when we got there and the male nurse took him into a room, he must have thought he had been captured. He escaped out a window before the nurse came back with the bandages to help him.

I don't know what happened to him after that, but I believe that on the way to Moroto, Dodoth men extracted information from him, because right after we got back to Morukore, they said another raid was coming. The Teutho in the hills had started the alarm.

The men of Lomurri's neighborhood held another sacrifice. This time there was a problem with the ox. The previous sacrifice had indicated that the next sacrifice should be a red ox, and they knew of a red ox, but the owner didn't want to give him. Only after much pressure did the owner very reluctantly agree, and the herd was brought near. The ox was identified, and some men then tried to drive him to the sacred tree. But he ran in a huge circle around the tree and back to his herd. His owner then insisted that he wasn't the right ox, but the other men believed differently and tried again to bring him to the tree. Again the ox made a big circle around the tree and ran back to the herd. All this time the owner was violently protesting, saying that such behavior showed that the red ox was not the ox to sacrifice and that the men should find another, but by then some men had gathered a few other cattle to accompany the victim and drove them together to the tree. With the other cattle at his side, the red ox wasn't as frightened. He came to the tree and the men there were able to kill him. The owner was a mature man and a seasoned warrior with scars on his upper body to show he had killed enemy warriors, but when his ox died, he burst into tears.

Despite the sacrifice, a raid took place that same afternoon, again not at Morukore, but at a neighborhood out on the plain. Raiders killed a man and a woman and made off for the Rift Valley with perhaps fifty cattle. The next day at Lomurri's *etem* I asked the gathering if this meant the sacrifice had been unsuccessful.

Not at all, the men said. The benefits came just at the right time. If the people had not bargained and argued with the owner of the ox, or if the ox had been killed the first or second time he was brought to the tree, the benefits would have come too soon. Instead, the ox was speared just as the Turkanas were approaching. Also the ox of his own free will had run in a circle for almost half a mile, casting a widespread circle of protection which saved the dwellings of all the people present by keeping the Turkanas away. As for the man whose dwelling was raided, if he hadn't refused to come to the sacrifice, he would still be alive.

Soon after that, early one morning, we again heard the alarm call in the distance. It came from a hill in the north, then from another hill, then from a third hill, then from a fourth. Then it passed by us to the south. Someone far away was shouting "Ngimoe," which means "enemies," and at the top of Morukore a little white dog named Emuthugut, which means "white person," began to bark and then to howl. He knew that danger was coming.

The doorways in the stockade dwellings were only about three feet high — you had to go through on hands and knees, vulnerably presenting the back of your neck — and in the early morning light we saw Lomurri crawling out of his stockade dragging his spear and an ox horn. The horn was a trumpet, which he blew, a call to assemble. Already about thirty men were massed in a grove beside our camp, their spears stacked against a tree just as soldiers stack rifles. The men had been waiting for Lomurri, and when he appeared they started off.

Lomurri called some of them back and asked me to drive them to the north. The vehicle would get there sooner, he said, and he wanted to cut off the raiders before they got anywhere near the Morukore cattle. I was somewhat worried, but I would have done anything for Lomurri, and I still thought that cars were bulletproof, so I asked the men to get in the car with their spears pointed backward, if they didn't mind, in case we had to stop suddenly. They didn't mind. "Hurry, Mother of John," they said, and we went.

After twenty minutes we came to a place called Kalapata, a hilltop on which were three tiny shacks that were stores whose owners sold a few small items such as beads. There we stopped and looked around. Several groups of armed Dodoth men passed by and went into the bush to the east. The men in the Land Rover climbed out, and just then the other men from Morukore caught up with us. Dodoth men on foot can travel almost as fast as a Land Rover on a bad road. We all waited by the Land Rover because the men who had gone into the bush were coming back. They hadn't seen the Turkanas.

The raiders' surprise had been spoiled, some of the men said. They thought the raiders had retreated into the hills and were planning to attack later. The men from the Kalapata area started off for the hills in question, but the men from Morukore didn't join them. The cohesion that the men would have felt if the raiders had been near no longer applied. The men from Morukore didn't want to be off in the bush if the raiders came to their neighborhood.

We were standing around, thinking of going back, when six strangers came out of one of the little huts. The men were not Dodoth, I saw, because the Dodoth are tall and lean and these men were short and stocky, and also wore undershirts and khaki trousers. They were, I learned, the

Kaabong police force, and had come to Kalapata to forestall the expected raid.

They looked at the Dodoth contemptuously. One said to me in English, "Don't worry, madam. These people always think there'll be a raid." He then told me that he and the other police would "just go to have a look," and they all went into the hut. They soon emerged in uniform, wearing helmets and carrying rifles. They asked if they could use my car. I said they could, although Lomurri seemed angry. The police got in, telling Lomurri that he couldn't come. He ignored them. But by then they had taken all the seats, so he had to sit on the tailgate with his feet dangling.

When we left Kalapata, by then empty except for a very old man and some chickens, I thought we might seem formidable, but the old man laughed at us. A few unknown guys in a car driven by a woman were not as formidable as a group of twenty or thirty Dodoth warriors with nine-foot spears — not even close.

The hill where we were going was farther than I'd thought. Soon we were out of sight of any other people — just the empty plain and the forest around it. I felt exposed and perhaps in danger. I had also lost confidence in the Kaabong policemen, who seemed unsure, but by then I felt responsible for them. I didn't know what to do if we saw raiders.

In a valley we noticed a young boy in the distance with a little herd of goats. The sergeant asked me to stop, and when I did, he sent the youngest corporal to talk to the boy. The corporal left his rifle in the car. I asked the sergeant what was happening. He said that he and the other policemen wanted to get a goat. "Or buy one," he added vaguely. The corporal began to talk to the boy, but then a man, probably the boy's father, ran down from his lookout and took over the talking. After a very long time the corporal came back to the car empty-handed. The sergeant asked him why he didn't have a goat. "They were all sick," said the corporal.

We drove on. At last we came to the hill where raiders were expected. The top of the hill was bare but its sides were forested. It began to rain. The policemen with their rifles got out and walked together to the top of the hill, leaving behind the youngest corporal to guard the car. Lomurri with his spear slid off the tailgate, and watching the ground for footprints and looking intently into the bushes, he went by himself into the forest.

The policemen sat down in a cluster on top of the hill. Though the hilltop was bare, the road was in a dense bush that went on for miles to the south. The policemen may have been right not to stay by the car, a decoy plainly visible among the leaves, and while we waited beside it in silence I began to realize how unwise it had been to go there, and how frightened I was. Thunder was rolling in the hills behind us, the only sound. The young corporal stood by the fender, straight and tall, with his face expressionless, and showed his fear only in that he could not keep his hands from shaking. I think he was fifteen or sixteen, but not more.

Just then, in the woods, we heard a branch crack. "What was that?" cried the young corporal, leveling his rifle. We then heard a cowbell, then trampling feet and more branches moving, then nothing, as the herd we were hearing was made to stop.

The profound silence that followed was broken by a whistle, not that of a bird, and then a rustle, which we saw was caused by the bushes swaying, nearer and nearer, as something made its way toward the road. It was very frightening. "Let us get in and drive on," whispered the corporal. I was very glad to go. We went forward until we came to a place where the car could turn around, only to find that the police on the hill had come down to meet us, perhaps afraid that we would leave them behind. "Did you find anything?" I asked the sergeant.

"Absolutely nothing," said he.

"We heard cattle being driven over there," said the young corporal.

"Oh?" said the sergeant.

"We can return to Kalapata," said the older corporal.

But we couldn't leave without Lomurri. "What to do?" I asked him when, shining with rain, he finally appeared.

The sergeant answered for him. "Drive back to Kalapata," he said with contempt. "Nothing here." So we did, as fast as possible through the hollow where we heard the sounds.

What had we heard? I have no idea, except that the sound was made by cattle. Had they been captured by Turkanas who perhaps did not have rifles and decided to show discretion when they saw the Land Rover and the police?

Near Kalapata we came upon a group of twelve Dodoth men, walking casually, spear tails dragging. They parted ranks to let us by. Lomurri wanted to speak with them, so I stopped. They told him that the raid had come and gone. A group of Turkanas had attacked a neighborhood north of Kalapata and had escaped with three herds. A large group of Dodoth men had followed and had not returned. As for the twelve, they had done what they had come to do and had made the scouting foray, and now they were going home. Not one of them as much as glanced at the police, who had turned their backs and were talking together in Swahili. I knew one of the Dodoth men quite well, and when I had a chance I asked him what he thought of the police. "Nothing," he said. "Where were they?"

I never learned more about what happened that rainy day, but I did learn why Lomurri came with me. David told me that when Steve was leaving, he had asked Lomurri to protect me. Lomurri had promised to do so, and was as good as his word.

That police were in Kalapata meant something, however. Police had not been up there before, so it seemed that the protectorate government was trying to do something more forceful about the raiding. This, I thought, was worrisome, because the police would be just as hard on Dodoth raiders as they would be on Turkana raiders, and since the Dodoth and Turkanas looked alike (although they spoke somewhat different languages), how would the police know who was who?

Raiding was a terrible thing, of course, and the Dodoth were suffering—the neighborhoods near the escarpment had been abandoned, the people had been forced to move away from their crops, and some people faced starvation. But the police were not effective, and soon the protectorate army—the King's African Rifles, better known as the KAR—took over.

One day a group of army trucks drove up to our camp and many soldiers got out. Not for them the dinky little rifles of the policemen. These guys had automatic weapons. The commanding officer asked why we were there and I told him. Everyone got back in the trucks and drove off. But not far. They summoned a group of Dodoth men, Lomurri among them, and questioned them. Then the trucks and the soldiers went north and the Dodoth men followed. Even the army trucks could not speed on that road. The men on foot kept up with them.

I learned what happened from the Dodoth men who followed the soldiers. The trucks went to the escarpment, which was so steep and dangerous that the soldiers got out of the trucks and walked. The Dodoth were right behind them. At the bottom of the escarpment was the border of Kenya. The soldiers were not authorized to attack the citizens of another country, which would be an act of war. Yet the commanding officer led the soldiers on into Kenya, where they attacked the first Turkana settlement they came upon. Why did they cross an international border? Why did they attack Kenyan citizens? Because, as I learned years later, the commanding officer was Idi Amin.

Just a few cattle were at the settlement, and the Dodoth men, who knew almost every cow in the country, recognized none of them as Dodoth cattle. So not only were the villagers in a different country, they also did not seem responsible for any raiding. Even so, Idi Amin mowed them down with his automatic weapon. Then, in the resulting mayhem, he noticed a weeping little girl clinging to her dying mother. He grabbed the little girl, forced her down on the ground, and broke her back with a stone.

He then had his soldiers throw the body of a Turkana man in a fire and burn off most of his skin. Without the skin, a corpse is white, which is probably why in at least one African language the word for "white person" is "peeled person." The few cattle owned by that settlement were nearby. Idi Amin ordered the soldiers to shoot some of them. They did. The soldiers then dragged the dead cattle and the burned corpse up the escarpment.

Tim Asch, the photographer who had come with us, was at the top of the escarpment when the soldiers arrived. I had stayed in camp because under the circumstances, I didn't want to leave my children. But as the soldiers loaded the corpses into the trucks, Tim took photos. The first I learned about any of this was when the army trucks came back to my camp. Idi Amin got out of his truck, walked over to me, and demanded that I drive the skinless corpse fifty miles to the government post in Moroto.

What to do? Take my children in a car with a corpse? Leave them behind with Idi Amin? I looked at him. He was a scary guy—the portrayal of him by Forest Whitaker in *The Last King of Scotland* was amazingly accurate, especially by someone who perhaps had never met him—and standing in front of me, much taller and more massive in every way than I was, staring at me with his feet apart and his arms folded, he seemed the ultimate in machismo. *I could appeal to that*, I thought, and with a sorrowful, feminine expression on my face, I looked up at him and told him that the road was muddy and my car was not strong, not like his powerful army trucks. I wasn't sure I could drive well enough to get all the way to Moroto. I said I'd like to help but I didn't think I could and I was sorry.

It worked. Men such as he are glad to hear about the weakness of women. He turned on his heel, got back in a truck, and they left.

A few days later, two businesslike British gentlemen, obviously with military connections but dressed in plain clothes, came to our camp. They asked us to give them the film Tim had taken at the top of the escarpment. We asked why. They said they wanted photos of Turkanas whom they would identify by their tribal markings. We thought the two men didn't know what they were talking about, because the Turkanas didn't have tribal markings. Neither did the Dodoth or any other of the related people. Those were the days when cameras used rolls of film that had to be developed, so we didn't have prints or copies. Believing that our film would do them no good, we said we couldn't give it. The two men made their farewells and left.

Now I wish we had given them the film. The two men had lied to us, and I wish they had told us what I think was the truth, that they wanted a photo of Idi Amin with the corpse of a murdered citizen of Kenya who had nothing to do with the current raiding. At the time, Idi Amin was the only African with high rank in the King's African Rifles—I believe he was a colonel—and because of this, the other soldiers were loyal to him. So he was on his way up politically, eventually to begin his reign of terror in Uganda by means of a military coup. The two men and whoever they represented must have known how dangerous he was and wanted to stop him. As government agents, the two men could have confiscated the film, if not that day, then later with a court order. I wish they had. I'll bet they do too.

While writing this chapter I saw on the Internet a photo posted by Brian Jones on a website called thecompassedge.net, a photo taken in 2004 of Dodoth men driving a large herd of cattle through Kaabong. From the photo, I gathered that Kaabong had changed very little. The men had changed, however. They were wearing Western clothes, and at least one of them carried what seemed to be a Chinese assault rifle. I e-mailed Brian Jones to ask about the other men in the photo, and very helpfully he told me that all of them were armed with guns of one kind or another. Earlier I had spoken with an anthropologist who had been in Dodoth County, and she told me that every man and boy in northern Uganda had at least one AK-47, if not two, on his person, and also belts of ammunition. For this, I learned, the Dodoth could thank Idi Amin, who had kept a storehouse near Kaabong filled with thousands of weapons and millions of rounds of ammunition. The storehouse was just a big tin shed, which the Dodoth men easily broke into. From then on, virtually all of them had weapons, and after Ugandan independence, nothing stopped them from acquiring more. When I was there, the fathers of those men would chant, "Our enemies will meet a spear." Those days were gone forever.

I doubt that the wildlife has survived the automatic weapons — certainly not the large predators — but back when I was in Dodoth there were still quite a few. I didn't get much chance to consider them except to wonder how they managed, because thanks to overgrazing by the livestock, especially by goats, there seemed to be few antelopes or any other large prey. That left mostly baboons, warthogs, and hyraxes as potential prey, and of course the livestock, but the predators almost never preyed upon Dodoth livestock, and wisely so.

Now and then I had to go to Moroto for some reason, and David would go with me. We were always the only car on the road, which ran for fifty miles through wild country. Usually we'd come home in the dark, and often enough we'd see lions. They'd be walking along the road, as lions do, but would move off in a subdued manner, ears up but not stiff, facial expressions calm but cautious, body language saying *No worries — we're just getting out of your way.*

One night on that road, soon after seeing lions, we got a flat tire. I stopped the car and would have gotten out to change it, but David said not to. He said we were too close to the lions so I should keep driving and he'd tell me where to stop. So I did, despite the damage to the tire. The place he chose to stop was flanked by a dark forest, but nevertheless we got out to change the tire. Then I noticed a tiny, darkened hut about thirty feet from the road. Somehow David had known about it. He said we were safer near a human dwelling.

I was surprised, but then it came to me that the northern Uganda lions took pains to avoid people. I saw them a number of times, always at night, but never once heard them roaring. In the Kalahari, lions had roared themselves hoarse whenever they felt like it, even roaring when they heard thunder, as if they thought more lions were up in the sky. In contrast, the Dodoth lions hid from people by being inconspicuous, and considering the people they hid from, no wonder.

This was not true of leopards, because leopards, being solitary and also much smaller than lions, had less trouble coexisting with people. If cattle and goats denuded an area, making it uninhabitable for the larger antelopes, the resident leopard could live on hyraxes and monkeys. As for the leopard who sometimes visited our camp, I didn't know what he was eating, but obviously he was finding something and I was happy for him, just as long as he wasn't after one of us.

One afternoon I accompanied some of the Dodoth to a dance in a settlement two or three miles away, but not until after dark did I learn that the people with whom I'd gone were planning to spend the night. This meant I would be going back to camp by myself. Since I had been counting on my companions to find the way home, I hadn't taken a flashlight, and of course no weapon, but I thought, *Oh well,* and started walking.

The moon was low in the west, the night was dark, and I had a long way to travel. I got lost in the heavy bush, but with the help of the constellation Orion I was trying to go east, hoping to cross a north-south track made earlier by my vehicle.

Instead, I crossed a footpath. I stopped and looked around and noticed the outline of a hill against the sky. There were plenty of hills in the area, but the hill I was looking at seemed to resemble Morukore. If so, my camp would be on it and the path led toward it. Without a better idea of where to go, I started up the path. If it wasn't the right hill, I could always keep going east in search of the vehicle track.

Suddenly, just ahead of me, a leopard coughed. This was worrisome. Evidently I was walking toward him. But since I didn't know where I was except that I was very near a leopard, I had no idea where else to go. I didn't want to stand still in the dark, in case, not hearing footsteps, he might approach me. I also didn't want to turn and walk in another direction, because then he'd be behind me, and leopards attack from behind. At least he was trying to tell me where he was. Hoping that I was right about the hill and my camp, I took the only option left to me and kept walking slowly toward him.

He coughed again, louder. *What are you doing? I'm a leopard.* Well, I certainly knew he was a leopard, but could think of no other plan except to keep going. I believe he became exasperated, because after a moment of what seemed like astonished silence as he listened to my slowly advancing footsteps, he coughed three times, as fast and forcefully as he could. *You're not listening! Now you're too close!* But I still didn't know what else to do except keep going.

He didn't cough again, so perhaps he decided that his warnings were useless. As I approached the place where he'd been coughing, I got the feeling that he had left. If he hadn't, at least he lay low and let me pass safely.[2]

It was the Old Way. He never would have coughed if he was hunting me, in which case I'd be nothing but the dust of a dried-up leopard scat by now. Surely he coughed so that I wouldn't come up on him, get scared, and take the offensive in close quarters. For all their predatory skills, leopards are cautious. Evidently he wanted some distance between himself and a potential passerby.

Old rules govern the Old Way, and he was keeping one of the rules as it applies to cats. Do not fight and risk injury if you can help it, as an injury will decrease your chances for survival. You can warn and threaten, but don't attack unless you must. Animals have all kinds of methods for avoiding unnecessary confrontations. I think of the neighborhood cats that vocalized in my parents' basement without actually fighting—the cats I observed when I was five. The leopard's method, it seemed, was to alert me to his presence. When I didn't seem to understand, he took the initiative and left.

The hill was Morukore, my camp was on it, and I reached it in a fairly short time. This was not because I ran, but because the camp was near. There is nothing worse than running from a predator unless you're sure you can get to safety before he gets to you. Better to show confidence, as if you feel so strong and competent that the predator is of no concern. If you can't do that, then it's often best to face him and try to make yourself seem bigger—by holding your coat or your backpack over your head, for instance, as hikers facing cougars are advised to do. This is why our skin prickles when we're scared. We're raising our hair to seem bigger, although we don't know this consciously. We do as we would have done when our body hair was long and thick, back when we lived in the trees, back when our raised hair would make us seem much bigger, and I find it quite touching that we humans with our tiny body hairs continue to do this. Obviously the leopard was the one who watched our camp. My body hair rose when I heard his first cough. I was, in a sense, trying.

After our six-month sojourn in Uganda, we all went home and I wrote *Warrior Herdsmen*. William Shawn published it as a series of articles, and Knopf published it as a book. I sent a copy to David, who liked it. Mr. Shawn then wanted me to write another piece for *The New Yorker*. I'd written about hunter-gatherers whose lives were reminiscent of the Paleolithic, and also about pastoralists whose lives were somewhat reminiscent of the last part of the Neolithic, so I thought my next subject should probably be one of the precolonial African cities. Ibadan in Nigeria met that description, so I thought I'd try it. This was fine with Mr. Shawn, who again gave me lots of money.

I sometimes think of the cattle I was offered for my daughter. Had I accepted, I might have over 20,000 head by now. Sometimes I feel the tiniest pang of regret—not that I don't love my daughter dearly, but she lives in Texas, which as far as I'm concerned is almost as far away as Kaabong. We wouldn't have lost touch, or not completely, because I'm sure that by now there's a phone in Kaabong. I thought of this years ago when she told me she was getting married. I remembered the wealth that had slipped away from me, and suggested that her husband-to-be give me at least something, maybe a cat. He said he would, but he is Jewish, and unlike the northern Ugandan pastoralists, Jews don't give animals in exchange for women, so in the end he forgot. It served me right for having such thoughts.

9

NIGERIA

NIGERIA HAD BEEN INDEPENDENT for five years when we arrived. One of the most significant political figures in the country, Chief Obafemi Awolowo, was in prison. We didn't understand the importance of this at first, nor could we foresee what would happen as a result.

Steve came with me. Tom Johnson came too, just to be with us because, to our infinite sorrow, Kirsti had died of a stroke two years earlier. Also with us was a young American woman whom I'd hired as a nanny for our children, who by then were six and eight. The children, of course, came with us, as did our two little dogs.

We went to Ibadan, a Yoruba city that was the capital of Nigeria's Western Region, where we bought a car, rented a condo in a layout that belonged to the University of Ibadan, and enrolled our children in the English-speaking school that served the university community. Our kids seemed to be the only Americans, at least in their grades, so they were fair game for the other kids, and also perhaps for the teachers.

We had named our son John for my brother, never dreaming that he would one day attend a British school or that the Brits call their penises John Thomas. Not only that, but he was the youngest, smallest boy in his class. The other kids bullied him so mercilessly that on one occasion he came home with a black eye and on another occasion he ran away. His British teacher didn't seem to notice the bullying or his departure, and she phoned us to ask why he wasn't in class. Surprised because we had taken him to school ourselves and had watched him trudge unhappily into the building, we went to look for him. No one from the school seemed to care that he was missing.

Luckily the Yoruba groundskeeper cared, and showed us which direction he'd taken. We found him very sensibly climbing along a steep embankment above the only highway, rather than walking in the traffic. He was almost a mile from the school by then, and obviously had a sense of direction, as he was only six and the route to the school was complicated. Probably that made no difference, though, because in the back seat of our car on his way to school, crouched down with misery, he couldn't have seen where we were going. But he had made no mistakes and was almost home.

Many people — certainly many westerners — can't orient themselves without equipment, so I was exceptionally proud of him. A cougar could not have done better.

We didn't like to see our children suffer, so in time we developed a what-the-heck attitude. They could go to school if they felt like it, but they didn't have to. Some of the neighbors felt as we did, so our kids could play with theirs.

Eventually, as a young adult, our son dropped his first name and used his middle name, Ramsay. This was due to some issues with my brother, not because of the British slang for *penis*, which by then was forgotten. So at first he was John, later he was Ramsay, and hereafter I refer to him as Ramsay.

One day the young nanny borrowed our car and drove off to do a little sightseeing. Alas, in one of the villages along the road, she ran over a man and killed him. Sometimes when such a thing happened the villagers would kill the driver of the car, but the nanny was so broken by the experience that they took pity on her. They said it was the man's fault. I don't remember all that happened after that, but the nanny soon went home. So things began rather badly.

But if the Nigerian experience was lukewarm for our children and dreadful for the nanny, it was good for Steve. He made friends with the editor of the *Nigerian Tribune*, Ayo Ojewumi, and also with Olu Olofin, editor of *Irohin Yoruba*, then a highly political Yoruba-language weekly paper in Ibadan. Olu became one of the closest friends Steve ever had, so close that they became known as "the twins," and thanks to him and Ayo, Steve came to know every person of interest in the progressive political spectrum, from the leaders to the thugs, who, as it happened, were known as "field assistants." Young women found the dignified title attractive. The wide political spectrum fascinated Steve and awoke his love of politics.

The political situation was complicated and has been written about by various historians with varying amounts of bias. Here I will just paint the broad strokes. The large picture, of course, began with colonization, when the colonizing powers drew lines on the map of Africa and declared the enclosed areas to be nations. The lines creating Nigeria enclosed no fewer than 453 different tribes, each of which had its own culture and language. Little attention was paid to the tribes themselves, so in some cases the national borders cut across their areas, leaving part of a group in the newly formed Nigeria and their relatives in the nations that were to become Cameroon, Benin, Niger, and Chad. Also the northern part of the new Nigeria was savannah, the southern part was rainforest, and the middle part was mixed, so the regions had totally different economies. It was as if some authority in a big city had captured a crowded subway train and tried to force the passengers to behave like a family.

Because of the cultural issues, Nigeria was then subdivided into three main areas — the Northern Region, where the largest ethnic groups were Hausa and Fulani; the Eastern Region, where the largest ethnic group was Ibo; and the Western Region, where the largest ethnic group was Yoruba but was divided into different tribal units which in the not-so-distant past had made war on each other. Some of the enmity lingered.

Then during the colonial period people began to move around, so that each region gained communities of ethnic minorities in addition to the indigenous populations. A large Hausa community went to Yoruba Ibadan, for instance, complete with its traditional culture. In all this there seemed to be no unifying element. Each group looked after its own.

At the time of independence, a struggle arose as to which group would dominate. Representation in parliament was based on population, so the census-takers, being of the same ethnicity as those they were counting, exaggerated the figures so greatly that the census was considered a joke. This was most flagrant in the Northern Region, which was getting the highest numbers, so the party of the Eastern Region joined with the progressive party of the Western Region in an effort to have representation. Even so, the conservative, authoritarian party of the Northern Region came out on top, controlling the federal government as well as the Western Region by means of a conservative but not very popular Yoruba party that was allied with the north.

Widespread rioting resulted. Chief Awolowo, leader of the large, progressive Yoruba party (the Action Group), was imprisoned. Not surprisingly, this caused profound resentment among his party members and clouded the prospects for the next election, which was upcoming when we arrived. I was about to get a lesson in the New Way — the politics of mankind rather than the appeal of nature.

Most of the Yoruba people in Ibadan belonged to the Action Group, which gave them considerable unity. This came home to me when we tried to get a telephone. We went to the phone company to apply and learned that the waiting period was six months to a year. Steve mentioned this to his friend Olu, and Olu, a member of the Action Group, took Steve to meet a certain chief, also a member of the Action Group, who had connections to the phone company. Three days later a crew was at our condo installing the phone, and that evening we had phone service.

As for political unity, this was not a rare example. Far from it. Now and then Steve would telephone the leader of the Action Group, Alhaji Dawodu Adegbenro, the man who replaced the imprisoned Chief Awolowo. The alhaji[1] lived in Abeokuta, a small but important city about forty miles southeast of Ibadan; thus the phone call was long distance, for which one needed the operator.

On one occasion Steve gave the operator the alhaji's number. She too belonged to the Action Group, or so it appeared when she asked, "Do you want to speak with the alhaji himself?"

Surprised, Steve said he did.

"He's not at home," said the operator. "He's in Lagos. Will I ring him there?"

Steve said please do, and moments later he and the alhaji were talking.

---

1 Alhaji is the title taken by those who make the haj, the holy pilgrimage to Mecca.

The alhaji and Steve became friends, and Steve and I would sometimes visit him in Abeokuta. I was wowed by him — not only was he a brilliant, congenial person, but he liked dogs. His three wives, also brilliant and congenial, were equally awesome, each of them strong and self-sufficient like most Yoruba women, each with her own successful business which she ran herself, with no involvement by the alhaji. I'd listen while all of them talked politics.

This, of course, fed Steve's interests, but I learned something that fed mine when the alhaji told us how he had determined Eid al-Fitr, a three-day festival at the end of Ramadan. A feast had been prepared but could not be enjoyed until the right people saw the new crescent moon, the sign that Ramadan had ended. That year, as often happened in the forested parts of Nigeria, the new crescent was hidden by clouds. So the alhaji called an imam in Kano, five hundred miles northeast of Ibadan in northern Nigeria, to ask if he had seen the crescent. Kano is in open country and the sky is usually clear, but that night Kano was also cloudy and the imam had not seen the moon. The alhaji then called an imam in Maiduguri, six hundred miles northeast of Ibadan, still in Nigeria but at the edge of the Sahara. Even Maiduguri was cloudy, so the alhaji called an imam in Khartoum, two thousand miles northeast of Ibadan, in the Sudan. And yes, in Khartoum the imam had seen the crescent. Ramadan had ended, and in Ibadan the feast could begin. The alhaji said that if Khartoum had been cloudy, his next call would have been to Mecca. That's almost three thousand miles away in Saudi Arabia, and the call would have been costly, but by then Mecca would have been the only option, because the moon had to be seen.

We didn't have much to do with the expatriate community, which was mostly British, mostly tied up with the university and the arts, and far above the ongoing hassle of politics. But Steve was different. Within a fairly short time, his friendships expanded so widely that he found connections not only in the Western Region but also in the Eastern Region. In the evenings he would join various groups of men at a nightspot called the Rose Catering Club or a bar called Total Gardens, part of the gas station that sold Total gasoline, where they would drink beer and eat tree snails while talking politics. The people at the American consulate in Ibadan became aware of Steve's connections and now and then would phone him if they needed information.

This too was interesting, because almost any English-speaking man could have done what Steve did — any man who was politically inclined and fun to be with — because almost everybody spoke English and nothing about the political scene was confidential. Far from it. Most people spoke of nothing else, and that Steve was an American bothered no one because if people thought about America at all, they were perfectly happy to know that at least one American took an interest.

Steve was not only interested, he was fascinated. Originally we had gone to Nigeria with the plan of working together, but very quickly our objectives diverged, and I seldom saw him. The understanding he acquired and the friendships he formed remained a high point in his life, so much so — interestingly — that fifty years later, after I wrote this chapter and showed it to him, he was astonished that our experiences had been so different. "Were we in the same country?" he asked.

We were, of course, but we didn't seem to be because I had no involvement with politics. My task was to get a sense of a traditional African city. Ibadan dated from the nineteenth century, so one of the first things I did, with an interpreter, was to meet the chief priest of its patron goddess. The chief priest was a kindly, elderly man who with other members of his family lived in one of the traditional compounds of Ibadan, and he was generous enough to talk with me. But all he wanted to talk about was the political situation!

I soon became aware that he was probably the most conservative person I'd ever met, even though he seemed to lean toward the liberal Action Group. This would be because he was from Ibadan and didn't like the fact that the party in power in the Western Region was associated with Oyo, a city that at one time had been at war with Ibadan. He chose the Action Group because it was not associated with Oyo. But that didn't make him a liberal.

The political situation was riveting, but I wasn't there for that and I kept trying to turn the conversation. My best success came when I asked the chief priest what was wrong with his leg, which was swollen and which he kept propped on a pillow. A guinea worm was in his leg, he told me, and showed me the hole from which the worm's head would sometimes emerge. Guinea worms are huge, two or three feet long and as thick as cooked spaghetti noodles. The worm made a bulge under his skin, and he experienced burning pain whenever it changed its position.

I was horrified, and as soon as I got home that day I consulted my medical handbook, because I thought that western medicine might help. From my handbook I learned that you get guinea worms from drinking contaminated water. That came as no surprise but wasn't enough information, so I consulted a Nigerian medical doctor, who told me he would treat the chief priest without charge if I took him to the Ibadan hospital.

I rushed back to the chief priest and told him all this, but he just smiled in a patronizing manner. He wouldn't go to that doctor, he said, because he didn't believe in western medicine. I praised the medical doctor, which did nothing to alter the chief priest's opinion. Then I turned to the question of water. He should boil it, I told him. Again he smiled. "Boiling kills the life in the water," he said. I felt a surge of hope. "That's right," I cried. "And guinea worms are part of that life." But again my information was worthless. The kind of life he had in mind was of a spiritual nature.

He was always polite and gracious, but he had a habit of looking at the ceiling and talking with someone else while I tried to talk about guinea worms and water, and I soon saw the hopelessness of someone like me changing the mind of someone like him. Foreign, white, and a woman, I was not the kind of person he'd be likely to believe, so I could understand his position. If the situation had been reversed and he had tried to persuade me not to boil water, I would have been interested and respectful and I would not have looked at the ceiling, but he was a priest, not a scientist, so I wouldn't have believed him either.

In time I gave up. Now and then on later visits I'd beseech him to let me take him to the medical doctor, but I soon saw that this also was beginning to annoy him, so I gave it up too. Even so, every time the guinea worm moved it would hurt him, and he suffered. One day I saw that someone had managed to capture a few millimeters of the guinea worm and wrap it around a matchstick with the idea of slowly rolling it up until all of it was out, but at about that time the political situation overtook us and my visits with the chief priest ended. He was a wise and very interesting person, so this is one of my regrets.

No doubt I wasted the chief priest's time, but he certainly didn't waste mine, because, perhaps in hopes of diverting my attention from boiled water and western medicine, he agreed to talk about religious ceremonies. Often a sacrifice would accompany them.

At many of the important ceremonies, animals were sacrificed. I'd seen goats and even a dog sacrificed at various altars. Sometimes I was there and sometimes I saw the sacrifice on television, because the Nigerian broadcasting station covered the local events. On one occasion the sacrificed animal was an ox.

I was somewhat surprised, as I didn't understand how an ox could be traditional. Cattle didn't live in Yoruba country because the area is forested, and in the forest are tsetse flies, which are lethal to cattle. Cattle appeared in the Western Region only because Hausa or Fulani people drove them down from the north and sold them at a market just outside Ibadan.

It seemed unusual that people from an ancient culture would import sacrificial animals, because normally if people are going to sacrifice something, the sacrifice has cultural significance. In Uganda, the Dodoth sacrificed cattle because cattle were the most highly prized, most precious offerings. Nothing had more value than an ox as far as the Dodoth were concerned. So did cattle also mean something to the Yorubas?

I asked the chief priest, who told me that cattle had no traditional meaning. They were substitutes, he told me. When he didn't want to take this further and changed the subject when I asked what the substitute was for, I realized that cattle were substitutes for human beings.

Human sacrifice, a time-honored practice, has occurred all over the world, from the land of the Aztecs to the Holy Land. The Bible tells us that Abraham was prepared to sacrifice his son, which is not something one would do unless it were culturally tolerable — and that was two thousand years ago. The practice was common in West Africa — most notably in Nigeria during the early 1900s, when a woman whose father was the king of Oyo and whose husband was the king of Ibadan was sacrificed to enable warriors from Ibadan to cross a swollen river. One thinks of the warriors of ancient Greece planning to sacrifice Agamemnon's daughter, Iphigenia, again for the purpose of crossing water. In Nigeria the British colonial powers forbade human sacrifice, but the memory of it was still fresh in the minds of anyone born in the precolonial period. That would include the chief priest.

I found this very interesting. Respect for humanity makes a person the highest possible offering. Christians would say that the most valued person in the world, God's own son, became a sacrifice to save humanity. I remembered the Episcopal boarding school I attended, where every Sunday we were expected to take communion in the form of a wafer which represented the body of Christ and a sip of wine which represented his blood. (Actually we took a sip of grape juice, which represented wine, which represented blood.) With cattle representing people, the Yorubas were doing something similar. Fourteen hundred years ago, a deer was substituted for Iphigenia, so the concept of substitution was not new. I asked the chief priest what kind of offering the Ibadan goddess wanted, but he didn't answer. I had made him uneasy with my interest in sacrifices.

One day the Nigerian Broadcasting Corporation televised an important ritual for which an ox was sacrificed. A big crowd was present, me in the middle of it, and many other people tuned in, as there was nothing else to watch. Thus this event was witnessed by many, and soon gave rise to a rumor about the death a few years earlier of the alake of Abeokuta, ruler of the Egba Yorubas. Traditionally when an alake died, a person was sacrificed, and when this greatly respected ruler died, an ox should have been substituted. But perhaps that didn't happen.

A taxi with Abeokuta plates was seen trying to get a fare near the University of Ibadan. Students from afar attended the university and would not have known of the Abeokuta custom, or of the alake's death, for that matter. A student was rumored to have hailed the taxi and was never seen again. If a student did indeed become a victim, he or she would have been thrown off a famous cliff known as the Rock of Abeokuta.

Or that's what I was told. The rumor was not for me to judge, but plenty of Yoruba people believed it, and I was tempted to believe it myself when something similar happened. I had a book, *Religion in an Af-*

rican City, by Geoffrey Parrinder, an authority on comparative religion, in which I read that on Easter Monday a human sacrifice was offered in a lake near Ibadan. So on Easter Monday morning I went to that lake.

Swarms of people were gathered on the shores, looking at the water as if they were waiting for something. Two or three men were swimming, and eventually one of them went under. I had been watching him from a distance, and right before he disappeared his expression was troubled, or at least preoccupied. He didn't come up. The crowd was absolutely silent. He still didn't come up. Then a deep, excited murmur went through the crowd and someone called the police, who came and made the crowd disperse.

Later I went to the police station and learned the name and address of the drowned man. On my behalf, Steve's friend Olu went to visit the man's family and learned that a few days earlier he had given away his motorbike and other personal items. Olu would have pressed the matter further, but the family didn't like his questions and in a threatening manner told him to leave.

The drowning was considered an accident, or at least not a homicide, and I was sure that the latter was true. I'd seen the whole thing not forty feet away, and I knew no other person was involved. Even so, I told the police what I had read in Parrinder. They were not from Ibadan and hadn't known about the annual sacrifice but were interested, and took Parrinder's information seriously. But they said that if the death was a sacrifice, it must have been a voluntary self-sacrifice, perhaps through the action of a crocodile, because at least one crocodile lived in the lake. The police also decided that the lake should be fenced off.

The fence went up, a massive construction, but I never learned if it was effective. By the following Easter, Nigeria was in a state of anarchy and was about to erupt into civil war. It was this that ended my conversations with the chief priest, which was unfortunate — not that he would have offered any insight, necessarily, as any spiritual matter above the fact that water has life was not what he cared to discuss. Yet few things would have been more informative than inquiry into the Easter Monday drowning. Human sacrifice was certainly traditional, but for Christians? Did Jesus inspire the custom? Jesus is said to have accepted his role, as did the man in the lake, evidently, so was the Christian story deeper, more real, and more immediate to Yoruba believers than it is to western believers? Millions of Christians in the western world and elsewhere ardently believe in Christ's sacrifice, but none of them offer themselves in a similar manner. Nigerians did, or so it seemed, and had done so for years, according to Parrinder. But with all that was happening between that Easter and the next, I had no hope of exploring the issue.

Before the election, I didn't see much campaigning as we in America know it, except that now and then a passing truck with a loudspeaker would remind the public to vote. After all, the political parties, not the candidates, were at issue, and the likelihood of persuading a voter to change parties was almost zero. Best just to get them to the polls. And people seemed eager to get to the polls, even though most assumed that the election would be rigged. I attended several sessions of the regional legislature, and during one of them a legislator leaned over to Chief Akintola, the premier of the Western Region, and said ferociously, "If you rig this election I will kill you."

The assumption that rigging would take place brought voters to the polls in large numbers, but to no avail, as the election was evidently rigged successfully and plenty of thought had gone into the effort. For instance, an important political figure whose surname was Fani-Kay-ode—also known as "Fani-Power"—was said to have dressed as a nun and transported a coffin filled with illegal ballots in a hearse. The story was generally believed but not confirmed. Fani-Kayode granted Steve an interview, so Steve might have asked, but in the end he decided not to. Nonetheless, so many people did believe it that rumors of Fani-Kayode's death began to circulate. This confused the American embassy. "Fani dead, Kayode safe," they reported in a written message, evidently unaware that Fani and Kayode were one person.

Despite the extensive, widely recognized rigging, the election itself was quiet enough. As I remember, I barely noticed it, although Steve certainly did. For a day or two after the results were announced, nothing happened. Few people had access to a newspaper or the radio, and it took time for word to spread. But when it did, the region erupted. People began killing each other and setting fire to cars and houses.

The following is from a letter I should never have written to my parents:

Violence and sorrow are everywhere. This region, and (it follows) our fieldwork, are by now almost entirely involved with violence and fear. I recently visited a town where one man, for political reasons, was beaten to death and two others were locked in their burning houses and burned to death, and another man had his hand chopped off before being soaked with gasoline and immolated (according to one story) or else pushed back in his house and burned with it (according to another story). The maimed and the dead were supporters of Chief Akintola's party. That party had opposed the Action Group, and its members were getting revenge.

I didn't mention another visit to a village where killings had taken place the night before. The person I had gone to see showed me the blood of the victims splashed on houses all up and down a street. He didn't seem to know the reason for this, or so he said, but I suspect it was because these victims too belonged to the wrong party. My host hadn't anticipated such violence, however, so it left him horrified and shaken. Another day, on a visit to a different person in a different village, I learned that an hour earlier a man and his wife had been rolled up in rugs and burned with their house. The ruins were still burning.

Much of the violence was against Hausas. Some of it might have been to settle scores, but most of it was because Hausas were from the Northern Region, home of the dominant political party, which apparently had rigged the election in its favor. Those who lost the election wanted revenge, not just against the higher-ups but against anybody. Once a teenage boy — who as I could see from his white clothing was a Hausa — dashed across the road in front of my car, a few feet ahead of a gang of tough-looking Yoruba men with clubs who were chasing him. I would have taken the boy in the car, but he was gone in an instant. To this day I think about that boy. My mind's eye still sees him.

Because of the general anarchy, the police had more than they could handle, and not a few people looked for ways to profit. Everywhere, gangs of crooks tore down the telephone lines to sell the wire. And everywhere, gangs of thugs — not the political party's "field assistants," just self-employed thugs—put up roadblocks, mostly of rocks or burning tires, and when the oncoming cars had to stop because they couldn't pass, the thugs would demand money from the drivers.

Often enough my fearless Steve would meet such a roadblock, but with his unfailing sense of humor he'd get out of the car and make friends with the robbers. They'd all laugh for a while, and then he'd give them some money. They would thank him and wave as he drove away. Often enough they'd let him go back the other way without paying. One of our neighbors wasn't so lucky, perhaps because she had an attitude problem common to white people, especially those such as herself, a British expatriate. When she came to one such roadblock she got out of her car, marched over to the leading thug, and ordered him to let her pass. The leader beckoned to another thug, who brought a five-gallon can of gasoline. The leader poured the gas over her car, lit a match, and said, "Money." Of course she quickly gave him money and the thug blew out the match, but the event left her permanently shaken.

One day Steve and I went to the Northern Region with our children. We started home the next afternoon. Just at dusk, we came around a bend in the road and saw a young man carrying a large rock. This must have been heavy work—he seemed tired and moved slowly because he had already brought about twenty other large rocks and had piled them up across the road. He was bringing the last rock when we came along. About two feet of open road were left, so we sped through the open place with the right wheels on the pavement and the left wheels on the roadside grass. The young man dropped his rock and sagged with disappointment as his unbelieving eyes watched our escape.

We were the only people who seemed to be traveling, and we could probably expect more bandits farther along, so we decided to spend the night nearby and travel in the morning. But where to go? We found a large excavation pit with mounds of earth which would hide our car unless someone actually came into the pit, and we slept there. Or we tried to. We got home the next day.

Every morning the radio announced itself not with words but with talking drums. These drums said clearly and in English, "This is the Nigerian Broadcasting Corporation." It worked as follows: This is (*tum ta*) the Nigerian (*ta ta-tum-ta-ta*) Broadcasting (*ta-tum-ta*) Corporation (*tum-ta-tum-ta*). The drums had tones, though, as does the Yoruba language, and the tones seemed to clarify the message, which without them might have said something else. To hear this was a sort of bright spot in my otherwise anxious and sometimes terrified life. But there was very little news. As far as the radio was concerned, it almost seemed as if nothing much was happening, although the roadblocks, the fires, and the killings were spreading.

Even so, everyone tuned in, hoping to hear something official, something better than the many rumors. Mostly we heard the usual highlife and juju music. But one memorable morning in January, we turned on the radio and heard Schubert's Unfinished Symphony.

Uh-oh. That wasn't right. In fact, it was terrifying. The radio station seemed to be under new management, which must have happened during the night. People whose phones still worked began to telephone each other feverishly. Eventually it emerged that soldiers had killed the prime minister, also the premier of the Northern Region, also Chief Akintola, premier of the Western Region, as well as other soldiers and important political figures. The rebels had taken over the government buildings and the radio station and God knows what else. In short, there'd been a coup.

We didn't know this early that morning. We just listened with horror to the Unfinished Symphony. But I am here to tell you that if unexplained western classical music comes over the only radio station of a third world country, the feathers have hit the fan.

Because Steve was so knowledgeable about the political situation, the American consulate called him up to see if he had learned anything, but for all his connections, he was as surprised as they were. Then someone from the Peace Corps called to report a rumor that Akintola had been killed, but no one could confirm it. *What do you mean, can't confirm it?* I said to myself. *I'll confirm it.* And I got in the car.

On the way to the premier's residence, I made up a story to explain my visit. I would tell whoever wanted to know that I had an appointment with one of the premier's assistants, and would feel safe in doing so because I had already met that person and was sure that at the first sign of trouble he would flee. As I approached the premier's driveway, I saw a searchlight—the kind used to find planes at night during World War II —still on and pointed at the sky. That it was on in the daytime, or for that matter that it was there at all, seemed sinister. The lights in the residence were on too and the doors were open, which also seemed sinister. And when I drove up in front of the residence, I saw the premier, naked except for his jockey shorts, lying dead on the lawn.

So the rumor was true. Evidently he was shot inside the residence and dragged outdoors. As I was taking in the enormity of what I was looking at, a soldier with an automatic weapon ran up to my car, wide-eyed and very excited. "What are you doing?" he shouted. He seemed frightened. I started to tell him about my fictional appointment, but before I could finish he was screaming that I was in great danger and should leave at once. So I did.

Steve called the consulate and I called the Peace Corps, but by then they probably knew about the coup, because the prime minister's body had also been found, as had the body of the premier of the Northern Region.

The coup was said to be bloodless because not many people had been killed. For a day or two everything was quiet. Even so, the radio continued to broadcast classical music by Brahms and Beethoven, which seemed even more dire than the Unfinished Symphony, no doubt to remind us of the gravity of our situation.

But there wasn't a single word of real news. Instead, rumors kept coming. We heard that the United States and Great Britain were angered by the coup and planned to invade Nigeria with paratroopers to restore the displaced government. Having lived at Fort Bragg, I didn't like the sound of that, as nobody would want to be in a place invaded by the 82nd Airborne.

At this point Tom Johnson wisely decided to go home, and not a moment too soon. As Steve drove him to the airport, a gang of thugs stopped them, and Steve had to joke them out of burning his car. Not an hour after Tom's plane took off, the airport was closed, along with the ports and all the borders. We expatriates learned that we were hostages, to be used unless the United States and Great Britain changed their minds.

I should have gone with Tom, taking the children and the dogs, but I didn't. I thought that perhaps after the coup the country would have a new government and things would settle down. They didn't, but at least some people were benefiting from the confusion: we learned that at the morgue where Chief Akintola's body had been taken, the attendants were selling views of his corpse. At first the price was high, but day by day the price went down, until the body could be viewed for a shilling. But even at that price I didn't go there. I'd already seen the body.

A rumor began to circulate that American citizens would be evacuated by plane. I went to the consulate to get on the list. I then went home, and as I was going into our condo my neighbor, a woman from India whose husband taught at the university, ran up to me because she too had heard the rumor. She was frantic with fear, with which I could certainly empathize, and she asked for my help in getting her and her family on the plane. Yes, they were from India, but her infant son had been born in the United States. *Hooray!* I thought, and told her I'd do everything in my power, and with that I went back to the consulate and insisted that there was an American in our neighborhood who was not on the list and was too young to leave without his parents. He and his parents should also be on the list. Miraculously, the consulate agreed and added their names. I went back and told our neighbor, who wept with relief. I wept too, but it was all for nothing—the plane never came.

Soon after that I heard that soldiers were massing at the school my children attended. Why were my children in school at a time like that? Because all the other children were also in school. The parents wanted to keep an air of normalcy, and everybody thought the school had no military importance.

We were wrong. I rushed to the school, where I saw soldiers with machine guns all over the place, some digging trenches across the lawns and walkways, others positioning huge artillery pieces as if they were expecting something. I didn't know who these soldiers were or what side they were on, which is certainly the down side of being a civilian in another country's war, but on the other hand, what did it matter? I grabbed my children and shoved them in the car.

Just then the headmistress, an Englishwoman, marched up to the commanding officer, who was loading an automatic weapon. She coldly informed him that he and his soldiers were on school property and they must leave at once. *Good God, woman, what are you doing?* I thought, starting my car. The officer gave her the briefest possible glance and went on loading his weapon. I later learned that the soldiers were establishing a perimeter. They were expecting an invasion from the north.

Needless to say, that was my children's last day in the school, if only because I realized that the headmistress had very poor judgment. Thus my children may have been the only people in Nigeria who found a silver lining in the very heavy cloud. Well, perhaps not the only people. By then the radio station had resumed its broadcast of highlife and juju music, and introduced a new highlife song called "Machine Gun," pronounced *Mochine* (with the *o* as in *mop* and the accent on the first syllable) *Gon*. I hope the musicians made some money.

I wanted to go home, but the borders were closed. I thought of trying to get near the border of Niger by car, then abandoning the car and crossing the border on foot through the bush at night. I planned, of course, to take my children and the dogs, but the walk across the desert to the nearest community would have been difficult for the children and could have put them more in harm's way than they were already. So I didn't do it. Anyway, it wasn't really a plan. It was more of a fantasy. All this time we heard gunfire and saw smoke from burning buildings.

Steve learned about one of the fires, not in Ibadan but in Lagos, where he'd been staying with two men, both good friends, in hopes of meeting a certain lawyer who had taken part in the coup. Steve had requested an appointment, but the appointment didn't materialize, so Steve spent the night in the house of one of his friends. There was only one bed, so the three men shared it, with Steve in the middle. All of them were asleep when the lawyer burst into the room. "Where is this man Thomas?" he shouted. Steve sat up and reached for his tape recorder. The lawyer grabbed the microphone and delivered an oration concerning the coup, during which the governor's house had been consumed with fire. Steve later learned that the lawyer himself had burned the house—he had sent some thugs to set the fire—but being a lawyer, he hadn't mentioned his involvement.

One day an army jeep pulled up in front of our house. Two soldiers with automatic weapons got out and banged on our door. To say I was scared doesn't describe it, but I opened the door. The soldiers were from the Northern Region, and one was an army officer, a very good friend. His name was Lieutenant Ogli, and he was from one of the small tribes in northern Nigeria—a man whom we knew very well. The other man was his driver, a sergeant. They had been fighting insurgents in the north, but the fight had spread to the army itself and non-Ibo soldiers were killing their Ibo comrades. Lieutenant Ogli was unwilling to do this, so he and his sergeant were transferring themselves to the south. He came to see us, he told us, to show that he was still alive.

When the army jeep appeared, our neighbors hid in their houses. Suddenly the street was deserted, with every door shut and every window covered. But there was one exception. Our neighbor Phil Stevens was in the Peace Corps and therefore more courageous. He came straight to our house because he was concerned for our safety. Glad to see that we were okay, he shook hands all around and joined us for coffee. I will never forget his honor or his courage. I had freedom from fear, at least for the moment.

Steve continued to travel around, visiting political activists, and I did too, as by then even I was involved with the political situation. Steve and I came to an agreement. We would not travel together or at the same time, so if trouble came while he was traveling and I was at home, I would try to escape with the children, not waiting for him. If I was traveling and he was at home, he would do the same and not wait for me. This was no way to live, but it was the best way we had, so, secure in the genuinely comforting knowledge that Steve would abandon me if necessary, I drove to Enugu in the Eastern Region to interview an Ibo gentleman, a colonel in the army and also a government official. He had a story to tell and he wanted someone to hear it, and as we sat on his sofa in his pleasant, western-style living room, he carefully explained what had happened to Ibo people after the coup. I liked him very much and wrote down everything he said, although his accounts were horrifying. A few days later, after I was back in Ibadan, I learned that he too had been killed.

In all this fear and trouble, certain events seemed very important. Lieutenant Ogli's visit was one of them. Another happened later, when our daughter got sick with a high fever. I put her in the car to take her to a doctor—a white South African whom I had never met but who ran a clinic at the university and to whom the university had assigned us. But on the way I came upon a long line of stopped traffic, perhaps seventy or eighty cars, which soldiers were searching for weapons and ammunition. Some of the soldiers were taking everything out of the cars, including the seats, from which they sometimes ripped the upholstery, while other soldiers stood by with their automatic weapons trained on the drivers and passengers.

I got out of my car and just looked at all this. My daughter was lying on the back seat, twisting from side to side with her eyes rolled up into her head, and my distress must have showed. Have I spoken earlier of the intuition, sensitivity, and empathy of many African people? I saw a young soldier looking at me from a distance. Then he walked up to me and asked what was wrong. I took him to the car so he could see my daughter and told him I was taking her to the doctor. He took one look and understood. He called to the other soldiers to let me through. In tears, I tried to thank him, but in an urgent voice he said, "Go with God" and waved me out of the line of waiting cars so I could pass them. This was the good part of the experience.

The bad part came ten minutes later, when I carried my daughter into the clinic. By then she wasn't moving and may have been unconscious. The Nigerian nursing assistant jumped up from her desk to call the white South African doctor. He was in his office and hurried out. But when he saw me standing there, he said he wouldn't help me. At first I didn't understand, and thought perhaps my daughter was so sick that nothing could be done. I must have asked a question to that effect because the next thing I heard, to my unbelieving ears, was the doctor saying that I once had taken my children to see the Peace Corps doctor, an American woman whom I had come to know as a friend. Somehow the South African doctor had learned of this and it angered him. If I didn't want him then, I couldn't have him now, so I should leave, he told me.

I couldn't make sense of this. Did the doctor want my daughter dead because long before I had consulted another doctor? I begged him, saying I hadn't meant to offend him, and the visit to the other doctor wasn't my daughter's fault. She was only eight, I told him. But the white South

African doctor was firm. Whether I meant to or not, I had done him wrong and I would pay for it. He went back to his office and shut the door while his nursing assistant watched him dismally. I had no choice but to take my daughter home, back through the line of cars that were being searched for weapons.

The Peace Corps doctor had since moved to Lagos or I would have taken my daughter to her in the first place. I would also have taken her to the Ibadan hospital, to the doctor who had offered to help the chief priest, but I couldn't get there because the road was blocked. Anyway, by then I had lost confidence in that hospital. Here's an excerpt from another letter I should never have written to my parents:

> *Close friends of ours, a Nigerian couple at the university, came home one afternoon and found their daughter with a fever. The fever was high; they took the child in a taxi to the hospital. The child was examined but not admitted, and was discharged at about 4:00 AM. The parents took her home, and by 7:00 AM she was dead.*

So my daughter had to make do without medical help. I brought down her fever with cold compresses, helped her drink water and take aspirins, and by morning she seemed a little better. Within a week she had recovered. God knows what sickness she had.

A few days later we heard that the coup had failed and the army had taken over the government. Steve learned from one of his many connections that the coup leaders had expected the army to be on their side. But for that to happen they would have had to neutralize the commanding officer, Major General Aguiyi-Ironsi. They meant to capture him or kill him if necessary, and they sent a lieutenant to do this. Aguiyi-Ironsi was a big, imposing person, brimming with authority, and when the lieutenant came around a corner pointing a gun at him, he commanded the lieutenant to hand over the weapon. His authority was such that the lieutenant hesitated just long enough for Aguiyi-Ironsi to grab the gun and wrestle it away from him. Thus Aguiyi-Ironsi remained in charge of the army, and when the new, post-coup military government was formed, he became its leader. Because he continued to control the army, his new government could appoint whomever it liked, and did not appoint the coup leaders. The decision may have partly appeased the Northern Region, but it inflamed many people in the Eastern and Western Regions, and the violence and killings got worse.

Perhaps the new unrest unnerved some leaders in the north, or perhaps Aguiyi-Ironsi unnerved them. They secretly planned yet another coup, but didn't quite keep the secret. Steve learned of it one evening while in the barracks with an army friend. He and his friend planned to visit a bar, but before they went, the friend wanted to change into civilian clothes. And while Steve sat on his friend's footlocker, waiting, two soldiers sitting on the next bed began to chat about the new coup that was coming. It came two days later. Many soldiers were loyal to Aguiyi-Ironsi, so the new coup leaders had to kill him, which this time was done successfully, and with him gone, the Northern Region again took power.

The countercoup brought some of the military action to a halt, but in the Western Region it only increased the anarchy. Groups of men began stopping all traffic that went through their villages, pulling the drivers and passengers out of the cars and buses and killing those who didn't have local tribal markings. These were the facial scarifications that had begun in slavery times so that slave raiders from friendly groups wouldn't capture those who wore them. Since then the scarifications had been traditionally worn by many Yorubas. Needless to say, expatriates didn't have tribal markings, so sometimes the slaughter included them. An expatriate neighbor of ours with his family went through such a village and was mauled. His attackers wanted revenge, not money, but at least they didn't kill him or maul his wife and children.

These killings took place in roadside villages, so we learned of them only by rumor. As there were constant, terrible rumors about all kinds of things, one couldn't make all decisions based on them, and one day our wonderful neighbor, Phil Stevens, who was an anthropologist, decided to go to the Northern Region to continue some research that had a time constraint. He invited Steve to go with him. Our little son, by then seven, wanted to go with his dad, so taking Steve's car, which was roomier than Phil's, the three of them went off together.

The next day I was told by a horrified neighbor who had just come from the north that on the north-south road that Steve and Phil had taken, the men in one of the villages were stopping all cars, murdering those who lacked the right facial scarifications, and throwing their children down a well.

The village was near Ibadan. I didn't know which village, but there weren't many of them, so it might easily have been the one in which our nanny had killed a pedestrian. The people who saw the accident hadn't blamed her, but a crowd of people would have gathered at that point, and who knew how they felt about it? They'd remember the car.

By then Steve and Phil were beyond that town, but because they had no access to a telephone, nor was any such news reported on the radio, they would be coming home along that road knowing nothing of the danger.

I've never known such terror. I'm not happy to say this, but it's one thing to fear that your husband is at risk and another thing to fear that your child could be thrown down a well. Your mind's eye sees him struggling in the water. Your mind's ear hears him calling.

I thought of going to warn them, to get through the town as best I could or die trying. But what about my daughter? I certainly couldn't take her with me and I couldn't leave her behind. I tried to phone a police station north of the town, believing that the police could possibly find Steve and Phil and warn them, but the phone lines had been cut and I couldn't get through.

Here again, a phone operator helped me. I told her why I was so frightened, why I had to reach my husband, and she tried another police station farther north. She couldn't get through to them either, so she tried a third. This time it worked. I was crying with relief and gratitude when I told the police what was happening. They hadn't heard about it. I told them what kind of car Steve and Phil were driving, and the police said they'd keep a lookout for it, but reluctantly told me that they were not on that north-south road so they weren't hopeful.

I had no idea what else I could do. The travelers were not expected home for forty-eight hours. I would just have to wait. I was consumed with fear so strong I couldn't bear it, so I went to the kitchen, filled a teacup with gin, and drank it. I will always remember that moment. My fear receded a little. I drank another cup of gin.

Unknown to me, Steve and Phil had changed their plans. At their first destination, Phil learned something related to his work that sent them to another destination on the opposite side of the Northern Region. So rather than coming back on the road that passed the town where the massacres were occurring, they came back safely on another north-south road on the far side of the region.

One thing I learned from the Nigerian experience was what it's like to be a civilian in a war zone. You never know what's happening, or who is shooting at whom. You just hope with all your heart that they won't do it near you. I would sit up at night, wide awake, and one night, mixed with distant gunfire, I heard a song coming from a neighbor's house. It was "Moonlight in Vermont."

My body actually began to ache because I wanted so badly to be in Vermont. I still can't hear that song without pain. I began to hope that my dad would come in a helicopter and rescue us. I was like someone in a Pacific island cargo cult, wherein people believed that somehow a plane would appear, loaded with things they desperately needed. They would clear a landing place and wait beside it for the help that never came. Interestingly, as I learned later, my dad at home also thought of rescuing us with a helicopter, but such an effort would not have been possible — an approaching helicopter would have been shot out of the sky.

Steve didn't want to go home, but I did, and when at last the borders opened, I got on a homebound plane with the children and the dogs but without enough material for a book. A series of scares was not what *The New Yorker* had sent me to write about, nor did I have any intention of trying. I just wanted to erase the whole thing from my mind.

But I did go home with three perfect memories. The first came about because I loved highlife music, and also learned to dance the highlife, which I'd do when we went to a nightclub. Steve didn't like to dance, but his Nigerian friends did, so they would dance with me. One night my dancing partner told me I was the best expatriate dancer in Ibadan. Wow! The Nigerian women were much better, of course, but it was nevertheless good to hear.

The second perfect memory came from before the rigged election, while the country was still relatively stable, and concerned a performance of *Danda*, a stage production based on a recently published novel by Nkem Nwankwo. The production was mobile and took place outdoors at night when a large truck arrived and people began to unfold things from it—the stage, a ramp, powerful lights, the scenery, and a strong metal barricade to surround the area so that people who hadn't paid for tickets couldn't get near enough to see the play. The production had little to do with the novel, as far as I could tell, but the audience loved it. What I liked best about the evening, though, was that some people saw it for free.

A swarm of twenty or thirty tiny children gathered outside the barricade. One or two might have been as old as six and a few were just two or three, but most were four or five. The stage managers kept chasing them away, and they'd all run off together, but soon enough they'd be back. When the lights went down and the play was about to start, they crept between the bars of the barricade, and by the time the lights went up again, the play was in progress so nobody was available to chase them. They stood near the stage and watched the play, enraptured—all but some of the very tiny ones who by then had fallen asleep in the arms of the slightly older children who carried them.

When Danda's baby, a life-sized doll, was carried offstage, the children crept around behind the stage in hopes of seeing it. They came back looking a bit disappointed. When the play was over and the whole cast, singing and dancing, piled down the ramp in the grand finale, the tiny children, very subdued but wide-eyed and excited, clung to the sides of the ramp. Some of them danced. One tiny girl in a ragged dress lifted both arms and waved at the performers.

The grown-up audience went home, the stage was folded up, the ramp was folded up, the wings of the stage were folded up, the lights were packed in boxes, then all was put on the truck and the sides of the truck were folded up. The little children watched all this with wonder. Then someone in authority got out of the truck to chase them and they ran off into the night.

The third perfect memory arose from the trip that Steve and I and our children took to the Northern Region—the time we were nearly stopped by the bandit and his roadblock. We had gone to the Northern Region to meet the emir of one of the smaller tribal areas, an extremely nice man who gave us three dozen eggs as a gift and asked us about a "tail-star" he had been watching. It appeared suddenly, he told us, and he wondered if we knew about it.

We knew nothing about it. We didn't even know what a "tail-star" was. But we were sorry to have no information because the emir had been awed by it. We talked for a while about the stars and the mysteries of nature, and when we parted he told us to look at the eastern sky a little after midnight.

By midnight we were in a motel and Steve was asleep, not particularly interested in the tail-star, but the children and I went to a nearby hill. Stars, in my experience, were tiny, and I wondered if we could see the star without binoculars.

Binoculars? On the far side of the hill was a blinding pillar of light that took up a quarter of the sky and reached from the zenith to the horizon. It was a monstrous comet, the brightest ever seen for a thousand years. It came to be known as the Great Comet of 1965, which is an understatement, and it was worth the whole trip to Nigeria.

After I went home with the children and dogs, Steve went to Enugu, capital of what had been Nigeria's Eastern Region. The massacre of Ibo people, by then called "the Jews of Nigeria," had been so intense that the Eastern Region seceded, to become Biafra and declare its independence from the rest of Nigeria. While Steve was there, the Nigerian army massed at the border to invade. I was at home by then, and learned from a newscast that the Biafran government had declared that all non-Biafrans found in Biafra would be shot. Steve later told me that this wasn't true, as reporters from England were there and not in any more danger than other people, but the border was closed, so he couldn't go back to Ibadan.

However, he was offered transportation in a government vehicle which would take several important Biafrans to Cameroon, from which they would go on various missions for their country. Steve couldn't take his car with him, so he gave it to the Biafran cause and left it at the barracks. He then got in the government vehicle with the others, among whom was the Nigerian author Chinua Achebe. Steve was a huge fan, so he and Achebe went to Cameroon talking about *Things Fall Apart*, Achebe's famous novel.

Because of road conditions, the government vehicle could go no farther than central Cameroon, so everyone got out and waited until a plane could come for them. Central Cameroon gets 140 inches of rain a year, also plenty of fog, so the plane took a while to get there. But come it did, and they all got in. It was raining hard, and the windshield wipers didn't work so the pilot had to work them manually. The plane took off and flew for several hours through high mountains buried in clouds. Every so often the passengers would get a glimpse of a rock cliff just beyond the plane's wing. But then the clouds parted, the plane flew into beautiful, bright sunlight, the shining ocean appeared before them, and they landed in Port Douala. Steve came home from there.

❦

10

DARK

A S THE FIRST WORLD WAR was to my father, as Vietnam was to my daughter's husband, so was the Nigerian experience to me, in that I didn't talk about it. Needless to say, I couldn't write the book that *The New Yorker* had sent me to write. Nor did I want to. Nor did I want to write about anything.

What I did at first was drink. My children spent most of the day in school, and Steve, still enamored of politics, worked on the national campaigns of various political candidates until he joined the Council for a Livable World, an arms-control organization involved with getting like-minded people elected to the Senate. One of the council's biggest successes was to appear on Nixon's "enemies list," which brought in a flood of new contributors. Before going to Nigeria we had moved from Manhattan to Cambridge, to a house across town from my parents, but Steve's work took him all around the country. I seldom saw him. I seldom saw anyone except my dogs, because for most of the day I was alone at home, somewhat buzzed but functional throughout the day and getting drunk after my children went to bed.

While I was growing up, alcohol was an essential part of everyday life, or it was for my parents' generation — the people who came of age during Prohibition and the Roaring Twenties. My two grandmothers, in contrast, were from the generation that felt the need for Prohibition. They never drank. Everybody else did, though, including my parents and their dozens of friends. Drinks were consumed at cocktail parties, at dinner parties, at weddings, christenings, funerals, and engagement parties, at parties for book publications and other triumphs, at consolation parties for friends who had mishaps, at farewell parties for travelers even if the travelers weren't going very far, and at welcome-home parties when the travelers returned.

There were rules, though. For morning celebrations, the celebrants drank champagne. For noontime celebrations, they drank sherry or vermouth. Before dinner they drank cocktails, during dinner wine, after dinner brandy or cognac, and after that beer or highballs. But a formal celebration was unnecessary; people drank when the sun passed the yardarm and happy hour arrived, in which case there were no rules—they drank whatever they liked best.

Neither my parents nor their legion of friends were alcoholics. Despite the overwhelming number of available beverages, they never overdid the drinking and never got drunk or even very high. They knew a few people who had problems with alcohol, but these people were not considered to be alcoholics because they didn't fit the image. Alcoholics were homeless men—always men—who lived under bridges. Alcoholism was the deepest of disgraces, unthinkable to the degree that my honest, honorable mother and one of her highborn friends responded untruthfully to the questions of a judge during a court trial concerning the mental instability and possible alcoholism of a woman who belonged to their social circle. The woman in question was no longer living, but while she lived she was strange indeed, and had disinherited one of her children, who was contesting her will. But my mom and her friend calmly testified under oath that the woman showed no sign of alcohol misuse or mental confusion.

Hello? I was present at the trial and in my mind was shouting, *Good Lord, Mom, you perjured yourself!* However, I'm sure these ladies had no intention of lying, nor did it occur to them that they were doing so, because a lie is a purposeful misstatement and these ladies were truthful according to their code. A Cambridge lady would never suggest that anything was wrong with another Cambridge lady. A Cambridge lady would not speak against the dead. A Cambridge lady would not acknowledge a friend's dysfunction, at least not to a stranger like the judge, because her friend's troubles were none of his business. So they answered the judge's questions in keeping with their sense of honor. Their faces conveyed their integrity. Their voices conveyed their heartfelt sincerity. Their gracious manner conveyed their respect for the court and the gravity of the occasion. The judge was awed by these Cambridge ladies and found against the plaintiff.

When I was in college everybody drank, to the point that my classmates and I had many terrifying rides in cars with some of the drunken guys we dated. Failing to connect the terror to the alcohol, we drank on our own as an afternoon's amusement, when we would leave the dormitory together and head for the local bar. One day a drunken student rode his motorcycle into the bar and zoomed around all the tables. Every woman present fell in love with him, hugely impressed with his daring.

Thus alcohol seemed to be a good thing. We weren't supposed to drink in the dormitories, of course, but sometimes we did. One memorable evening the women in our dorm, which was small, broke every rule the college had. All of us were drinking and smoking, and two boys were in bed with their girlfriends. One was my roommate, so I had to sleep somewhere else. During the night the dorm matron, who lived in another dorm, got wind of the partying and came to see what we were up to, and she was so taken aback by what she found that she decided to pretend she hadn't seen it. No doubt she would have lost her job and most of us would have been expelled.

Aside from things like that, I didn't feel that alcohol was doing me too much harm until I came home from Nigeria. Then I'd get drunk at night and fight with Steve if he was home. One night I yanked off my wedding ring and threw it in the fire. It was gold, and it melted. The next day in a serious mood we went together to a jewelry store, where Steve bought me a new gold ring and put it on my finger. But soon enough we had another fight and that ring too went in the fire. Steve patiently bought me a third ring, but not a gold one this time, just gold-colored.

In spite of all this, I was more or less functional. I had two dogs who had four marvelous pups. Two of these became sled dogs who formed a racing team, thanks to the help of a friend in New Hampshire. I then bought a dog known as an Indian dog—a young, mixed-breed husky who had been the leader of a dog team in a village in northern Canada. She was to be the leader of our team, which raced so successfully with my son as the driver that they won everything that could be won in the regional three-dog races.

Other racers hated to see them coming. My son accumulated a collection of trophies the like of which few can imagine — golden statues of angels with dogs at their sides or golden statues of dogs with angels at their sides — and almost all were first prizes.

The lead dog's name was Coke. I don't know why, except that sled dogs were often named for alcoholic beverages such as Budweiser and Brandy. But perhaps the folks from whom I bought my dog had run out of alcohol-related names, or perhaps, considering the community she came from, Coke was short for cocaine.

I called her Cokie. We loved each other deeply. She knew substantially more than the rest of us about the down side of alcohol, as I learned one evening when I took her to meet my parents. My brother joined us. He'd come from a party where he'd had a drink or two, but not many. Perhaps his breath smelled of alcohol, or perhaps the alcohol sounded slightly in his voice. I remember wondering if he had come from a party, but he certainly wasn't drunk, so I thought nothing of it.

But Cokie, who had never met any of these people before, bristled the moment he entered the room. Every hair on her body stood on end. Her eyes blazed. She bared all of her chattering teeth and trembled so violently that she seemed about to fall. But she didn't run — terror had rooted her. Never before had I seen such terror in anyone, let alone in a dog. I put my arms around her and took her to another room, where she calmed down a little, but she wanted us to go home, so we did.

Terrible things must have happened to those chained-up dogs in that northern Canadian village, but the horrors must have happened at the hands of men. Women who were drinking bothered Cokie not at all. She would sit beside me in the kitchen while I drank my evening highballs and curl up peacefully beside me on the bed when I lay down.

One afternoon when I was resting on my bed, mildly drunk but with Cokie right next to me, my mom appeared in the doorway. She had come, I later learned, to tell me not to drink so much, but she didn't have a chance to say so because Cokie leaped up and stood over me, her hind feet on one side, and her front feet on the other. She bared all her teeth and roared *Go!* My mom stepped into the room and

Cokie roared again, snapping her teeth and leaning forward—*Any nearer and I'll bite,* she said—and would have launched herself if my mother had come any closer. I was holding Cokie's collar, of course, but I didn't need to restrain her because my mom got the picture and left. I hated to think what happened to helpless drunken women in that northern Canadian village. But Cokie knew, and whatever it was, she wanted to save me from it.

A few months later, the alcohol was making me sick. I was only in my thirties and shouldn't have felt so sick. I went to our doctor, who asked how much I drank. I told him. He asked why I drank. I said I drank because I was always anxious and depressed. I wanted to escape my situation, but to do that there was no way up. The only escape was downward. I'd think of suicide and drink to erase that feeling, I said.

The doctor asked if I knew that alcohol caused such feelings. I hadn't known. He suggested that I stop drinking, so I did, right then in his office, almost miraculously, with no difficulty and no wish to drink again.

A few days later I felt wonderful. Gone were the depression and anxiety. I became happy and stayed that way for many years, despite a few disasters that almost broke my heart but didn't reactivate the depression or the drinking.

Interestingly, before I saw the doctor I had been seeing a psychiatrist. I would go to my appointments drunk—maybe not falling-down drunk but certainly with alcohol on my breath. This the psychiatrist often mentioned, but he didn't connect the alcohol with the depression. Instead, we examined my near-perfect childhood and my uninteresting dreams, none of which shed light on my problems, and when I told this to my doctor he said, "Fire that psychiatrist."

So I did, and I told him why. This made him angry. He phoned my doctor to blast him for meddling with his patient. But if I had stayed with that psychiatrist, and if not for my doctor, I'd be dead by now, or under a bridge with the proverbial alcoholics.

However, I didn't join Alcoholics Anonymous. I knew nothing about it. I wasn't even sure I was an alcoholic, but what difference did it make if I didn't drink?

•   •   •

Many years later, when my children were grown up and married and my dad had died, my mother came to live with me in New Hampshire. She still enjoyed a glass of wine before dinner, and in the distant past when I was drinking less, she and I would have a drink together in the evenings. So I thought it would be nice to share happy hour with her.

I had yet to join Alcoholics Anonymous and had no understanding of addiction. I thought I was a different person than I'd been so long ago. My life was going fairly well, I was healthy and happy, and years earlier I had started to write again. I also had forgotten about depression, so I saw no reason not to drink. Soon I was drinking with my mother every evening before dinner, not realizing where this would take me.

Four months later I was looking at myself in the bathroom mirror. I saw a strange-looking woman with uncombed hair wearing a ragged sweatshirt. She was all alone and she was drunk. The house was cold and quiet. Night was coming. The woman in the mirror was me, to be sure, but she didn't seem like me. The real me was a healthy writer with a manuscript to finish. If I couldn't stop drinking, what would happen to the manuscript? I couldn't write when I was drunk. I'd try, but the result was hopeless.

I remembered a woman I'd met who was a prostitute. She used drugs. She couldn't help it, she said. "I need the drugs to whore and I whore so I can buy them. I can't whore when I'm straight," she said, crying.

I'm as far down as she was, I told myself. *If I can't be a writer, maybe I could be a whore.* But I looked again at the woman in the mirror. I saw the aging skin, the ragged sweatshirt. It wasn't clear that such a woman could make it as a whore. *Maybe,* I thought, *I'd better stick to writing.*

I looked out the bathroom window and in the distance saw the lights of Beech Hill, a drug and alcohol rehab center in Dublin, a town west of Peterborough. I went downstairs and asked Steve to take me there. We got in the car and we went.

What an experience! I've never had such a good time in my life. I slept for twelve hours and awoke to meet a collection of people as smart as they were funny, brimming with insight, experience, and good advice. Beech Hill had a large glassed-in room—probably a former conservatory—that was known as the Lung and was where the smokers gathered. I didn't smoke when I arrived, but I soon resumed the habit because the funniest, most interesting people were smokers. I loved being with them. Some of them were there because of a relapse, just as I was, but they had been in AA in the meantime and had learned about addiction. Why did they drink or take drugs? For the same reason I did: to erase emotional discomfort. What did they want? The same thing I wanted: to somehow rise up, to feel well and happy. But that didn't happen. Then what? Just as I had done before I looked in the mirror, they sank down and down toward the bottom, the place you find yourself when you no longer can keep doing what you're doing. Some people try to conquer their addictions when they hit bottom, and some succeed. Most of the people at Beech Hill were succeeding. But in the bottom is a trapdoor. If you don't stop drinking or drugging, the trapdoor opens and you fall through. You die from an overdose of drugs or from liver failure or wet brain or some other complication, and if those things don't kill you, you kill yourself. I'd thought of suicide a few times, as had most of the other people. And most of them knew someone who had made that choice.

Why would I discuss this? It's not necessarily a good idea, as alcoholism looms large in the minds of many people. Once a friend asked what writer I liked best, and I said John Cheever. My friend said, "Cheever was an alcoholic."

I was impressed. Millions of people are alcoholics, but Cheever was unique as a writer. Yet to my friend, his alcoholism was more important than his brilliance. Once you're known to be an alcoholic, that's how many people identify you, which could be a reason not to talk about it.

Interestingly, the same kind of disgrace does not seem to be attached to drug addiction, or not as strongly. If my friend had asked which comedian I liked best and I'd said Richard Pryor, I'm sure she would not immediately have said he was a drug addict. People stoned on drugs tend to be quiet while drunks yell and fight, which is why alcoholism is more conspicuous and also more disgraceful, and that's another reason not to talk about it.

A third reason is that after all this happened, I joined Alcoholics Anonymous and learned that AA has twelve traditions, the twelfth being that you don't talk in public about your AA membership. But I have learned much about addiction from reading some of the many published accounts of my fellow addicts, and I'm following their lead here rather than adhering to a concept of the 1930s when the Twelfth Tradition was written. Anyway, as a brilliant member of AA once said, secrecy doesn't fit alcoholics. "They let it all out when they're drunk," he said, "and let it all out again in the AA meetings."

One man at Beech Hill made a deep impression on me and gave me an insight that will last me forever. He was a massive guy in his forties with broad shoulders and a deep masculine voice. He wore jeans, work boots, a blue work shirt, and a ponytail. He worked for a blasting company, dynamiting mountains to make way for construction projects. He hitched up his pants and looked us over carefully. Our eyes burned from the testosterone coming off him. Then he began his story.

He was driving his pickup down I-95 with a twelve-pack of beer beside him. As he drained a can, he'd crush it in his fist and throw it out the window. A police car was following him. A can bounced off the police car. The officer tried to pull him over. He floored it. The officer gave chase. Soon many police cars were speeding behind him but he went even faster until, at a curve, the pickup left the road and wrapped around a tree. Enraged, he hauled himself out of the wreckage, attacked the police, and fought so hard that it took six of them to wrestle him down and get the handcuffs on him. They dragged him to Manchester, to the Valley Street jail.

My goodness! What a story! I'd never wrapped a car around a tree or fought with police officers or gone to jail, or even lost my driver's license, for that matter, and when I heard the story, I saw no similarity between this man and me. But there was one—a very close one—though it would take me some time to realize it.

I left Beech Hill on New Year's Eve after a stay of two weeks. Because Beech Hill was in sight of our house, I told my fellow addicts that when I got home I would signal to them with a flashlight to show I was thinking of them. But when I got home I found our house full of guests who were waiting to have New Year's Eve dinner, which I then began to prepare, and I forgot to signal with the flashlight. My friends at Beech Hill waited in the Lung for hours, but I failed them. Although years have gone by, some of them still remind me of this. It's one of my deep regrets.

Why did my friends want to see the flashlight? Because of the fellowship. We had achieved a closeness unparalleled in any other setting. When I see one of those people on the street I get a little squirt of joy. We stop and chat. We hug each other. I think the reason I forgot to signal was that I felt out of place in my own kitchen. I was there with my family and our closest friends, but although they knew I'd been in Beech Hill, they had no idea what had happened to me there, or how much the experience had changed me.

Of course I stopped drinking, but that seemed like a relatively minor change, because the real one was greater. All of us there had known important darkness. I'd thought the darkness was my own, but I learned that others also knew it. They said things I'd never heard before. I said things I'd never said before. Many of us, perhaps all of us, emerged as different people. My friends and family in the kitchen were not those people. I don't remember ever feeling so alone.

A few weeks later I went to a party where I met a woman who once had been a counselor at Beech Hill. She was sipping a glass of wine, so I assumed that she wasn't an alcoholic, and I wondered how effective her counseling might have been. I'm sure she'd taken a few courses on the subject, but that's something like trying to learn to swim by reading a book. I've never heard anything useful about addiction from anyone who has not experienced its difficulties, and it's the same with swimming. You need to get in the water.

We chatted for a while. She had gone to Wellesley. I had gone to Radcliffe. We were about the same age, and wore the same kind of clothes. Obviously, we were social equals. She asked if I knew of Beech Hill. I said I did, adding that not only could I see it from my house but that I'd been there as an inmate.

The woman was astonished. This, from a social equal? "You're not an alcoholic," she said in disbelief.

"If I'm not, nobody is," I told her. Then a question struck me, and with it the abovementioned insight that I'd gained from the man in the pickup with the beer. With whom did I have more in common, this woman who had gone to Wellesley or the man in the pickup? I sometimes tell this story in AA meetings, and the response is always the same. Unanimous agreement. Of course and without question, it's the man in the pickup.

That makes me happy. He was stronger than his addiction and I'm glad to be stronger than mine. And the lawless aspect of his story detracted nothing from his narrative but made me admire him all the more. After I got my driver's license (first thing in the morning of the day I turned sixteen) I would drive into town and make a U-turn in front of the police station. This wasn't alcohol-related, as at the time I didn't drink, but at sixteen I didn't need any help to be lawless. I was a fearless, independent spirit, showing the law my upraised second finger. Imagine, then, my disappointment to learn that a U-turn was perfectly legal. But at least I'd had a tiny whiff of what it might be like to drive at ninety miles an hour throwing beer cans at police cars.

For many years after that I didn't drink. Then Steve got sick. He experienced weakness in his legs and feet, collapsed a few times, and couldn't get up without help. We went to a clinic. A neurologist examined him, and when she finished she said, "There is no good way to say what I must tell you."

Then she told us he had amyotrophic lateral sclerosis, better known as ALS or Lou Gehrig's disease. There is no cure. People with ALS live for three to five years after diagnosis, she said.

Long ago I had said "until death do us part," but not until that moment did I know what it meant. I saw white light and felt myself fainting. I stayed on my feet but must have turned pale, so the doctor left us alone to absorb what she'd told us. Steve, in contrast, has never been unnerved by any situation, not even this. Judging from his reaction, the doctor might have said that it looked like rain. But I began to cry. Then I heard Steve saying he was sorry. He put his arms around me to comfort me. He was apologizing! He was sorry to be the cause of my crying.

In some people, the illness moves more slowly and the people live longer. Steve turned out to have the slow-moving kind. Death would not part us quite so soon. When it became clear that Steve would probably be with me five years later, I'd tell people that he was doing fine, and he didn't worry about his body anyway. All he cared about was his scholarly brain, which was functioning perfectly. He needed his body to keep his brain off the floor and focused on the book he was writing about ethnic conflicts in Czechoslovakia after World War I. This had been the subject of his graduate studies, and since his retirement from the political scene he had been researching those issues.

With that, we settled into our new lives, Steve writing his book, me doing all the things I'd already been doing, plus the all the things he had been doing, plus all the things I gladly did for him, such as making special meals and bringing him things that he needed. I too had been writing a book, but I gave that up, because my office is far from the house and I didn't dare stay there for long because I was afraid that Steve might need me.

Meanwhile I wasn't doing as well as I'd hoped about fighting off the thought that he might not survive this illness. We were just barely grownups when we began our lives together. I had long since forgotten where he began and I ended, because over the years we had more or less become one person. Now all that was crashing. I was fully aware that something similar faces all people — especially older people — who have emotional attachments, but somehow this fact didn't help.

I can't do this, I told myself one cold winter morning, leaning on the snow shovel to rest for a moment. *Fuck AA. I'm going to drink.* And I did. Gin and water. Nor did I need to look far to find the gin, because for all those years, Steve had enjoyed a martini in the evening. When he became ill, I bought the gin for him. We had plenty of gin.

Alcohol helps when nothing else will, at least for a while. The relief was enormously welcome. I remembered the life-saving relief I'd gained from those teacups of gin in Nigeria. But soon enough I was drinking as before, and of course the relief disappeared.

A friend has since asked why I even considered drinking, knowing from experience what would happen. Her question surprised me. Isn't that why it's called addiction? And it's not confined to our species. I was told of an article, perhaps from the *Journal of Science,* about male fruit flies who, if spurned by female fruit flies, turn to alcohol to solve their emotional problems, and these flies become addicts too. If fruit flies, so far from us on the evolutionary tree, share a problem with us, the problem must be fairly powerful. I've heard addiction expressed in memorable ways by people in the AA meetings. *We have minds we can't trust. The pilot light is always on. I know the alcohol is there and it knows I'm there. Alcohol waits for us — it's very patient.*

· · ·

But for those of us who are lucky, help may be at hand. One day I went into our kitchen, where, to my surprise, I saw a man named Jack.

He had come to save me. The reason he did is a story in itself and began when we met in Beech Hill. The police brought him in on the night I got there, so we were due to leave together. We became friends while talking and laughing in the Lung as if we would always be there, safe and happy, and nothing would ever go wrong. But then I learned that when he left Beech Hill, he had nowhere to go. After years of drinking and drugging, combined with a deep, unmanageable rage, he had alienated everyone he knew. When I learned that his worldly goods amounted to $15, a plastic trash bag with a shirt in it, and a rusty old pickup that had been impounded, I brought him home with me.

All this was before Steve got sick, of course, but both of us were getting on in years; hence the fact that Jack wanted to be helpful was welcome. He mowed the lawn, shoveled the snow, and fixed all the things that were broken. He later moved to an apartment in town but our friendship continued. I was grateful.

He was a contractor by trade, a very good one, and like me he loved the woods. Of course he took every construction job that came his way, but when he wasn't working he was hunting or fishing. He spent much of his time on a nearby lake, fishing from a canoe in summer and from a bobhouse in winter, when he fished through the ice. Sometimes I'd go to the lake with him, and I loved it. The breathing forest, the water or the ice, the open sky, the wind, the silence. I'd think of my dad, and how much he would have liked this. In fact, except for Jack's rages, he sometimes reminded me of my dad.

I'd roam around the woods with Jack just as I'd done with my dad, which to me was very important. Jack's interests were the same as mine, he was even more skilled at walking quietly, and he showed me places I hadn't noticed before, like a certain microclimate where the deer go when it's cold.

One day in the woods we happened to pass the embankment beside the wetland where, so long ago, I sat with my father and saw a towhee, the place where I learned to sit quietly for hours. I mentioned this to Jack, who said, "Your dad must have been a hunter. This is exactly where I'd wait for deer."

I was greatly surprised. As has been said, I was slow to realize that my dad knew about hunting before he went to the Kalahari, and this moment with Jack was when the truth first struck. Of course my dad had been a hunter. That's why he knew so much about the woods. That's why he knew how to say "The moose saw us first" in Micmac. (It sounds like *dyam mukduk numinumkwe.*) And that's why he was such a good shot. I sometimes assumed that he had learned to shoot from serving in the field artillery during WWI, but aiming an artillery piece is not the same as aiming a rifle, nor is the target likely to go bounding away. All this came in a flash of comprehension, and if not for Jack, I might never have seen it. I wished that my dad had known Jack. They would have liked each other.

Jack told me about his childhood. It may have been something like my father's, and it was certainly like my dog Cokie's. From infancy all through his childhood until he left home at seventeen and joined the coast guard, he suffered fearful abuse of the kind that results in ER visits and broken bones at the hands of his angry, alcoholic father. His mother did not protect him. But that's how he came to know the woods. Children who suffer as he did have few resources, so he stayed in the woods as much as he could. He was safe there, and he wasn't alone. His only friend, a dog named Spook, went with him.

Perhaps that's why I felt protective of Jack. Perhaps because he sometimes reminded me of my father, it was almost as if he were one of my children, hence one of my father's grandchildren, perhaps by way of a spiritual gene.

Then too, a person such as he who doesn't have a helpful mother sometimes looks around until he finds one, and for Jack I may have been that mother. He was every inch a grownup — a big, tall guy with a mustache, dark hair from a Micmac grandparent, and *Don't fuck with me* written all over him — but for me he didn't fit the image of a grownup. I happened to know where he had lived as a child, and one night I dreamed I was driving on that road. In my dream, I was in my twenties. It was late at night and very dark, and the road was empty except for a ghostly boy about seven years old but big for his age, walking alone by the roadside. I knew the boy wasn't mine and that I might be accused of kidnapping if I took him, but I picked him up anyway and brought him home with me.

Before Jack got back the driver's license he had lost for drunk driving, I would sometimes give him a ride somewhere and, much to his annoyance, find myself flinging out my right arm and pinning him to the seat if we came to a sudden stop — a reaction left over from my own kids in the days before there were seat belts. I never did that to other people. In an earlier life, I probably was Jack's mother.

Like me, Jack was in AA, and he came to our house that day because he hadn't seen me in any AA meetings. He also learned that I'd been thinking about a rifle in my upstairs closet and the bullets in a drawer. How did this happen? I must have said something to someone — perhaps to him — as I never would have said anything so dire to Steve. "Hi, Jack," I said when I saw him in the kitchen. "I'm drunk."

He said, "I know," and went upstairs to get the rifle.

Soon after that I got a conference call from my two kids — my son, who lived across the road, and my daughter, who lived in Texas. Jack must have alerted them. But they didn't sound like anyone's kids. They sounded like full-fledged, power-mad grownups insisting that I go to a drug and alcohol rehab center. Beech Hill was long gone by then, but they had found two other centers, one in Arizona and one in New Hampshire. I was to choose, they said.

I refused. I apologized for drinking, told them I knew I shouldn't be doing it, and promised to stop right then by returning to AA. I'd do it for Steve and for them, but no rehab center, not then, not ever, and that was the end of it.

They paid no attention. They told me the only choice I had was which rehab center and if I didn't choose one, they'd choose for me.

Jack arrived and the discussion grew heated. I yelled that I was a freaking adult and their freaking mother and was freaking well running my own freaking life. This went right past them. And finally, exhausted and outnumbered, I caved to those full-fledged, power-mad grownups, especially since Steve had joined in on their side. The next thing I knew I was in the New Hampshire rehab center, standing in a circle of hand-holding people, saying the Serenity Prayer.

As with Beech Hill, I had a wonderful time at the center. My son and his family moved in with Steve and the dogs and cats, so I had little to worry about. I especially enjoyed the other women over fifty, some of them staff and others residents. One was my roommate. These freewheeling women were emotional giants, wise, brave, and unendingly funny. Other people called us the Golden Girls, but I preferred the names that one of our own circle chose for us — the Drunken Bitches and the No-Uterus Club. (Actually, one of us still had a uterus, but she was an honorary member.) And all but one of us smoked. To be with people like them was all I ever wanted. It was great to be sober. I was exceptionally happy.

Many people ask why the twelve-step programs are successful — not for everyone, to be sure, but for those who stay with them — and a number of theories are offered. But in that rehab center, I was struck with a theory of my own, which came from the Old Way, from the Ju/wa hunter-gatherers when they lived on the savannah.

The twelve-step discussion meetings were similar to the Ju/wa encampments. The most important similarity, of course, was that belonging to the group enabled everyone's survival. But there were other similarities too. Both kinds of groups had roughly the same numbers of people — not exact numbers, to be sure, but on the same scale. Somehow that kind of number seems right. Neither group had chiefs or leaders. Men and women were equal and nobody was more important than anybody else. In both kinds of community, the equality feels right. Why might this be so? Because all members of these groups are in the same situation with similar amounts of knowledge. The individuals are their own leaders and they make their decisions together.

One more factor seemed important. A few months after the No-Uterus Club left the rehab center, we met there again one Sunday when the center held an open house. We had no special reason for going except that we wanted to see one another. The rest of our club had gone the night before, but I couldn't spend a night away from Steve so I joined them in the morning.

About fifty other people were present. Some of them were staff, some were residents whom we knew, some were residents who came after we left, some were former residents who left before we came, and some were local people there to attend an AA meeting. Everyone who knew me gave me a big hug and began to tell me the news of current and former residents, some of it good but some of it bad, about people who had "gone back out" (which is AA-speak for drugging or drinking) and had incurred all kinds of trouble, from jail to detox, all of it upsetting but none of it surprising, as any of this can happen when someone goes back out.

Three things struck me. The first was the tragedy of the bad news. The second was the speed with which I learned it. And the third and most important was that I learned it at all. This was due to our unity. The deep, personal news I got at the rehab center was of the kind that's spread around by a close, functional family in which every member expects to know the facts about everybody else and to know these facts immediately. Most certainly the people in the Ju/wa encampments expected nothing less.

Thus a twelve-step group and a savannah encampment would appear to be similar. Or so they seemed to me. And why might that be? Like all other mammals, we carry a certain amount of inherited information. Perhaps we carry an inherited memory of some of the ancient behaviors that helped our survival for hundreds of thousands of years. If so, such memories may still work for our survival by way of twelve-step programs, all over the world and in many different cultures. To be with like-minded equals promotes serenity, the loss of which left me filled with fear and canceled my sobriety. But I got smoothed out at the rehab center when, after a few days, my stressful life with all its problems receded, and I began to know the other residents. We achieved a sense of community unlike any other except perhaps those of the Paleolithic savannah — and the ease I felt among these people made me calm.

There with the others, I was in the moment. I saw that I should live in the moment. If not, I would spend the rest of my life worrying about terrible things that might happen, everything from a decline in my husband's health to the predicted eruption of the Yellowstone volcano, which, according to the geologists, will end life as we know it. Or I could simply experience each moment as it came. I saw that if nothing bad is actually in progress, most moments are quite pleasant.

A dear friend of mine, the anthropologist Megan Biesele, once pointed out something that I found very important, which is that post-Neolithic people are different from hunter-gatherers in the way they experience daily life. Most of us are required to focus on the future, a mindset that began with the Neolithic farmers. The seeds they planted in spring produced food in the fall. Their cow would not give milk until she had a calf, and it took nine months for that to happen. The early farmers were compelled to look ahead, and the concept holds. Today, for all kinds of reasons, most of us continue to focus on the future.

But hunter-gatherers focused on the present. They paid constant attention to everything around them, from a rustle in the grass to vultures in the sky, as every little thing told them something, usually something important. Of course they were aware of the future and of course they thought about it, but they lived in the present — in the moment. Megan might compare my former way of thinking to that of the post-Neolithic people and my new way of thinking to that of hunter-gatherers. And there's no one I'd rather resemble.

I have a parting thought for people who don't belong to a twelve-step program. They'd be astonished to know who does. Down in those church basements are some of the best and most respected people in anyone's community. I speak from considerable experience when I say that recovering addicts of all kinds tend to be substantially wiser and better informed about life and humanity than is the general population. It has been my great privilege to hear what they have to say.

❦

11

WARRIOR

To live in the moment was not my only useful lesson from the Ju/wasi. Another was how to raise children. I wrote about this extensively in *The Old Way*, saying:

> *The Ju/wasi were unfailingly good to their children. An infant would be nursed on demand and stay close to its mother, safe in the pouch of her cape, warm in cold weather, shaded in hot weather, complete with a wad of soft grass for a diaper. Ju/wa children very rarely cried, probably because they had little to cry about.* [This, I believe, was true of our species from the earliest times, because crying tells a predator that somewhere a helpless child is in distress and no one is paying attention.] *No child was ever yelled at or slapped or physically punished, and few were even scolded. Most never heard a discouraging word until they were approaching adolescence, and even then the reprimand, if it was a reprimand, was delivered in a soft voice. At least the tone was soft, even if the words weren't always. We are sometimes told that children who are treated so kindly become spoiled, but this is because those who hold that opinion have no idea how successful such measures can be. Free from frustration or anxiety, sunny and cooperative, and usually without close siblings as competitors, the Ju/wa children were every parent's dream. No culture can ever have raised better, more intelligent, more likable, more confident children.*[1]

I don't claim to have been a perfect mother — certainly not while I was drinking — but at least I adhered to the Ju/wa principles, and this alone must have overridden my sins, because if I say so myself, my children turned out quite well.

The first one—the daughter in Texas who forced me to go to the rehab center—was born in Manhattan on the hottest night of the year. Steve drove me to the hospital in our rattling Volkswagen bug. Then he went home, as someone told him the birth might take a long time and men were not allowed to stay with women in labor. So I was left alone in a tiny, windowless cubicle with no one to talk to, nothing to read, nothing but bare walls to look at. Music was playing on some in-house public address system—sprightly Elizabethan tunes along the lines of "Greensleeves." The music tinkled away as the pain grew worse, then grew unbearable—more than I'd ever experienced—then swelled into the horrible, blinding pain that's said to be the most the nervous system can transmit.

By then the music seemed inappropriate, piping merrily away while I was smelling my own blood and losing control of my bowels. This went on for nine hours while I swore I'd never look at a man again as long as I lived and certainly not my husband.

At one point someone tried to give me a spinal anesthetic but was unable to insert the needle. Thus I felt the whole thing, just as the Ju/wa women did, just as my ancestors had done before me. But because of an atavistic, prehuman fear of attracting attention while in so much trouble, I never once screamed. Interestingly, neither did the Ju/wa women alone in the bush, crouched down and grinding their teeth as the baby was coming. The last thing one wants to do at a time like that is to attract a predator.

The next thing I knew, I was holding a little baby girl. The past nine hours vanished from memory as if they had never been. The hospital people wanted to put my baby in the nursery, the standard procedure back then, but I remembered the Ju/wasi, who would think this was madness. A newborn baby away from her mother? There could be no such thing. Maybe in fifteen or sixteen years I'd let go of this child, but not much sooner, and certainly not then. I refused to hand her to the hospital people. So they put a crib from the nursery beside my bed.

Steve had returned by this time, and we took turns holding her. We named her Stephanie Kirsti, Stephanie for him and Kirsti for my beloved

Finnish surrogate mother. Then visiting hours were over, Steve had to go, and I was alone with my new daughter. Getting born must be a rough experience, and giving birth is even worse, so both of us were tired. But being a grownup, wanting to absorb this marvelous thing that had just happened to me, I was still wide awake. Not so my little daughter, who had fallen asleep.

By then it was after midnight. I still didn't want to let go of her. Nor did I think she would want me to. I'd noticed that her tiny hands had a viselike grip, ready to cling to the long dark fur that would have covered my body if we were still in the African rainforest. Evidently giving birth was nothing new.

But it seemed new. I took her to a window. She opened her eyes. We looked out at the night. We were in the Presbyterian Hospital on Morningside Heights, one of the highest points in the city, and it came to me that somewhere among those miles of dark streets and buildings was a boy who would marry my daughter and take her away from me.

That was true. He was in the Bronx, eleven years old, and his name was Bob Kafka. At that moment he was probably asleep.

Interestingly, just as I was writing the above paragraphs, the phone rang. It was Bob, so I told him what I had just written. He was intrigued. Then he asked, "Were you looking at the Bronx?" I said yes. He said, "Are you sure were looking *right at* the Bronx?" I said I was positive. "That explains it!" he cheered. "At exactly that moment I knew I was extremely lucky. I ran down to the street to play stickball and hit a two-sewer."

"What's a two-sewer?" I asked.

"In stickball," said Bob, "a *home run*."

Stephanie was a dream child, very beautiful, an excellent student, loved by all. She also was tough, as she proved one autumn day when we, with her brother and some of their friends, were going camping. We had put our gear in backpacks and were about to leave for the camping area when Steve, who at the time was involved with a political campaign, learned that he couldn't come. Elections were at hand. The candidate needed him.

What about Steve's pack? It weighed about fifty pounds, and mine weighed forty. I thought we should cancel the trip, but Stephanie said she'd take the extra pack. I told her that the packs were too heavy, but she tried mine and said she could do it. So her brother took her pack, she took my pack, I took Steve's pack, and we went camping after all, no worries. She was only nine years old, and weighed not much more than the pack she carried, but she carried it all the way without stopping to rest and of course without complaining.

I thought I was proud of her then, but more was to come—much more—so we skip forward eight years—right after she graduated from the same boarding school I had attended—to the day that she was paralyzed for life. The accident involved a man who, with the help of Stephanie and her friend Jana Schweitzer, was doing some work for Tom with a tractor.

We had been staying with Tom in Peterborough and I was in the kitchen when the tractor departed with Stephanie and Jana standing in the bucket attachment on the front. I didn't know they were riding in the bucket, which I would have considered unsafe. A few minutes later the phone rang. It was our neighbor's son, Andy Peterson. He told me that Stephanie had been hurt. I rushed to Andy's house. Stephanie was lying on her back in the road, looking somewhat apologetic for the trouble she was causing. Evidently she fell forward out of the bucket and the tractor ran over her.

Andy called the ambulance. The ambulance people pricked her legs with a pin to see if she could feel it. She couldn't. Then they loaded her in and took her to the local hospital. No one at that small community hospital could do anything to help her except arrange for the ambulance to take her to a larger hospital in Boston. I made a frantic phone call to Steve, who at the time was at work in Washington, D.C. His assistant told me he was in a meeting. I screamed, "I need him now!" and the next thing I knew, he was saying he was on his way. I also called my parents. They said they'd meet me at the hospital. When Stephanie was moved back into the ambulance, I got in with her and we went.

The trip from New Hampshire took almost two hours, so by the time we got there not much could be done. Waiting for me was Dr. Sensitivity in a white jacket. As I came into the waiting room he yelled, "She's paralyzed for life." Then he added that her life wouldn't be that long anyway, because paralysis would shorten it by one third. "Most of them die of kidney failure," he added. Would I like to talk to a clergyman? There was one in the next room, he said. But I didn't want a clergyman. Just then a door opened and Stephanie came through on a gurney.

She was on her way to the operating room. I grabbed her hands and told her I'd stay with her no matter what and that she'd be okay, although at the time that seemed unlikely. She looked a bit scared but was very brave anyway. She told me not to be afraid.

My parents were in the waiting room. Other relatives began to gather. I felt as hard as granite. I couldn't cry. I could laugh, though—my name wasn't Kothonjoro for nothing. I know what I was like from a photo taken a few days later, with Stephanie again on a gurney, one of my brother's girlfriends leaning over her sadly and sweetly, and me standing by, wearing sunglasses and grinning a hard-ass grin that shows all my teeth except the rear molars.

My sister-in-law Pamela was with me in this—she doesn't cry either. When she joined us in the waiting room, we joked along the lines of "Aside from that, Mrs. Lincoln, how did you enjoy the show?" And ever after this I've had great sympathy for the unfortunate victims of television news to whom something terrible has happened that they don't cry about. The newscaster finds fault with them for not crying. Their failure to cry casts doubt on their story. But I know why they don't cry—they don't because they can't, because some things, many things, are far beyond crying.

Steve arrived while Stephanie was in the recovery room. We couldn't see her until she was taken to the intensive care unit in a Stryker frame, a device in which she was like the filling in a sandwich. This was her second experience in a hospital. The first was the night we had looked toward the Bronx where her future husband slept. The doctors had stabilized her spine but told us that her spinal cord was cut between the twelfth thoracic and first lumbar vertebrae. Her upper body was okay but her lower body was gone. Or that's how they put it. She would have to wait for her bones to mend before she could transfer to a rehabilitation unit.

When we first saw her she was facing the ceiling, but soon an attendant came in and turned the frame with her inside it so that she faced the floor. We lay on our backs on the floor and looked up at her, scaring the hospital people, as they thought we had fainted side by side. No, we were just visiting our daughter with a severed spine.

Interestingly, an event of this kind sorts out your friends. Most of them, of course, were very present for us, offering us places to stay and help of any kind if needed. But several of them dropped us. We never heard from them again. I didn't care that a few of our erstwhile friends did this to us, but I cared plenty when one of Stephanie's friends did it to her. That friend, a former teacher whom Stephanie adored, promised to visit her on a certain day. Stephanie asked me to buy a potted plant, the most beautiful one I could find, and bring it to the hospital so she could present it to her teacher during the expected visit. I bought a gorgeous azalea and Stephanie waited and waited. She waited all day, but the woman didn't come. She didn't call either. We thought perhaps we had the day wrong, but we didn't. The woman never came and never called to say she'd changed her mind. A few months later I saw this woman at the airport on a bus. She said she had just been thinking about me. "So that's what happened," I said in a voice that wasn't too friendly. "A moment ago I was in my kitchen, then *whoof!* I'm here on a bus." *You're a witch* was my message, and she got it. She looked down at her hands.

On balance, I'd say that the people who avoided us had problems with injuries, or else they didn't know what to say when they heard our news and then felt guilty because they hadn't responded—all of which I could understand because I'd done such things myself, before I knew what really bad things felt like or how to react to them.

But oh, the people who stood by us! One friend, Alan Forbes, went to the hospital to visit Stephanie. He was a scholar of ancient Greece, doing research for a paper on images of Hercules portrayed as a lion on Greek vases, and he knew that Stephanie was interested in mythology. She had been accepted at Harvard, where she planned to major in mythology. So Alan offered her a job as his assistant and she took it. He brought her a huge pile of books and other publications with photographs of Greek vases and she began a search for images of a lionlike Hercules.

I never found the words to thank Alan for this. A job! When everyone else was in mourning, when everyone else believed that her life was as good as over because this terrible thing had happened to her. But Alan didn't bring a sympathy card or flowers. He told her that she had a future, that she had value, that she was needed, that her interests were important, that she could help. There was nothing in this world I would not have done for Alan. I would have aligned with the devil on his behalf, and in time I did. I heartlessly betrayed a trusting friend for his sake, a terrible, almost unspeakable deed which I did without regret. I won't say what it was because it involves other people, but I did it coldly and gladly for Alan. And I'd do it again.

That was not my only alignment with the devil. Someone sent me an article about stem cell research and how scientists had severed a rat's spinal cord, then injected him with cells from another rat's fetus. The experiment worked, and the spinal cord regenerated. At the time the concept of stem-cell research was new, so I took the article to my gynecologist. I told him that I was going to get pregnant and that he would remove the unborn child and inject his or her cells into my daughter. I told him that he was the only person who knew my plan and he had to help me.

He said we couldn't do it. I said we had to. He said we couldn't possibly do it, that even if it were to become an accepted medical practice, the research was just beginning and he had no way of knowing how to do it. Therefore we didn't, but I would have done it. A hunter-gatherer woman of the Old Way, a woman living with hunger and with a nursing baby who needed all her milk, would be required to commit infanticide if she bore a second child too soon after the first, thus losing just one of her infants but not both. Among the many Bushmen we knew, a few women — very few — had been forced to kill a newborn child to save a toddler, although they suffered terribly because of it. But the Ju/wasi were my lodestar. When the idea of the stem cells came to me, and of killing an unborn child to save another child, I was thinking of them.

Obviously, I had a negative view of spinal cord injury. And I was not alone. Just a few days after our daughter's accident I read a news story about a boy in Georgia who was the same age as our daughter and had been injured at the same time in the same way. He too faced life in a wheelchair, but that was not to be his fate. One night soon after his injury, as he was lying in his hospital bed, his father and some of his brothers came in and shot him. My efforts to help my daughter had taken a different turn, but the feeling behind these efforts was the same: paralysis is more terrible than death, and everything possible must be done to mitigate it.

But then I had an interesting conversation. The rehab unit where Stephanie was placed was mainly supported by workers' compensation. For a while Stephanie was the only woman. The others could be divided into two groups as to the cause of their injuries — the young men were injured by bullets or in vehicle accidents, and the older men were injured in the course of their work. A man employed by a power company had fallen out of the cherry-picker bucket that was lifting him up to the power lines, for example. All of the younger men were newly injured, but some of the older men were at the unit for checkups.

During my visits, I couldn't help but notice one of them, a middle-aged gentleman who was very handy with his wheelchair, spinning it around, whisking it through doorways, as if he had been using it for a long time. I decided to seek his advice and asked if I could talk with him. "Of course," he said.

I looked around for a chair to sit in — he already had a chair — and when I found one he rolled up beside me. I told him that he seemed very experienced and asked him what lay ahead for my daughter. I don't know what I expected to hear — perhaps something tragic and dark. So I was hugely surprised, even shocked, by his answer. "It's a nuisance," he said. "It takes longer to do things. But other than that, there isn't much change, so it's really not very important."

Oh my God. Not a fate worse than death? Merely a nuisance? It was if a light came on. I saw it. And this wonderful man, my benefactor, proved it. There he was, going about his business, making phone calls, reading the paper, getting ready to go back to his job and his life beyond the rehab unit. He knew what he was talking about. I hadn't. I thanked him very much. He said I was welcome. "She's a nice girl," he added. "She'll be fine."

He was right. She was fine. I doubt that in those days Harvard would have accepted a paraplegic, but it was too late, she had already been accepted, so when classes began the following autumn, she was ready. She majored in folklore and mythology and graduated with honors, and in the meantime became something of an activist, working with Harvard to make some of its buildings and even some bathrooms accessible to people in wheelchairs. I once had occasion to visit the Harvard infirmary — I don't remember why — and when the doctor learned whose mother I was, he threw his arms around me. He told me stories about Stephanie — one of them about how a young man in her dormitory had overdosed on something late at night and she had taken him to the infirmary on her lap. That was her, though. Strong.

After her graduation, which Steve and I attended, all dressed up, me weeping, Stephanie and I went to Australia to visit my brother's ex-wife Heather and my niece Sonya. My mother gave us the money to go — it was her graduation present to Stephanie. After the visit we took a little tour on our own. I rented a small car in which we drove from Heather's home in Melbourne all the way to Darwin via Alice Springs, having adventures on the way that I wouldn't have minded not having.

One night, for instance, we arrived at the campground at Ayer's Rock, only to learn that a dingo had just carried off a baby. People were shouting and rushing around with flashlights. I assumed that the parents had killed the baby and made up the story about the dingo. Because child abuse is only too common in the United States, other Americans might make the same assumption. When I heard that the officials at Ayer's Rock intended to exterminate the local dingoes, I made a phone call to Heather's husband, a much-respected biologist who knew people in high places. He said he'd do his best to stop the slaughter, but I was told that the authorities killed a great many dingoes before the parents were considered. Soon enough the event became international news, and in time the baby's mother went to prison, but if we could have chosen a sensational, newsworthy event to attend, we would have chosen something less distressing.

After that, on our way through northern Australia, we found ourselves in the middle of a forest fire that was moving so fast it was on us almost before we saw it. It was a firestorm, really, with the eucalyptus trees around us exploding into flame. In the blink of an eye, the fire crossed the road behind us so there was no choice but to step on the gas and speed forward as fast as we could. It was our good luck that the trees ahead were just catching fire. We whizzed by them and lived to tell the story.

A day or two later we camped beside a river. Had we known it was called the East Alligator River we would have camped somewhere else. We didn't have a tent — we just put our sleeping bags on the ground. During the night we heard something very large come out of the river, as if a sunken, overturned boat were being lifted straight up from the water. The biggest crocodiles in the world are in northern Australia. They can be forty feet long and are responsible for more human deaths than any other kind. I wasn't sure we'd heard a crocodile, but anything big enough to displace all that water would not be good, so we got in the car. There we spent a miserable, bug-bitten night listening to something dragging slowly around on the gravel until, what seemed like hours later, we heard a second, more modest splash, and then silence. No doubt whatever it was went back in the river. We stayed in the car.

We also went to Kakadu National Park, because Stephanie had learned of a certain cave or rock shelter where there are classic examples of Aboriginal art. She wanted to see them. But we were told by a park ranger that the cave was almost a mile away over soft sand and no road led to it, just a trail. He didn't think that Stephanie in her wheelchair could get there. But she wanted to try, although the day was very hot and the sand would have been difficult for anyone, let alone someone in a wheelchair. Nevertheless she pushed through the sand all the way to the cave and saw the paintings. When we returned to the car, hot and tired, we found a group of park rangers who had gathered just to look at her. With considerable respect, they told her that they had never thought she'd make it, that they were planning to rescue her, and that she had surprised them. Their hats were off to her, they said.

Australia wasn't the only place where remarkable things happened. On our way there we stopped in Fiji, where her favorite teacher, an anthropology professor, had done fieldwork. He had given Stephanie an introduction to an important Fijian healer, who, when we met him, offered to mend her spinal cord. The healer said he often did this and had cured many people. We knew it wasn't possible, that the people he had cured probably had different kinds of injuries, but we felt that the anthropological opportunity was too good to miss, so we agreed.

The healer hadn't mentioned payment, so we asked around and were told that a large fish might be appropriate. We bought a very large fish and went to his village, which was on a mountainside. There he lent us his sister's house. The sister wasn't there but her late husband was—in a large, concrete tomb just outside the window. The healer treated Stephanie twice a day, rubbing her spine with a dark-colored liquid which he carried in a gourd. For modesty's sake, he brought his granddaughter with him. She was a sweet girl about twelve years old whom her grandfather was training to be a healer. It was she, not her grandfather, who treated Stephanie below the waist.

The treatment was supposed to take two weeks, but for the last two days the healer couldn't be there, so he empowered me to rub in the liquid. We continued the treatment on the first day, but on the second day we didn't bother because we knew it wouldn't work. And then, thinking no more about it, we went on to Australia and back to the United States.

There Stephanie saw her neurologist because she was having phantom pain. Ever since the accident she'd had phantom pain—it had nothing to do with Fiji. But when the doctor examined her, he found that when he pressed a place on her thigh, her foot moved. He couldn't believe it. Supposedly, movement in her legs was gone for good. He scratched his head and reviewed his notes and said that she'd had no such reaction the last time he'd examined her.

What to make of this? I left it to Stephanie to tell the doctor about the Fijian healer, but she didn't want to. Later I wrote to an ethnobotany professor to ask if the Fijian healer might be on to something. The professor wrote the nicest letter in return but didn't know about the medicine. I also asked Stephanie's anthropology professor what he thought and he said, "I would never exclude the intervention of a god."

Well, that's what happened. Stephanie had a tiny amount of return. We were later to learn that paraplegics do experience such things without Fijian medication, but I kind of wish we had finished the treatment. We'll never know what might have happened if we had. None of us think for a minute that she might have been cured, but that's just guessing.

However, she didn't necessarily want to be "cured." She had come to feel that she was fine as she was. That same year she went back to Fiji by herself, not because of the healer but because while there she'd met a woman doctor who, like the Kakadu rangers, was impressed with her abilities and offered her a job teaching the skills of independent living to newly disabled Fijians.

She worked in Fiji for about a year. When she came home, she bought a Honda sedan with hand controls and drove herself to El Paso, Texas, where she'd been offered a similar job. She also met the man who had been sleeping in the Bronx on the night she was born. Since then he had been drafted into the army, served in Vietnam, become a quadriplegic in a truck accident, done his rehab in the veterans' hospital in New York made famous by the film *Born on the Fourth of July* (which truthfully showed rats running around under the beds), and been elected president of the Texas branch of the Paralyzed Veterans of America. When Stephanie met him, he was working at two centers for independent living while volunteering for VISTA with the Coalition of Texans with Disabilities. He lived in a mobile home near Austin.

Stephanie called me up one night to tell me she'd met someone. She had never said a word about any of her former boyfriends. Evidently this was serious. A few nights later she called again. She really liked him. She'd found a job in Austin and was moving there. Who was this man? I had no idea, as Stephanie, who likes her privacy, did not describe him.

So all I knew about him was that his name was Bob. But when the phone call ended, I said to myself, *Well, Bob, whoever you are, if I know my daughter, your bachelor days are done.* And so they were. Bob and Stephanie moved into a modest, bungalow-type house near the University of Texas in Austin. They were married later by a judge in the yard behind the house, followed by a party with beer, food, and live klezmer music. Stephanie insisted on paying for the wedding herself, despite the fact that Steve and I wanted to pay for it. She'd come to carry self-reliance to extremes.

And then, in Austin, together with large groups of other disabled people, most of them in wheelchairs, Bob and Stephanie began the work that would change public transportation.

Their organization is called ADAPT. They were among its leaders. "We Will Ride," said the people of ADAPT, and if today you see trains, buses, and subways with disabled people on them, it's because ADAPT, with my daughter, her husband, and many others like them, stopped traffic in cities all over the country, chained themselves to the fronts of buses, got roughed up, got arrested, got dragged off to jail, went back to the streets, chained themselves to different trains and buses, and otherwise pointed out to the higher-ups of public transportation that their vehicles weren't going anywhere unless disabled people could ride them.

I was moved to learn of one of their actions, which took place in St. Louis and was particularly rough but won them the admiration of the police chief. When he appeared on television to be interviewed about the demonstration, he wore an ADAPT headband.

ADAPT became a force to deal with. ADAPT of Texas was such a force that the Texas state legislature began to consult it. I was privileged to attend two back-to-back legislative hearings with Bob, who was representing a splendid group called Not Dead Yet. This group opposed physician-assisted suicide and also a tenet called "futile care," by which physicians can terminate the care of someone they believe to be hopeless. Why would Not Dead Yet hold these views despite the seeming lack of political correctness? Because disabled people are more likely than others to be the victims of these practices. The leader in this matter, the well-known professor of bioethics Peter Singer, had recommended that certain disabled people, such as infants born with disabilities as well as adults who acquire severe disabilities, be put to death or allowed to die because, according to Singer, their lives will be miserable, and anyway, if they lack cognitive abilities as newborns do, in Singer's view they are nonpersons.

Oh really? I think of our son's brother-in-law, Ben, who was born with spina bifida. The obstetrician believed that the baby should not live. But Ben's mother was a tigress when it came to protecting her children. Horrified by the doctor, she left the hospital with her baby very much alive and raised him to adulthood. By the time he was in preschool he had his own wheelchair and could handle it. He grew up to be a brilliant, well-educated young man with strong political talents, living independently and holding down a good job in Washington. He's also witty. A gay man, he said that if Sarah Palin became president of the United States, she would change our name from *Homo sapiens* to *Hetero sapiens*. On the humor scale, that has to be a ten. And Ben would be nothing but dust if his mom had trusted the doctor. So much for Peter Singer.

Bob didn't particularly want to attend the hearings. He'd already attended dozens like them which produced no results, and on our way there, he predicted that nothing would come of these two either. Even so, many of the legislators were very glad to see him and hurried over to thank him for coming. I sensed the esteem in which he was held by the warmth with which people greeted me when they learned I was his wife's mother. Women are seldom praised for being someone's mother-in-law. I was honored and delighted.

But I soon began to see his point. The hearings went on for hours. Doctors lined up to say why they, rather than the families of their patients, should decide whether the patients should live or die. Not Dead Yet argued that disabled people would be the victims of questionable decisions. Someone brought up the fact that in Texas at the time, the parents of a disabled girl were trying to prevent her care from being terminated. Another often-mentioned case was that of Terri Schiavo, the young woman who was deep in a coma whose parents wanted to continue her care although her husband wanted it to stop. The husband testified that while she was still in good health, she had said she didn't want to be a vegetable. Would any healthy young person say anything else? Her husband was already dating the woman who would replace her, so why couldn't he have left her to her parents? Perhaps he no longer wanted her, but her parents certainly did. She was responding to them, they insisted. But the courts sided with the husband. Terry Schiavo is dead.

Thus I found myself clearly on the side of Not Dead Yet. Like Schiavo's parents, I too would do everything I could to preserve the lives of my children, and I also saw how the disabled people in our own family could fall victim to such reasoning. The one with spina bifida almost did.

As Bob had predicted, nothing was resolved by the hearings. This sheds a bit of light on why ADAPT took its battles to the streets. Direct action had been more successful. Once when Bob and Stephanie were involved with the Texas legislature on another matter, Stephanie lost patience and said privately, "Oh, why don't we just have an action? That would get their attention." She wasn't serious, but what she said was true. Civil rights are not given to those who need them. They are wrested by force from an uncaring public when large groups of people take to the streets and fight until they win.

That was why ADAPT had actions. All were planned in an unusual but admirable way, in that ADAPT had no formal leadership — no president, no underlings — so that its members worked by consensus. This reminded me of the Ju/wasi, who did the same. Like the Ju/wasi, everyone at the ADAPT meetings who wished to speak was heard and taken seriously. It was nice, noting that someone who had joined recently was being heard with as much respect and attention as were the long-time veterans.

All the actions I attended were highly memorable. The most grueling action that I was privileged to see involved the American Public Transportation Association — the lobby group for the transit industry — when it held its annual convention in Montreal. A large group of ADAPT activists, Bob and Stephanie among them, set out for Canada to join with Canadian activists, and on the way Stephanie phoned to say where she was going. By then I'd been elected to the board of selectmen of our town, and I had been on my way out the door to attend a meeting. So after her call I got in the car. But on the way down the driveway I began to wonder. Would I rather turn left at the corner and go to the meeting? Or would I rather turn right, go north, and see my daughter do her thing? I turned right and went to Canada.

The demonstration at the Montreal convention had been so enormous that traffic was gridlocked for miles outside the city. It took me several hours to penetrate the outskirts of Montreal, and by then night had come and the demonstration was over. I asked a passing policeman where the demonstrators might be found. Of course he knew what demonstrators I had in mind, and he directed me to the courthouse, a tall midtown building where my daughter and many others were jailed on an upper floor.

I went in. The prisoners were not allowed visitors, so I waited. During the night I talked to the guards and to a lawyer who I had been told was the prisoners' lawyer. He was actually the prosecutor, but he was a man of honor, and when the trial began — at three o'clock in the morning in order to avoid media coverage—he did not mention some of the things I had carelessly told him about my daughter while trying to learn if I could bail her out. I'd said she'd been in jail before for the same reason. The prosecutor admitted to the judge that he had additional information about one of the demonstrators, but because he had obtained it in an improper manner, he wouldn't reveal it.

The prisoners in their wheelchairs were massed in the courtroom. The trial took less than an hour. One young man popped a wheelie—the term for riding on the rear wheels only—that brought him in front of the judge. "I did the crime, I'll do the time," he called out over his shoulder, banging down his chair and wheeling away before the judge could ask how he pleaded. All the demonstrators pleaded guilty and all were sentenced—not to jails this time but to prisons, the women to Tanguay Women's Prison and the men to Bordeaux Prison, both outside the city.

I saw my daughter in the crowd but couldn't speak to her. So the next day I went to Tanguay Prison. Again I had to wait, this time sitting on cement steps in a freezing entryway, not allowed inside because escapes were in progress. According to a radio on the far side of a door—a radio I could barely hear—a group of prostitutes had climbed out a window and onto the prison roof. Some had managed to shinny down a pipe and hide in the bushes, but others were apprehended on the roof. These women were handcuffed with their hands behind their backs and made to walk facing forward down a steep fire ladder. I could not imagine walking forward down a steep ladder with my hands behind my back. Evidently this prison treated women harshly.

At last a guard opened the door. I was led to the proverbial thick glass window with the telephone. After another long wait, my daughter appeared on the far side of the glass. She was naked except for a tablecloth that was wrapped around her like a sarong. They had taken away her clothes, she told me, and had no prison clothes left to give her. The prison was cold, her lips were blue, and she was shivering. I told her I would get her out of there if I had to sell my blood and body parts to do it. She told me firmly not to bail her out. She refused to abandon the other imprisoned demonstrators. I begged her. My plea went unheard. She was adamant.

What do you do with a daughter like that? She was iron-hard, no question. Everyone knew it. One of her friends named her "Stalin with Tits." She also was loyal. Many disabled women were imprisoned for their part in the demonstration, some for the first time, and they were depending on each other. They found strength in their numbers. Stephanie had been imprisoned before. She knew the ropes. The others needed her experience.

However, she was afraid for her husband and the men with him. Some required medication to prevent seizures, but prisoners are not allowed to have medications. I later heard that one of the prisoners, without his medication, had such violent seizures that he almost died.

A guard arrived to take Stephanie back to her cell. I told her I'd come in the morning. And I did. By noon, more prisoners with their wheelchairs and their disabilities had arrived. The first batch was released with time served. They went back to the streets and took over the Montreal subway.

The subway trains were down a flight of stairs. One young man, caught up in the passion of the struggle, tipped his chair into a wheelie and went hurtling down the stairs. Others, such as my daughter, got out of their wheelchairs and crawled.

I've seldom seen anything so dramatic. Watching a young man rocketing almost out of control down a long flight of concrete stairs was heart-stopping, but the people who crawled were equally compelling. There were no ramps and no elevators. They had only one way to reach the lower level. The sight of a large group of people dragging their bodies down a staircase was so dramatic that right-to-lifers copied it later for their own demonstrations in Washington, D.C., and crawled up the steps of the Capitol. But when their demonstration ended, the right-to-lifers stood up and walked away. Not so the paralyzed people—not then, not ever.

Of course, crowds of regular subway passengers were also present, staring at the demonstrators and stepping on and around them. At a bend in the stairs, one of the demonstrators, a young African American man with cerebral palsy, began to spasm from being too long on the floor. A drunken white man began to punch him—I thought because he didn't like black people, although my daughter realized that he was trying to do forceful CPR. My daughter grabbed her young colleague and shielded him with her body from the blows. I grabbed the drunk from behind, pinned his arms, threw him off-balance, and yelled for a policeman. There were plenty of them nearby, and although they seemed confused as to what was going on, some of them hurried over. "Get rid of this guy," I told them. The drunk had no idea what was happening to him or what he had gotten himself into, and like an obedient child, he allowed the policemen to lead him away.

When the young man recovered from his spasm, he and Stephanie, with many other demonstrators, dragged themselves across the platform to the subway train, which just at that moment was opening its doors. They stayed in the doorway, and that was that. The door could not shut and the train could not proceed. Nor could any of the trains behind it. The Montreal commute had ground to a dramatic halt. Eventually the police removed the demonstrators, but by then the Canadian media were covering their story. Thus they emerged as the heroes they were, and the transit officials, who also were unable use the subway, "got a taste of their own medicine," said my daughter.

An equally stirring action took place when ADAPT took over a federal building in Atlanta. I attended that action too. The idea was to occupy the building and interrupt business as usual until a government representative of sufficient rank agreed to talk with ADAPT about an upcoming issue. The passage of the Americans with Disabilities Act, better known as the ADA, was pending. The question was whether the transit companies would use the time before the new law took effect to buy inaccessible buses which would then be in use for years to come. Earlier ADAPT had tried repeatedly to speak with government officials on this subject, but the government officials had refused. ADAPT had decided to force them.

Time magazine once praised the ADAPT folks as "wheelchair warriors," but the transit authorities called them terrorists. The demonstrators were never violent, and the name made them laugh. That morning in Atlanta, with their attendants, their power wheelchairs, their manual wheelchairs, their walkers, their oxygen tanks, their white canes, and their seeing-eye dogs, they assembled in a parking lot. "Terrorists?" said one. "Getting us out of this parking lot will take at least an hour."

But leave the parking lot they finally did, and moved slowly through the streets toward the federal building.

ADAPT had asked the leaders of several black civil rights groups in Atlanta to support them. But the civil rights leaders refused. However, when early in the morning the demonstrators filled the streets, it was the black community who cheered for them. Most were just citizens on their way to work when the demonstrators came by, but realizing at once that a civil rights demonstration was in progress, they cheered, blew their car horns, raised their fists in the power sign, whistled, and applauded. In contrast, most white people just looked puzzled, as if they couldn't imagine why several hundred disabled people were in the streets.

At the federal building, the guards did not let the demonstrators in. But the demonstrators had foreseen that possibility. Having studied the building in advance, some had gone around to the back, where they opened a door. In poured a few hundred people in wheelchairs, some to take possession of the elevators, others to bar the doors against the federal guards who would soon be swarming everywhere.

I had tagged along with the demonstrators, and once inside the lobby of the building, I noticed a pair of exterior doors that could still be opened. Nearby was an African American woman whose disabled son was also in the demonstration. Our eyes met. We took unspoken responsibility for the doors. Neither of us was particularly muscular, and as we learned later when we began to chat, both of us were grandmothers, but together we dragged a gigantic full-grown potted palm to block one of the doors, and then, noticing some federal guards approaching, quickly put our arms through the handles of the other door. The guards could still get in, of course, but they'd have to break our arms to do it.

And there we stood with the guards outside, knocking on the glass and shouting at us to open up. We pretended we didn't hear them. And this was partly true. Everyone was yelling; the elevators were stalled, jammed with demonstrators holding the doors open; the lobby was packed with demonstrators chanting "We Will Ride"; and on one of the floors above, ADAPT members, our own Bob Kafka among them, were trying to get the federal officials to talk with them. We didn't know if they were succeeding, because with all the noise, the scene was confusing. All I can say is that when night came, the lobby was still packed with chanting demonstrators and we were still holding the door.

George H. W. Bush was president then, and was informed of the ADAPT action. He asked his personal lawyer to speak with ADAPT representatives, which the lawyer did, by phone. By this time the guards had penetrated and were dragging out the demonstrators. But on orders from the White House, the demonstrators were allowed to stay in the building. Those who had been wrestled out to the police vans were allowed to return, and planned to spend the night. Someone in the White House then caused cots and blankets to be brought to the building so that the demonstrators would have a place to sleep, which I thought was exceptionally decent. As a lifelong Democrat, I didn't know if I should accept a cot from a Republican administration, but in the end I did. I looked around for Stephanie but didn't see her. I waited, but she didn't come. I lay down on a Republican cot, wrapped myself in a Republican blanket, and went to sleep anyway, grateful for our kindly Republican president.

The following day we heard that President Bush understood the issue. Top officials of the Federal Transit Administration flew to Atlanta, met with the demonstrators, and agreed to their demands.

At some point in all this I met a reporter who began a conversation. He asked if I was involved in the demonstration. I said yes, but just a little, as I was visiting my daughter. He asked if she was a demonstrator. I said she was. He asked if she had ever been arrested. I said she might have been.

But the word *might* didn't quite cover it. In reality, she had been arrested an extraordinary number of times and was jailed on almost every occasion. She'd been in jail thirty times, if not more. She'd been jailed more times than Al Capone, and exponentially more than any other Harvard graduate. She'd been shoved into inaccessible police vans without ramps or lifts and bundled off to inaccessible jails reached only by flights of stairs. She was a connoisseur of jails across the country. She could teach you how to act while being arrested, what to expect if you went to jail, and how to handle yourself while you were there.

But when I said she might have been arrested, the reporter looked at me with pity. "You have my sympathy," he said.

"No need," I told him. "Atlanta, Georgia, could be these people's Selma, Alabama." The reporter didn't know quite what I meant. I left it to him to figure it out, but added, "She has a great career."

I think of the middle-aged man in the rehab unit, remembering him with gratitude and affection. He told me that paraplegia was a nuisance, which was true. He told me that my daughter would be fine, which also was true. She learned how to manage her life, made important contributions to society, got married, and lived happily with her husband (Bob Perfect, I call him) in a house they bought in Austin. They continued to work with the Texas state legislature, which gave them awards of merit for their meaningful contributions. They testified in Washington before the House of Representatives, and they participated in passing the ADA, which, thanks to ADAPT, includes access to public transportation. In July 1990, President Bush invited them to the White House for its signing.

ADAPT created a bumper sticker as a tribute. It says, "To boldly go where everyone else has gone before."

How did Bob and Stephanie and many others like them develop lives of happiness and achievement? It took me a while to figure it out, but I think I know the answer. Miraculously, after they were injured they didn't experience self-pity. I don't present this as a virtue, because what person, especially a young person, is not entitled to a certain amount of sorrow when suddenly paralyzed for life? Self-pity is stigmatized, but in such cases it shouldn't be — people who are paralyzed in their teens and early twenties, or at any age for that matter, have lost forever the life they have known, and with it their envisioned futures. How can they not mourn this? Many do. But if they can shake off the sorrow, it's easier to let go of their former lives and move forward into new ones.

Those who can't often suffer from depression, which can be fatal. Some people who can't adjust commit suicide. Others die from substance abuse or from not taking care of themselves so that they develop infections or decubitus ulcers which drain their lives away.

I think of the boy in Georgia, the boy who was shot by his father. He too is in his grave. His family misunderstood paraplegia. Many people do. One woman shuddered when she learned I had a paralyzed daughter. She said she'd rather anything than become paralyzed. At one time I might have agreed with her, but by then I knew almost as much as the middle-aged man in the rehab unit. I told the woman that really the worst things about paraplegia were lack of access to the built environment, a lack which my daughter was addressing, and a negative social attitude, which one can easily ignore. The woman wiped away a tear and said that even if that were true, she'd just rather take her own life than live in a wheelchair. "There you go," I said. "That's the social attitude. What if someone said she'd rather kill herself than be like you?"

Once I read a scientific paper about the social attitude of rats. Rats live in colonies and protect themselves against the intrusion of rats from other colonies, whom they identify by their odor. An experiment was performed wherein a rat from Colony A was put in a small cage inside the enclosure of Colony B. The Colony B rats wanted to kill him, but they couldn't get at him. Eventually the scientists put him back in his own colony. He was greatly relieved and happy to be home, but his fur had absorbed the odor of Colony B. To his fellows, he seemed like an alien rat and they killed him.

Able-bodied people can be like that when it comes to disability. To avoid the perceived stigma, some paraplegics are encouraged to walk with braces and crutches rather than to use a wheelchair, just as many hearing-impaired people are encouraged to lip-read rather than to use sign language. The idea is to keep them looking like Colony A — the able-bodied, hearing population. But the practice is reminiscent of left-handed children forced to use their right hands, as if being left-handed were wrong, or gay people coerced into acting straight, as if being gay were wrong. Needless to say, a wheelchair is faster and more convenient than braces and crutches, just as signing is more comprehensive than lip-reading, but even so, the negative view of disability prevails in Colony A, particularly when little is known about the useful and productive lives of the people in Colony B.

A mindset can be laughed off. The built environment is the greater problem. On the twentieth anniversary of the signing of the ADA, ADAPT of Texas gave a party at a restaurant with games, food, and margaritas. The celebration was a great success, said my daughter, but the work wasn't done. A bit later, ADAPT people gathered at a loading area where tourists boarded vehicles known as Ducks, which give scenic tours on land and water. In some cities, disabled people could get on the Ducks, but not in Austin. There, in violation of the ADA, the only way to get on a Duck was by climbing a ladder.

The ADAPT people couldn't climb a ladder. They massed at the loading area to point this out. Someone had alerted the media, who were there taking photos and asking questions. One of the reporters asked a woman in a wheelchair why she wanted to get on a Duck anyway. She said she had a seven-year-old son. He wanted to get on a Duck. The reporter looked at her askance, as if wondering how a woman such as she could have a son.

The captain of the Duck, if that's what you call him, said there was no issue and no problem. Disabled people were welcome on the Ducks. Someone asked how a disabled person could get on. The captain said the person would be carried on. Some of the disabled people laughed. A power wheelchair, which many people use, can weigh two or three hundred pounds with no one in it. No way could something so unwieldy be carried up a ladder. Then what did the captain have in mind? Dragging its occupant onto the Duck and laying him on the deck? That didn't sound like fun to me, and I doubt that it did to the ADAPT people.

Back in her house in Austin, Stephanie called to tell me about the party and the Duck. ADAPT members were going to sue the Duck company, the twentieth such lawsuit of 2010, in honor of the twentieth anniversary of the signing of the ADA. ADAPT of Texas was following its star. They did this for every ADA anniversary, said Stephanie. Each year they added a lawsuit and also an action to correspond with the year of the anniversary. Thus in 2009, nineteen years after the signing, they had nineteen actions and filed nineteen lawsuits, and for 2011 they planned for twenty-one.

Stephanie said she'd been going around the city, enjoying what their work had accomplished. Formerly inaccessible stores and restaurants targeted by ADAPT had installed ramps. Disabled people could patronize these businesses. Years ago in Austin, there were few if any curb cuts. Someone in a wheelchair couldn't get on a sidewalk from the street, and despite the danger had to roll along among the speeding cars. With my heart in my mouth, I'd often watched my daughter do this. But after ADAPT had made its point, thousands of curb cuts appeared in Austin. Stephanie said it made her happy to see people use them — not just people in wheelchairs but also people with canes and walkers, tricycles and roller skates, shopping carts and strollers.

But best of all, she said, was the change in public transportation. When she first went to Austin, the disabled people had next to none. They more or less stayed home unless they had their own vehicles and somehow could drive them. They couldn't take taxis, as these were inaccessible, so if they didn't have cars with hand controls (very expensive), their only option was to request transportation by medi-vans booked far in advance. Then along came ADAPT and We Will Ride. Now they're riding.

On the night my daughter was born, the night we stood in the hospital window looking at the city, I wondered what was in her future — not just the boy in the Bronx but also her career and her adventures. I thought she'd get an education, which she did, and get married, which she did, but never in a thousand years would I have guessed what her work might be, or what kind of experiences would matter to her. Never did I think she'd be in a prison, naked except for a tablecloth, talking on a phone through a thick glass window. Never did I think she'd go to jail more times than Al Capone. And if I had tried to guess what sights would give her pleasure, I might have said the Grand Canyon or the Acropolis or a grizzly catching salmon. I'd like to see those sights and so would she. But her favorite? That's to see a disabled person — not someone she knows, just any disabled person — get on a bus.

☙

12

THE ICE MAIDEN

T HE ICE MAIDEN IS a mummified twelve-year-old Inca girl from the Andes, and the name applies to other things too because it's catchy. But these names derive from a spirit who lives among the peaks of the Alps, a cold-climate siren who inspires men to risk their lives by climbing up to find her. My second child, our son, whose name at first was John but now is Ramsay—the two-year-old who on all fours respectfully approached the widows of the late kabaka in Uganda, the six-year-old who navigated like a cougar in his escape from the school in Nigeria—heard this Ice Maiden's call and became a climber. Thanks to him I learned about a whole new part of the natural world—the upper part, the snow-covered part, the part with the glaciers and the avalanches.

Perhaps I also learned something about myself. Although I'm as far from being a climber as it's possible to be, his love of those breathtaking spaces above the tree line seemed something like my own love of the woods and the savannah. Perhaps the Ice Maiden is Gaia's second cousin once removed. They would seem to be related.

His fearlessness, however, must have come from his father, because it certainly didn't come from me. I sensed this when Ramsay was four and we were in a small plane on our way to Nantucket. Just as we were landing, we hit clear-air turbulence that hurled the plane around like a roller coaster gone wild. It was terrifying. The five passengers, including myself, lost all color and gripped the armrests. Then we heard joyous laughter. It came from Ramsay, who was sitting on my lap. "Don't you get it? We're going to die," I wanted to shout, holding him tight, preparing for the crash. But he was having the time of his life. When we landed, he was the only one smiling.

At first the Ice Maiden sent him rock climbing in the Quincy Quarries in Massachusetts, but he soon progressed to more difficult climbs in the White Mountains and the Colorado Rockies, then on to mountaineering and off-trail skiing in the Canadian Rockies, the Andes, the Alps, the Dolomites, the Alaska Range, and the Himalayas. He became an American Mountain Guide, then an International Mountain Guide, which was considerably more demanding, and then a French guide, or Guide de Haute Montagne, perhaps the most respected of all guiding communities. To be near his work he moved to France, to the Alps and the Chamonix Valley. He had found a way to make a living by doing what he liked best.

But it's not a profession a mother would choose. Why couldn't he just have been an architect or something? A number of his friends and colleagues have been killed in mountaineering accidents. One night after guiding a client, Ramsay came home to his apartment in Chamonix to find a man and a woman sitting on his couch in the dark. They were his friends, a married couple, both guides, and they began to cry. A terrible thing had happened to them and they needed to tell him about it.

They had been skiing in the Bernese Oberland when the wife looked back and couldn't see her husband. A crevasse had opened and swallowed him. She went to rescue him, but as she was readying her equipment, another crevasse opened and swallowed her. She shouted to her husband, but he couldn't hear her. Cell phones don't work under such circumstances. The crevasses were hundreds of feet deep, both people were wedged in such a way that they couldn't help themselves, and both would have stayed there, frozen forever like the Inca girl, if another skier, far away on the slope of another mountain, hadn't seen them. He had noticed them in the distance, but when a few minutes later he looked again, both had vanished. He guessed what had happened and he called the rescue helicopter.

They were very lucky. By 2008, so many guides had been killed in mountaineering accidents that the International Federation of Mountain Guides Associations held a conference in Geneva to see if they could sort out the reasons for this. Climate change was one — the formerly safe ice bridges weakened, the glaciers cracked, the steep slopes avalanched, and the melting ice on the upper peaks released stones and seracs to fall on whoever was below them.

Guiding agencies were also part of the problem. A guide would have a client who wanted to climb on days determined by his vacation and had hired the guide through an agency. But if, when the client arrived to begin his adventure, avalanches were likely or the weather was dangerous, the guide might decide that they shouldn't go up there. The client would be disappointed and might get angry. Having a limited time, he might insist on going anyway. The guide could then oblige the client and hope for the best, or he could refuse, in which case the client might complain about him to the agency and the agency would not call on him again. Sometimes, even in dangerous conditions, a guide would decide to please the client because his livelihood depended on it. This had led to several deaths.

Needless to say, I used to ask myself why my son decided to become *un guide de haute montagne*. At least he was a good, sensible climber. I was heartened to learn that on one occasion he had aborted a climb in the Andes because of dangerous weather, much to the disappointment of his client, who had wanted to summit. I don't know if the client hired him again, but even if he didn't, he was still alive and Ramsay had other clients. He found them himself, or they found him, so he didn't depend on an agency.

Even so, danger was always present, and I felt I was to blame. This was because when Ramsay was little, I read aloud to him an article from *The New Yorker* entitled "On Vous Cherche." It was about mountaineering. I thought the article might be too grown-up for him, and after reading a few paragraphs I asked if he'd rather hear something else. But no. He was enthralled. He was sitting up straight with his eyes wide open, listening with all his attention. He insisted that I keep reading, so I did. After that, he was fascinated with mountains. He had posters of them in his room. And as soon as he could, he began to climb them.

Years later I discussed this with a friend named Peter Schweitzer, who was also a climber. I told him I had lured Ramsay into danger with "On Vous Cherche" and thus was worse than the Ice Maiden, who at least didn't lure her own children. But Peter didn't agree. He said that Ramsay was already a climber when he heard the story. The story didn't persuade him to climb, it just woke the desire.

I thought that could be true. I have no idea how one can have a desire but not know it until one responds to it for the first time, but I do know what it feels like. I knew I'd always had the desire when I climbed the Needle of M, which I could see from Ramsay's house in the Chamonix Valley. When visiting him there, I would look at the Needle and the memory of the climb would come back to me. I had never felt anything like it.

Thus I could understand why Ramsay wanted to be a climber. I had done a little more climbing after climbing the Needle and loved every minute of it, so his climbing reawakened my own desire. And so, when he was about seventeen and had been climbing for a while, I asked to climb with him.

Ramsay had better climbing partners than his mother, but being an agreeable person like his father, he said he'd go with me. We lived in Virginia in those days, so we went to Seneca Rocks. There we began a three-pitch climb called Skyline Traverse. It was a Class 5 climb, rated at 5.3, the 5 for the class of climb and the 3 for the degree of difficulty. All Class 5 climbs require climbing equipment, but since at the time 5.13 was considered to be the most difficult category, a 5.3 climb did not present serious problems for an experienced rock climber.

Ramsay warned me that there might be some exposure, but never having encountered real exposure, I anticipated no trouble. I belayed him while he led the first pitch, but on the second pitch, I began to have doubts. We were up fairly high by then, the rope between us was twenty feet long, and I saw that if Ramsay fell, he'd fall twenty feet down to me, then twenty feet again when he went past me. I also saw that it was one thing to climb the Needle of M as an oblivious teenager with a professional guide and quite another thing to climb a towering Seneca Rock as an anxious, inexperienced mother belaying her youngest child. However, Ramsay was doing 5.10 climbs by that time, if not with his mother, so I'm sure he was doing what climbers usually do, which was to put in his own protection where he needed it.

The second pitch went well, although I was nervous. But on the third pitch, in a section of cliff that bulged out, we began to cross a narrow ledge that gradually became smaller. Soon we were on a little shred of rock, up in the sky above a valley stretching away for miles and miles with no help in sight. Hundreds of feet below us, the trees looked like toothpicks. I felt as if I'd been pushed out of a high-flying airplane with no parachute. My teeth were chattering. I thought my hair would turn white. My knees got weak so I sat down.

Ramsay didn't quite know what to do about this. He had been climbing with all the skill and grace of his primate forebears who lived in the trees. He looked as if he had been born on a rock face, as if he had never done anything else but climb. Now his mother was causing a problem. He sat down too.

I couldn't move. I thought that sooner or later, back at home, Steve would notice that dinner wasn't ready and the laundry wasn't done, and he would come to save me. I must have said this to Ramsay, because Ramsay patiently pointed out that Steve hadn't climbed since he was in college. "You're better off with me," he said kindly.

You're a child, I thought.

Ramsay sighed. But he said no more. We just waited. And waited. After a very long time he touched my arm and, still saying nothing, pointed up the valley.

Jesus! Black clouds flashing lightning were moving toward us. A storm was almost on us. Lightning would strike us. Rain would make everything slippery. We'd fall thousands of feet down to those tiny trees, which would not look like toothpicks when we reached them.

I had thought I could not feel more terror, but I was wrong. I jumped up and we kept going, across the rest of the ledge, up the third pitch to the top of the mountain and down the far side, which, as I remember, was just a steep downhill trail through a forest. The storm, by the way, went past us.

On the way we met two nice ladies who also had been climbing. They smiled when they saw us and said it was good to see people like us who climbed together. Well, they were wronger than wrong, I thought, and it was a sight they'd never see again and neither would anyone else, because by then I had resolved never to go anywhere near another mountain.

• • •

Years later, when Ramsay became a guide, I remembered the problem I'd caused him on Skyline Traverse when he was in his teens and just a rock climber. I also remembered how patient he was, and how splendid he had been about my panic — not a whisper of criticism, no blame, no irritation. These would be good qualities in a guide, I reasoned. So I was hopeful for him.

By then he was married and living in Boulder, Colorado, where he specialized in avalanche prediction. On skis, he taught the skill to others, and he told a scary story of showing a dangerous slope to his class. Up in the Rockies they had come upon a bowl, thousands of feet around its rim, with long, steep slopes thick with enticing powder. The class was thrilled, and wanted to ski down it. But Ramsay had already explained that avalanche conditions were bad that day, and told them they shouldn't even think about it. They didn't believe him, and would have launched themselves if Ramsay hadn't told them to wait until he showed them something first.

At the top of the bowl, the slope was fairly gentle. Ramsay went there, stamped his ski once, and thousands of tons of snow went thundering into the valley. The entire bowl emptied — the mother of all avalanches. As it happened, the snow that Ramsay was standing on slid too, but this was the tail of the avalanche, and on his skis he rode it down until he could ski off to the side.

His students applauded. They thought he was cool. But they also learned why it's best to listen to one's teacher. If they had skied on the slope, every one of them would have been buried. Thus it was a useful lesson.

Once during one of my visits, Ramsay offered to show me how to predict an avalanche. I welcomed the invitation, although I hoped I'd never need the skill. We went high up in the Rockies, where we planned to ski cross-country to a site where he would dig a snow pit and examine the layers of snow.

I could ski cross-country well enough on the stable snow of New England, but the deep powder in Colorado was beyond my skills. Ramsay wanted to go to a more distant location, but when I gave up with the skis, kicked them off, and simply plowed on foot through the hip-deep snow as best I could, he saw how long it would take to get where he meant to go and decided to dig his snow pit where we were.

All this time he had been explaining about different kinds of slopes and different kinds of snow, most of which I wasn't hearing because I'd been looking at a huge slope near us, wondering what chance there was of the snow sliding. I tried to warn Ramsay that this could happen. He said if it slid, the avalanche would go past us, not on us. I saw his point, as the slope wasn't over us, but what if the avalanche spilled sideways? We'd be buried. It's hard to accept reassurance from one's children, so I told him I was nevertheless concerned. "Oh, Mom," he said. "Don't worry."

What did he think a mother was for? "If you don't want a mother, why do you have one?" I asked him.

Ramsay began to dig the snow pit. When he finished, the pit was square, about four cubic feet in volume, and looked like a little white room. He showed me the many layers of snow, explaining their textures, also which layers might be stable and which unstable. He explained about temperatures and weather and how these affected the different layers. Under certain conditions, this layer might slide. Under different conditions, that layer might slide. The size of the avalanche would depend on how much snow had collected above the layer that was unstable. That's why one had to keep track of snowfall and temperature change, he told me.

He did seem to know quite a bit about the subject. He then pointed to the slope I'd been watching and said that judging from what his snow pit told him, the slope was indeed unstable.

My skin began to prickle. Hadn't I just warned him? Reassuring me that if it slid, it wouldn't touch us, he threw a snowball to see if he could set it off. Nothing happened. But I was scared. I asked him not to do that again. And so, not wanting a repeat of Skyline Traverse, he discarded the second snowball he was packing and asked if I'd like to leave. I said yes. He slipped gracefully away on his skis and I, up to my hips in snow, struggled along behind him. Again he had no words of criticism. He was the very soul of patience. Later he told me he hadn't felt patient but he hadn't let it show. Obviously I'd been a pain in the neck. But after all, I was his mom. He owed me a little patience. "Remember, I gave you life," I told him.

. . .

Another day we climbed a route called the Bomb in El Dorado Canyon, again a three-pitch climb but this time a 5.4 (although it has also been called a 5.6) and thus somewhat more challenging than Skyline Traverse. But it had no real exposure and therefore was not as scary, except for one place where I thought I couldn't make it. Maybe that part was 5.6.

Ramsay was leading again, of course, and when I didn't come up to him, he looked down. I told him the handhold was too far above me. I couldn't climb any higher. We had to go back, I said.

In his calm, matter-of-fact manner he said it would be difficult to go back. But he added that we probably wouldn't need to because he was sure I could reach the handhold if I shifted my position and tried again.

Difficult to go back? I didn't like the sound of that. So I moved as he suggested and tried a few times, until at last I gained the handhold and went up. At the top were several young men who perhaps were excited to have climbed something called the Bomb. But their faces fell when mine appeared above the ledge as I reached the top—the face of somebody's middle-aged mom, who, because she came over the ledge on her hands and knees, was clearly not much of a climber.

I had gone to ADAPT demonstrations to see my daughter do her thing, but clearly I would never see my son do his thing. The kind of climb I could manage would not take me up the towering mountains with their cliffs and glaciers, their seracs and crevasses, their avalanches and their whiteout storms, and thus Ramsay's life in that vast, frozen world that covered much of Europe was beyond me.

Even so, it was easy to see why he liked it. Once on a visit to Chamonix, Steve and I went with him up the *téléphérique* on Mont Blanc. The *téléphérique* was almost as big as a train and was jammed with hundreds of people, but as soon as it stopped, the people got off and vanished like a handful of peppercorns tossed in a lake. The enormous, timeless space with its ice and snow and silence swallowed them. Who wouldn't want to work in a place like that?

Most of what I learned about Ramsay's work I learned from the rare occasions when he'd tell his war stories. His worst client was a man who wanted to climb all the 14,000-foot peaks in Colorado. Other guides had taken this man up some of the peaks, but as Ramsay later discovered, any guide who had guided him once refused to guide him again.

Ramsay learned why. The client was a temperamental businessman from California who thought he knew more than he did. At ten o'clock one morning, he insisted on climbing a certain peak. Ramsay told him that to climb that peak, one had to start at six in the morning. To start at ten would take them into the afternoon thunderstorms, which would be dangerous, and even if they didn't find thunderstorms, they might be down-climbing in the dark, which, needless to say, is less safe than down-climbing in daylight.

If I were going to climb a dangerous peak, the very last thing I'd do would be to insult my guide, but the client wasn't as smart as I am. Furious and blustering, he kept accusing Ramsay of laziness and cowardice until Ramsay asked himself, *Why not?* And up they went.

After climbing a few hundred feet they came to a ledge where Ramsay suggested that his winded, red-faced client rest for a moment. And again the client got angry, yelling insults at Ramsay and flinging his arms about until the ice ax that he'd been using flew out of his hand and fell down, down, and down, almost all the way to the place from which they'd started. Without it, the client was helpless.

Ramsay tied the client to a rock. I don't know if the client agreed to this or not. Then Ramsay rappelled down to the ice ax, brought it up, and told the client they were going back to Boulder.

Ramsay and a climbing partner, Bruce Miller, made the first ascent of the north face of Lobuje East in the Himalayas. I have an account of that trip, not from Ramsay but from Peter Schweitzer, who sent an e-mail to tell me that after Bruce and Ramsay reached the summit and started to climb down,

> they used their only pot for something-or-other. As one sometimes does outdoors, when they were through, Miller grabbed the handle and swung the pot to empty out whatever was still inside. Oops! The pot went flying down the mountainside. Therefore they had no way to melt snow for their drinking water. Therefore they had better get off the mountain right away, no overnight bivouac. It was dark. Their flashlight batteries soon ran down.

Of course weight was an issue, which was why they didn't carry water, and they probably had brought less in the way of spare batteries (and for that matter, flashlights, bulbs) than I routinely bring when we visit you for a night or two in Peterborough. So they climbed down in the dark. Not, perhaps, the most delightful end to a successful climb, but actually the kind of thing that one treasures later.

When they came down they encountered an enormous, unseasonal snowstorm that was making international news, blocking the roads, filling up the valleys. Ramsay and Bruce went to a mountain village where they thought to wait it out. But there they were met by the Sherpa villagers, some of whom knew about Ramsay. Earlier he had become friends with a Sherpa guide who had summited Everest eight or nine times and who lived in the area, so word of Ramsay had spread. The villagers were concerned about their young children, five or six of them, who had gone down the mountain with their teacher but had not come back. They were not wearing warm clothes, so they were in danger. The villagers asked Ramsay and Bruce to find them, so, taking warm clothing, they went down through the blizzard, found the children and the teacher, bundled them up, and took them home.

Ramsay gave us a photo of himself and Bruce with the children. The storm has passed. They are sitting on sunlit grass. This may be the only photo ever taken of Sherpas who have been rescued by westerners, because it's normally the other way around. So Bruce and Ramsay made a first Himalayan ascent and then the first rescue of Sherpas by westerners. Yes, the Sherpas were small children, but a first is a first.

On one occasion Ramsay and two other guides took a party of twenty clients on a weeklong ski trip through the Mont Blanc massif in Italy, Switzerland, and France. Among the clients was a stunningly beautiful woman who had been a model. Her name was Heather McCoy. Heather was single, and Ramsay by then was divorced. They got to talking and found they liked each other.

Heather lived in Truckee, near Lake Tahoe. Her mother was the artist Stefani Esta, a delicately built woman who, with a welding torch and a welder's helmet, created huge sculptures in steel. She also made sculptures from large boulders. So Heather knew that there was more to womanhood than looking pretty. She hadn't much liked standing around in bathing suits while men ogled her, so by the time she went skiing in the Mont Blanc massif, she had left the lucrative modeling profession and become a chiropractor, with a practice so successful that she worked only three days a week and skied for the rest of the time. But soon enough she moved to Chamonix and into Ramsay's apartment, after which they came back to the States, got married in Yosemite Valley, went to India for their honeymoon, then bought a little house in Les Houches at a bend of the Chamonix Valley.

Beyond their front door was a heart-stopping panorama. To the right was Mont Blanc — the highest mountain in Europe[1] — also the Helbronner Peak and the Mer de Glace, and beyond these, towering on both sides of the valley, were the Needles of Médoc, Midi, and M, also three peaks called the English Sisters, also Les Drus and Les Grandes Jorasses, all of them thousands of feet high, most of them snow-covered. The view was stupefying.

That wasn't why they lived there, though. The neighborhood was an avalanche-free zone, one of relatively few in the Chamonix Valley. Now and then an avalanche would come thundering down off the Alps and engulf some houses or even a town, but Ramsay's neighborhood was immune. Other guides also lived there. The man whose house they bought was a guide. The entire neighborhood was favored by guides, and no wonder.

I loved everything about the Chamonix Valley. French food, of course, is the best in the world, but I would have traveled to Chamonix just for the cheese. It came from a goat farm on one of the mountains. And I could have spent the rest of my life on Ramsay's front steps, looking at the view. During the next few years on our visits I would do just that. But then one day when I was back at home, thinking of Heather and Ramsay, the phone rang.

It was Heather. She was crying. There had been a mountaineering accident and Ramsay had been badly hurt. She learned this while shop-

---

[1] Not counting Mount Elbrus in the Caucasus, which is in Asia and in Europe.

ping in Chamonix, where a storekeeper who knew her saw her passing on the sidewalk and came out to tell her. He'd heard about it on a radio that broadcasts calls for the rescue helicopter. The helicopter had taken Ramsay off a mountain and taken him to the Chamonix hospital. But by the time Heather got to the hospital, Ramsay had been taken somewhere else, and she didn't know where.

Heather was eight months pregnant. I told her to be strong. I told her I was on my way. I told her I'd call Steve, who was in Prague at the time and would get there before I could. We hung up. I called Steve. Then I called Stephanie in Texas—the person who would be the information center, keeping track of all of us, taking phone calls, communicating any news, and organizing whatever needed to be organized.

The phone rang again. It was my close friend Sy Montgomery, calling for our daily chat. I told her what had happened and that I was going to France. Believing that I consider myself too tough to ask for support, she announced that she was going with me. I arranged for someone to feed the dogs, found my passport, scraped up what money I had in the house, and put a few things in a suitcase.

The phone rang again. It was Heather, who had learned that Ramsay had been taken to a regional hospital in Sallanches. She also had learned how the accident had happened. Ramsay had been guiding a novice skier down a well-known off-trail slope when his ski caught on a ledge of white rock that was sticking up out of the snow. In the past the snowpack had been thicker and the ledge had been covered. Ramsay had skied there with clients many times before. But the world was warming, the snow-pack was shrinking, and the ledge was exposed. Ramsay flipped over. French guides didn't wear helmets while skiing, so Ramsay didn't have a helmet. His head hit the rock. He thought he was okay and stood up.

A man and a woman were skiing behind him and his client. They saw Ramsay fall. They skied down to him and saw that he was dazed and bleeding. They told him to lie down. As he did, he lost consciousness. The two people had a cell phone and called the rescue helicopter. After it came and Ramsay was carried aboard, these two splendid people led the client down the slope to safety.

The helicopter took Ramsay to the hospital in Chamonix, which dealt mostly with broken arms and legs. By then Ramsay was in a coma and the doctors couldn't help him. So they sent him by ambulance to the hospital in Sallanches. But even that hospital had no neurologist or neurosurgeon. The nearest neurosurgeon was in Switzerland.

Heather was calling from a cell phone while on her way to Sallanches. By the time she got there, Ramsay was in the operating room, where a doctor was performing surgery. In time the doctor came out, soaked with Ramsay's blood. He told Heather that Ramsay had less than a 50 percent chance of living but would be sent by ambulance to a neurosurgical hospital, part of the University Hospitals in Geneva.

Heather called a third time to tell me this, but spared me the thing about 50 percent. After the phone call ended, Sy came with a driver, who took us to the airport at eighty miles an hour, and we flew to Switzerland.

I remember nothing about the trip except that Sy was with me. We took a taxi from the airport to the hospital, where we found Ramsay lying on his back in the ICU, deep in coma, his face swollen and covered with dry blood that had come from his ears. There's nothing to say when you see that someone has been bleeding from the ears. You just know that things will never be the same.

Ramsay's eyes and mouth were shut. Steve and Heather were standing beside his bed, looking down at him. Sy and I looked down at him too. Quietly, Steve said he wanted to tell us something, but he'd tell us in the hall. From the expression on his face, I knew that what he had to say was nothing good. People in coma can sometimes hear things even if they don't seem to, so I was glad to be the hall when Steve told us that the doctors weren't sure that Ramsay would ever come out of the coma. We went back to his bed and continued to look at him. We stood there for hours in silence, not talking, just looking. There was nothing else to do.

Various monitors were attached to Ramsay. Sometimes we'd look at them. At one point a green light above his bed began to blink. We looked at that too. The blinking stopped but soon began again. A nurse came by and said that Ramsay was getting a phone call. Since he couldn't take the call, we just watched the green light. It eventually stopped, but again began blinking. This time Heather found the phone and answered it. The caller was a guide who had learned of the accident. Heather told him as much as she knew, and thanked him. In silence, we continued to look at Ramsay. But again the light blinked. Another guide was calling. A third guide called later. Word was spreading.

Heather and I went to the financial office to learn what we could about payment. We asked that the hospital keep Ramsay no matter what, because we would find a way to pay for it. Just then one of the doctors came by and heard what we were saying. He told us not to worry about payment. The important thing was to get the patient well, he said.

We then learned that even though Ramsay was in Switzerland, the French health-care system would cover his hospital bills. As a licensed French guide, Ramsay had a French green card and thus could receive the health care available to all French citizens, young or old, sick or healthy, rich or poor. The French took care of their own, which was more than the Americans did, and for which right-wing Americans scorn them.

Heather and I started back to the ICU. On the way we heard an orchestra playing Bach's Brandenburg Concerto No. 3. The orchestra was in the hospital lobby. The musicians were volunteers, playing for the benefit of the patients. The gorgeous music was going up the elevator shafts. We were enraptured. We would never have imagined an orchestra playing beautiful classical music in a hospital, and there we were, experiencing it. We stood there for a long time, just listening and breathing, while our souls absorbed the music. It felt like clear air after one has been suffocating. Then we went back to the ICU and stood beside the bed to look at Ramsay.

Steve found us rooms in a hotel, and late that night we went there. After we had gone to bed I heard Heather in the next room, crying. I knocked on the door and she opened it. She said that Ramsay was her closest friend. She said she needed him and didn't know what she'd do if he didn't get better. She put her hands on her pregnant belly. A little boy was in there. I remember wishing he was already born so that his father could have seen him. I also thought that Heather might rather be alone, so I went back to my room. Again I heard her crying. I'm unable to cry in such circumstances. Aside from this, Kothonjoro, how do you like Geneva?

In the morning we all went back to the ICU. Nothing had changed except that the blood had been washed off Ramsay's face. He was still lying on his back. His eyes and mouth were still shut. He hadn't moved since we had last seen him. He might be in a coffin, I thought. But he was alive — his heart was beating. We saw this from the monitor. We stood beside his bed and watched the monitor.

Several times a day we'd call Stephanie in Texas. She'd been taking phone calls from friends and family, giving them whatever information she had. She'd also been evaluating the various rehab centers for brain-injured people if and when Ramsay would be able to enter one. And if he were to come home, she'd been checking his American health insurance to see what it would cover. In short, she took care of everything related to this accident, and it gave us strength just talk to her.

One day Ramsay's eyes moved under his eyelids. The next day his lips and one of his hands moved. The neurologist measured his brain waves with some kind of machine and, based on what she found, decided that he could be moved from the ICU to the regular part of the hospital.

She was a kind and considerate person. She took time to explain to us that Ramsay was making progress, and she showed us what the machine had produced. Steve understood what she was showing us, but I didn't. By then my mind had gone as blank as Ramsay's. Steve was listening for both of us.

The doctors put Ramsay in a ward with two other people. He must have known he was somewhere else because he started to get up. Two male nurses hurried in and looped a tape around his hands to tie him to the bed rails. Although he was still in a coma and again lying on his back, I noticed he was working one hand loose. When it was free, he used it to free the other hand. A doctor came in, saw that Ramsay had freed himself, and tied his hands again, this time with twine using twenty or thirty knots for each hand. "Let's see him get out of that," said the doctor.

The twine had plenty of slack. Ramsay's hand moved down to feel the slack, then to feel the knots. Somehow, just from the way they felt, he must have understood what kind of knots they were, and he began to untie them. Although flat on his back, without looking at his hands, he did this efficiently, methodically, and without hesitation. To untie a knot with one hand and without looking at it was quite an ability. He'd acquired it from climbing, and it was still with him, deep in his brain. Although I knew he shouldn't be untying himself, it was a beautiful sight, and in my heart I was cheering.

As he opened the last knot I spoke to him. He gave no sign that he heard. I spoke again, but for him I wasn't there and neither was he. In the depths of his mind, he was far away, but he had purpose. With amazing agility for someone in a coma, he vaulted over the bed rail and started to leave the room. The two male nurses were talking in the hall and saw what he was doing. They walked him back to the bed and injected him with something. He sank to an earlier level of his coma.

After another week or so he could say a few words. He seemed to be getting better. Guides from different parts of Europe came to visit him, many of them bringing gifts of money. I hadn't appreciated the closeness of the guiding community, but why wouldn't they be close? Up there with the Ice Maiden, where most people will never go, they had little in common with the rest of us and everything in common with one another.

The neurologists and neurosurgeon who had been caring for Ramsay had a conference. They thought he should be moved back to the Sallanches hospital and from there to a rehab center. Steve and I wanted him to come home. So did Heather. Ramsay, who by then could talk a little, managed to say that he and Heather should stay in France. But if they did, what would happen to Heather? She'd be alone with a brain-injured husband and her first new baby. Not only did she want to go home, she wanted to go home quickly. The baby was due in less than a month, and if she waited much longer, the airlines wouldn't take her.

At about this time I thought I should do something about a phone call I had received shortly before Heather's fateful one telling of the accident. The earlier call had been from my doctor. It seemed that I had breast cancer. A biopsy had confirmed this, and I was supposed to have had a mastectomy. Instead I'd gone to Switzerland. One can't ignore such things forever, so I thought I should do something about it. Sy had gone home a few days earlier. I took a taxi to the airport and flew to Manchester, New Hampshire, where Sy met me. Steve and Heather went back to Les Houches, and Ramsay was taken by ambulance to Sallanches.

For a family to go through brain injury, breast cancer, and birth all at the same time only to experience a happy ending is more than one can expect. Yet that's what happened. When I got home, Stephanie flew from Texas to be with me, and she and Sy took me to Boston for what I thought would be essentially a drive-by procedure. A previous hysterectomy, every step of which I watched in the mirrorlike light fixture above the operating table, had been a walk in the park and was more than welcome because the pregnancy scares and the bother of menstruation were gone forever. But the mastectomy gave me a serious wound infection and made my chest look lopsided. Even so, it captured the cancer. As for the breast, I expect they gave it to the OR dog.

Meanwhile, Ramsay was discharged from the Sallanches hospital and went home to Les Houches. He'd been told to go to a rehab unit in the Chamonix Valley, but the waiting period was several months, so he listened to Steve's and Heather's advice and agreed to come home. At first his doctor wouldn't let him travel, and because of Heather's advanced pregnancy, things got a bit dicey with regard to time, but at the very last minute the doctor told him he could go. He had by no means recovered, so the long flight was difficult for him. But Steve and Heather helped him.

I thought of them as they were flying. I thought of wild geese because wild geese stay together and help one another. My mind's eye saw four wild geese, one of them as yet to be born, flying through the wind and night above the ocean.

Steve and I owned a house with a barn across the road from our house, originally a guest house or a rental property. Heather and Ramsay moved into it. Not long after that, the phone rang in the middle of the night. It was Ramsay. The baby was coming. Evidently he had driven Heather to the hospital despite his uncertain condition. Heather's mother had planned to be with her but was still at her home in California and couldn't get there in time. Would Stephanie and I take her place?

Normally the drive took forty minutes, but we were there in twenty minutes. Stephanie had to take the elevator, but it was long in coming so I ran up the stairs to the maternity section. On the way I heard singing. It was Hindustani music. Normally in New Hampshire one hears country music, so I assumed that the hospital had found an upscale radio station. But at the top of the stairs, people were gathered to listen to the song, and one of them pointed to one of the rooms. There I found Heather and Ramsay, Heather sitting on the edge of the bed with Ramsay on a chair facing her. Their foreheads were almost touching and they didn't look up. Together they were singing *Jaya Jaya Shiva Shambho Jaya Jaya Shiva Shambho Maha Deva Shambho Maha Deva Shambho Jaya Jaya Shiva Shambho,* over and over, on and on. They had learned such songs in India when Ramsay was designing a course about teaching avalanche prediction for the Indian army, and the song was a *dhun,* which means "resonance," in this case resonance with Shiva. It was working. With it, they sang Heather through her pain.

Heather delivered in a large tub of water. When the baby emerged, the midwife whisked him to the surface, where he took his first breath. That's how I met my little grandson, Jasper, dripping wet. Perhaps in honor of the time that Ramsay and Heather had spent in India, perhaps in honor of Ramsay's mountaineering in Nepal, or perhaps in honor of the *dhun* that helped Heather, Jasper's middle name is Jayashiva.

Ramsay's condition continued to improve. He received therapy at the Spaulding Hospital in Boston, got back his speech and most of his strength, and a year later it was hard to tell that anything bad had happened to him. He and Heather went back to France and sold their house (guides bought it, not surprisingly), then moved their things into the house across the road from our house with its view of the Wapack Range. The Wapack Range was not the Alps, of course, but at least Ramsay had his eyesight and could see it. Even so, needless to say, his guiding days were over.

Heather opened a chiropractic practice, which soon blossomed, and Ramsay with his lifelong friend Doug Frankenberger, both of whom were ardent musicians, converted the barn into a professional recording studio. The barn was a hay barn built by my father, but after its conversion it resonated like the inside of a cello. As for me, I got a rubber breast that looked something like the real one, and we all lived happily ever after.

To what do we owe this? To the skill and courage of the surgeon in Sallanches, whose name was Dr. Jacques Lemoine. He was an orthopedic surgeon, not a neurosurgeon, and he had never before done brain surgery. But he knew that someday he might be presented with a brain emergency, so he had done some reading and purchased some surgical tools. When he saw Ramsay, he knew that without immediate help, Ramsay would die or at best be left without brain function, so he performed surgery to relieve the pressure of the bleeding. Not many doctors would attempt brain surgery just from reading about it. But Dr. Lemoine did, and because of him, Ramsay not only lived but kept his intelligence, his eyesight, his speech, his memory, most of his strength, and all of his persona.

In Geneva, the neurologists couldn't stop saying how much they admired Dr. Lemoine. From what they'd seen during Ramsay's second surgery, they said he would have died without the first. As for our family, our gratitude is bigger than the Mont Blanc massif, and we will never find words to express it.

But Steve wanted to try. He went to Sallanches. "Vous avez sauvé la vie de mon fils," he told the doctor.

The doctor was modest. "Oui, c'est le travail," he said.

13

LOVE AND WORK

WASN'T IT FREUD who said that if you want to be happy, you should marry the right person and find the right work? I never doubted that I'd married the right person, even after Steve decided to spend six months of each year doing research in Prague, where he went after the fall of the Iron Curtain. I'm reminded of his value as a husband by a rose-colored pillow. It now sits on our armchair in New Hampshire and makes me happy every time I see it.

Steve had retired from his political career, claiming that he could no longer listen to a senator saying why he must be reelected, and wanting to address his early fascination with Central European history, the subject of his graduate studies, he went to Prague to search the archives. He could not have done this earlier in life, as much as he might have liked to, because while the Iron Curtain was in place, the archives were closed.

Knowing Steve, he must have been excited. Massive archives were stored in many different places. The information they contained would be as vast as it was valuable. Steve knew that his search would take a long time.

He was fluent in Czech to the point that Russians took him for a Czech and Czechs took him for a Russian, so he needed no interpreter or any other help to live in Prague, and he found an apartment near the I. P. Pavlova bus and subway stations, at the corner of Sokolska and Rumunská Streets, not far from the Dvořák Museum and the famous Wenceslas Square. He'd stay there for three months, then come home for three months, then go back for three months. While he was gone I missed him, so I'd visit him in Prague.

Prague is a marvelous city. I was thrilled that Steve's work took him there rather than, say, to Fayetteville, North Carolina. Steve didn't need a car, although he had a secondhand Škoda which he bought from a friend, because around the corner from his apartment were the bus and subway stations, from which he could go all over Prague by public transportation, also anywhere else in the country, even to tiny villages in the mountains, and also to the railroad station, from which he could go anywhere in Europe. The longest he ever waited for the subway was just over a minute, and just under three minutes for the bus. At home we could barely get from our house to the garage that quickly. On one of my visits, we walked from Steve's apartment to the corner and from there took public transportation all the way to a hotel in Berlin.

Memorable moments came from a trip we took to Austria, where right in the center of downtown Vienna I noticed an enormous sign with red letters saying THIS IS NOT VENICE. Most Austrian signs are in German, of course, but this was in English because English-speaking tourists, especially American tourists, are easily confused. Venice? Vienna? Anyone could mix those up and ask the Viennese where we could find the gondolas.

However, the most memorable moment, the moment involving the rose-colored pillow, came on the journey to Vienna. We went in Steve's car, leaving his apartment one morning to drive several hundred miles along a two-lane road. Scares came every few minutes. Often we'd see two cars coming at us, one in our lane, one in the other. And if that wasn't enough, the road was used by Czech farmers on their tractors and by Germans accustomed to the autobahns.

We would round a bend doing fifty miles an hour (which was almost too fast for that road) and come up behind a tractor doing five miles an hour. We would look back to see if we could pass, only to see a car with Deutschland plates hurtling toward us at ninety miles an hour. Steve would slam on the brakes, the farmer would look back at us with irritation, and the Deutschland car would swerve into the oncoming lane and whiz by with its horn blowing.

We did this all day, Steve driving. But our difficulties seemed about to end as we approached the Austrian border. Steve took his passport out of his pocket and asked me to get mine. I searched my tote bag, but my passport wasn't in it. I searched my pockets, and it wasn't there either. But by then I knew where it was — on the table in Steve's apartment. I didn't know how to share this information, and for a while I said nothing. But when we were almost at the border, I was forced to blurt it out.

And then came Steve's reaction, and this, not the drive, is why I remember the experience. He looked at me with a puzzled expression, absorbing the meaning of what he'd just heard. Then his face relaxed. Pleasantly, he said this could happen to anyone. He brushed aside my apologies, made a U-turn, and drove us back to Prague in perfect friendship. We got there late at night.

We still wanted to go to Austria, and decided to try again in the morning. As we were leaving the apartment, Steve asked to see my passport. I showed it to him. Then we walked to the corner, got on the subway, went to the railroad station, and took the train.

On our return, while walking from the subway, we passed a store window in which I saw the abovementioned rose-colored pillow. I knew it would look nice on an armchair at home and thought of buying it, but Steve thought it would be expensive. We certainly didn't need it, so I forgot about it. But the next day he bought it and gave it to me so I'd feel better about the passport. As indeed I did. Every time I see that lovely pillow on the chair, I remember how nice Steve was while driving back to Prague. I seemed to have taken Freud's advice about marrying the right person.

As for work, I liked it in almost any form except schoolwork, which I did but without enjoyment. As a child, I didn't see why I needed to know what my teachers were talking about, as my ambitions were to be a boy or a lion tamer or a firefighter, even though back then they didn't have girl firefighters. My attitude did not improve in college. I did the classwork only because I had to.

But I liked every other kind of work, for which I thank my surrogate parents, Tom and Kirsti Johnson. For all their intelligence and ability, they spent years of their lives working as servants. Their work did not have high status, but they nevertheless had high standards. They wanted to do everything well, and they had dignity, so when they told me that all work has dignity, I knew they were right.

When I was fourteen, they took over Dad's farm in Peterborough to raise chickens, and I stayed with them as long and as often as I could — all summer and on all school vacations. Tom was of course responsible for the outdoor work, but he had plenty of help in the form of me, my brother, and a boy my age named Arnold Autio, one of Kirsti's relatives, whom Tom and Kirsti more or less adopted after his parents died. Arnold and my brother helped Tom from morning to night, and I did too, but being a girl, I also helped Kirsti in the kitchen. Many kids who worked on farms didn't like it and moved to the city as soon as they could, but Tom and Kirsti could make anything fun, and we couldn't do enough for them. For years thereafter I welcomed almost any kind of work, and this helped me do things that might otherwise seem hopeless, and sometimes to finish projects I might otherwise abandon. It didn't seem to matter what the projects involved.

Here I must also thank my mother's mother, Gran, who, when I was very young, taught me perseverance with the following bedtime story. A princess must empty a granary before sunrise, but the piles of grain are so enormous she knows she won't be able to move all of them. Something bad will happen to her if she doesn't, so she starts to cry. An ant for whom she's done some service sees her. He tells the other ants and they help her. Since the story was supposed to put me to sleep, what I would hear after that little introduction was Gran's voice saying, "An ant came in and carried out a grain of wheat, then another ant came in and carried out a grain of wheat, then another ant came in" and so forth, ant after ant, grain after grain, into my dreams.

For me to go to sleep was the reason for the story, but the take-home was that the granary was empty by morning, and the moral is that a seemingly impossible task can be accomplished if you don't give up. Yes, the ants, not the princess, did all the work, but they didn't stop until the grain was moved. Since I must have fallen asleep hundreds of times with the ants and their achievement in my ears, the information got stuck in my brain at a rudimentary level.

. . .

The success of the ants was useful when I worked with Tom and Kirsti after they took over the farm, especially when I was weeding their enormous vegetable garden, and to this day the story enters my head if I take on a lengthy or difficult task. For instance, on the day before my eightieth birthday, frost was predicted, so I took apart a large vegetable garden that was planted by our son and a friend. They were somewhere else and the garden, which was near our house, needed immediate attention. I gathered all the vegetables that remained and brought them to the house, then drained the sprinklers and rolled up miles of hoses. I pulled up all the posts of the electric fence, making sure to keep all the little gizmos that held it in place, and rolled up miles of electric wires. I piled the organic matter into a wheelbarrow and dumped it on the compost pile. I then packed everything else into the garden shed, from which I first cleaned out many years' worth of mouse droppings. All that work took most of a day, but I did it without resting because my aim was to finish the job while I was still in my seventies, and by morning I'd be in my eighties. An ant came in and carried out a grain of wheat. Another ant came in and carried out another grain of wheat. In time the job was finished.

While I was at it, I also cleaned out the glove compartment of my son's Ford pickup so that anyone, not just him, could find the registration. He never asked me to do this, so I'm sure I was interfering, but I couldn't restrain myself, because the truck symbolized a similar experience that happened after a monstrous snowstorm when the man who normally plowed our driveway didn't come. Our driveway was ninety feet long and ten feet wide, the snow was three feet deep, I was seventy-something, Steve was away, and our son was still living in France so couldn't help me. But with the perseverance of those ants in mind, I shoveled the whole thing down to the gravel, meanwhile composing a rewrite of Gran's story: "Liz dug up a shovelful of snow and threw it in the woods, then another shovelful of snow and threw it in the woods, then another shovelful of snow," and so on. At least it was downhill.

When the driveway was clear all the way to the road, I walked back up the hill, went straight to my car, and drove into town to buy the Ford pickup and a snowplow. Price was no object. When our son came from

France to live across the road, we gave him the pickup, and from then on he plowed the driveway.

So I learned from my Finnish surrogate parents that all work has dignity, even sweeping up mounds of mouse droppings because the result is cleanliness, which is important, especially to Finns, and I learned from my gran that any task can be accomplished, even moving three thousand cubic feet of snow. But nobody told me that some kinds of work are better than others. That I found out for myself.

I'd always wanted to work with animals, and when I was in my early thirties, not long after we moved to Cambridge, I was offered a job in the monkey lab of a prestigious university. The scientists at the lab were having trouble with a monkey who was destined to be the subject of their experiments; I supposedly "had a way" with animals, and they hoped I could persuade the monkey to eat.

I went to the lab to see what I could do. A group of scientists and their assistants were gathered around a desk on which was an apparatus containing the smallest monkey I had ever seen, a newborn rhesus macaque who the day before had been delivered by C-section. The apparatus engulfed his body entirely. Only his tiny head was showing because the idea was that he should never see his hands.

Eyes wide, jaws clenched, lips pulled back in a horrified grin, he was looking up at the scientists, trembling with fear and also with cold, as he, like all macaques, was born naked. I gently stroked his forehead with my thumb. His eyes closed with relief and he slumped in his apparatus. The scientists murmured their approval. They could have done that themselves, I thought, but I took the part-time job they offered me. And yes, moments later I got the little guy to drink milk. In fact, all I had to do was to gently stroke his forehead, smile at him, and quietly tell him he was a sweet little, dear little monkey. He watched me with an alert, relaxed expression.

I don't know what those scientists eventually discovered about this infant, but when I smiled at him, I made a discovery of my own. He was only a day old, but he understood what a human smile meant. Just think. Naked, cold, straight from the womb, and alone in an apparatus surrounded by towering strangers, he understood what a human smile meant. He himself was grinning when I first saw him, but when a macaque grins, it's a threat.

If I draped him with a special cloth so that only his head was showing, I could hold him. And of course he liked that. The bad part was when I'd have to leave. He'd then be completely alone for sixteen hours, and when he saw me leaving, he'd be frantic. His wide eyes would follow my every move and he'd make little screams. It tore my heart. I couldn't stand it. I couldn't take him with me, of course, so I'd go home, get drunk, and cry.

The entire lab was joyless. The worst thing I saw was a cat strapped down on an operating table, alone in the room, lying on her back with her belly cut open for a C-section. The idea was to remove her unborn kittens and blind them, thus preventing them from seeing their front paws. Maybe the kittens had been removed already. I looked in the room because I heard the cat crying. She was coming out of anesthesia. I then noticed the female scientist who was supposed to be doing the operation chatting with someone in the hall.

The hierarchy in that lab was rigid, with the scientists at the top, their assistants next, and the lowly animal attendants like myself just inches above the animals in the cages. I pointed to the cat and said she was reviving. The scientist gave me a hostile stare and resumed her conversation. The cat kept crying, and I am as much to blame for that as was the scientist. I should have gone to the authorities. I should have called the ASPCA. I'd guess that after the kittens were removed, the cat would be killed and thus spared further agony — assuming that the scientist got around to it and didn't just let her die of pain. But I don't like to think about it, much less talk about it, and I've been racked with guilt ever since.

Another joyless sight was that of a male scientist trying to get an adolescent macaque out of a cage and transported to another kind of apparatus where his brain would be studied, or something like that. The macaque had electrodes implanted in his skull, so his brain had been studied before and he knew what was about to happen. For the longest time he successfully avoided getting caught. This amused the scientist. He laughed at the macaque's efforts and repeatedly called him "stupid." Finally he caught him, and off they went to the apparatus. No doubt the scientist made some kind of discovery, because later I saw a photo of that monkey, electrodes and all, on the cover of *Scientific American*. God knows what happened to him.

For a long time scientists questioned whether animals had thoughts, emotions, self-awareness, and the like, often assuming that they didn't. Thus it was amazing to be in that laboratory, where in every cage on every wall, the evidence that they did was overwhelming. The other animal attendants knew it — one of them showed me a female macaque who was cradling the corpse of her infant. The infant had died several days earlier, said the attendant, and the mother had been cradling it ever since. Her head was low and her shoulders sagged as she slowly groomed it.

The young attendant was an interesting person, a macho African American guy who talked street talk but beneath his tough exterior was deeply compassionate. He told me he would not remove the little corpse while the mother still had hope. He was waiting for her to give up.

The attendant thought she felt emotion. I thought she felt emotion. Darwin himself believed that animals think and feel emotion. But the scientists in that lab seemed to believe otherwise, including the scientist who, in saying that his macaque was stupid, seemed to know less about animals than an ordinary pet owner. Because scientists were just about the only people who doubted or denied that animals could think and feel emotion, and that to believe otherwise was sentimental anthropomorphization, they must have been misinformed in graduate school. (Today scientists are exploring these questions with fascinating, positive results. I learned of an octopus, for instance, who instantly found his way through a maze on the first try with no mistakes, because from his tank high on the wall he could look down at the maze and had seen how other octopuses, by trial and error, solved the problem. I doubt that most people could do that.)

As for the scientists in the monkey lab, their misinformation made me wonder about the results of their experiments. One question they addressed, and the reason for all the C-sections, was how the brain connects to the hands if the eyes can't see them. Were the scientists sure that the brain of an orphaned infant, alone, cold, and traumatized from the moment of birth, would develop in a normal manner?

Later, I'm glad to say, the laboratory went out of existence. I don't know what new form it took, but it didn't raise macaques. This wasn't because of compassion, however. Monkeys carry hepatitis B, and the scientists were afraid of catching it.

Aside from the monkey lab, which did not fit Freud's definition of the right work and which I left as soon as I could, I had little hope of doing anything with animals or any other fieldwork, if only because my children were no longer small and portable and they had to go to school. But one evening as I was sitting on our living room couch, my eyes fell upon a husky. He wasn't ours—he belonged to friends who were in Europe on sabbatical, but we were keeping him until they returned. And there he was in front of me, looking at me because he wanted me to let him out. I did. He came back a day later. I wondered where he'd been. I also vaguely wondered why he traveled so often—there were no leash laws then—and wondered if anyone had answered this question. I couldn't think of anything, though. All the books about dogs that I'd ever seen were about breeds, training, and so forth. And then it struck me. I wanted to study animals. Right in front of me was a wonderful animal. I could study him.

So I did. As I followed his travels on a bicycle, a world I hadn't dreamed of opened before me—the world of free-ranging city dogs, of whom at the time there were many. I didn't need to travel and I didn't need finances or equipment. I needed only a dog, a notebook, and a pencil. During the next few years I observed this husky and also my other dogs, and when I wasn't observing them, I'd hitch those who were huskies to a dogsled and go whizzing around in the woods in New Hampshire. It was paradise, even more for them than for me. If snow was falling, they'd rejoice and jump up to catch the snowflakes. Then they'd look at me. *Are we going?*

I took pages of notes but put them aside because I couldn't figure out how to handle the information. I'd figure it out later, I'd tell myself. And meanwhile, I just kept watching my dogs and enjoying them. I'm including this project in a discussion of work because I got a book out of it, *The Hidden Life of Dogs*, but in fact it was nothing but pleasure.

Soon enough, because Steve worked in Washington, we moved to Virginia, dogs and all, and then came Stephanie's accident. While she was in the rehab unit in Boston, I got an apartment in Cambridge to be near her. I took four dogs with me and lent three others to a friend who raced sled dogs. As I recall, it was illegal to have four dogs without a kennel license, but since one was a dingo and two of them were half dingo, and since dingoes are not the same species as dogs, I felt I actually had three dogs (the third was a husky) and thus didn't need a kennel license. The apartment was on the ground floor and had a little yard, but just to be safe, I never let all of them out at the same time, and I never let the dogs who looked like dingoes out together. Most people don't really see what they are looking at, so no one noticed that the apparent dingo was actually three creatures. I thought of starting to write about my dogs at that point, but I wasn't ready and decided to write another book I'd been thinking about that sprang from a story I had told my children. It had wowed them.

I scratched away at it for a while but couldn't concentrate. Then I thought a change of venue might be helpful. My apartment was just a few blocks from the Radcliffe Institute, which had been formed, I had heard, because many women who were scientists, artists, and the like were forced out of their careers by domestic issues. In other words, their educations were being squandered, and the institute wanted to help them. My education, such as it was, was certainly being squandered, and I was certainly subdued by a domestic issue, so seeing myself as the perfect candidate, I applied. The institute turned me down. I forget just why, but I think it was because they took only illustrious applicants.

Oh well. I had also applied for a grant from the National Endowment for the Humanities, and I got it. A few days later I got a flowery letter from the Radcliffe Institute inviting me to join. They had not reconsidered—they didn't realize I was the same person they had turned down. I had morphed into a woman with an NEH grant, thus bore no resemblance to that obscure earlier applicant with that daughter in the rehab hospital. I was tempted to scornfully refuse, but after thinking it over, I swallowed my pride and accepted.

They gave me an office, which was a better place to work than a crowded apartment, but I couldn't stop obsessing about my daughter. Every day I'd visit her in the rehab unit, where I would fuss over her constantly, hoping to get her to drink milk, which she hated. And try as I would, I couldn't write. Nor did I want to. I just thought I should. Nothing seemed to be working, so as soon as my daughter left the rehab unit and started college, I got three teaching jobs all at the same time, to keep myself too busy to think about my problems.

I taught freshman English at UMass Boston, also creative writing at the Harvard Extension, which is night school, and also a course that, if I remember rightly, was called "Communication" at the Massachusetts Correctional Institution at Walpole, better known as MCI Walpole[1] or just Walpole, a maximum-security prison where the bad guys go. After I went back to Virginia, I taught at George Washington University for a while, then worked for the embassy of the State of Kuwait.

One day while I was teaching at GWU, the head of the English Department came to my office. Perhaps because so many students seemed hopeless, or perhaps because of threats from their litigious parents because they got bad marks, she questioned the ability of their teachers and asked each of us to write something to prove that we knew how. So I wrote a truthful if somewhat emotional account of a dog who was shot by his owner for coming to my parents' house day after day, begging us to adopt him. Soon after that my boss came back to my office with my story in her hand, quite excited. "If you can write like this," she asked, "why are you teaching?"

I'd been wondering that myself. I'd been thinking about the book I did not write while at the Radcliffe Institute. By then I'd been offered the job at the Kuwait embassy, and because it provided health insurance that would have paid for some projected surgery for my daughter, something Blue Cross Blue Shield wouldn't cover, I took it. During the long commutes to and from the embassy, I'd think about the book I was planning. One day I discussed it with a friend named Nancy Jay. To her, it seemed important. "If you don't write it," she said, "it will never be written."

That did it. I was wasting the only life I'd ever have. The story was

---

1. The name was later changed to MCI Cedar Junction because of the negative image the prison shed on the town of Walpole. But the prison was famous, and at the time of this writing many people continue to call it Walpole.

no more than a kaleidoscope of thoughts, as vague as mist. Unless it was written, the images in all their detail would evaporate. Earlier in this book I've spoken of unrecognized desire. After talking with Nancy, I knew that I very much wanted to return to writing but had buried the desire. I suddenly felt like a different person. I suddenly knew what to do.

Tom and Kirsti had died. My dad had died. My mom inherited the house in Cambridge, my brother inherited half the land in New Hampshire along with the barn and the farmhouse, and I inherited the rest of the land and the house my dad built. By then my kids were in college. I still had the money from the NEH grant. My daughter wasn't going to have the surgery after all—we no longer needed the special insurance. I quit my job at the embassy and told Steve I was going to live in New Hampshire to start writing. If he wanted to come, I'd be overjoyed. But if he didn't, I was going anyway.

Steve had left the Council for a Livable World and was consulting. He could do that from afar, so he approved of my plan. We sold our house in Virginia, he got an apartment in D.C., and I went to New Hampshire to write my novel about the Upper Paleolithic. For a while Steve came on weekends, but soon enough he moved there with me. I made an office for myself in an old barn where John Leathers, the son of the Civil War soldier, had been living when he sold the land to my father. The barn had a space where I could work and an attic where bats and barn swallows slept in the summer and where millions of flies and ladybugs spent the winter. Once there, I wrote without stopping.

Many people were horrified to hear that I'd left a good job to take a chance on writing. I should have kept the job and written in the evenings, they said, to find out if my work could be published. But I knew my work would be published. I felt sure of my decision. I loved every minute of my working time and earned more money than I did from teaching or even from working for the Kuwait embassy. True, my pay rate was about twenty cents an hour, but I didn't need much sleep and I didn't take vacations. I just wrote.

14

RESEARCH

MOST OF WHAT I WROTE was informed by the natural world and the Old Way, not only by the Bushmen who lived it, but also by wild animals who continue to live it. This required research, much of which I had done, beginning when I was five and watched the cats in my parents' basement. Ever since then I've watched animals and tried to learn from them.

What seems to go on in their minds enthralls me. One day one of our dogs was having a bad dream, twitching and crying, so I stroked her gently to soothe her. Instantly she jumped up and attacked the other dog. Why was that interesting? Because the other dog tries constantly to dominate her, which she resents. The most interesting part is that to her, the dream seemed real.

In Namibia I loved to watch sleeping lions. They usually sleep in the shade of a tree, and often the patch of shade isn't big enough for all of them, so the latecomers lie down on top of those who got there first, creating a pile of lions. Unlike many animals who must always be vigilant, lions sleep soundly. After all, who is going to bother a large number of lions? Or even one lion, for that matter? As they sleep, their eyelids move, each lion in his or her own world, dreaming.

One day my friend Sy told me that she had been in the Boston Aquarium with the aquarium biologists, watching an electric eel. The exhibit provided a light that flashed when the eel discharged electricity. But now and then the light would flash although the eel was sleeping. He too was dreaming, said the aquarium biologists. I'd give all I possess to know his dream.

I think of my own dreams. From the time I came back from the Kalahari to the present, I've had recurring dreams of African lions. They come out of the woods at the edge of our field and I watch them, often with some concern, but they never come right up to the house and never try to hunt me. They seem not to know I'm there. The dream combines many of my experiences and most of my feelings—lions, the Kalahari, my love of my fields, my ambient anxiety as symbolized by unrestrained lions, and my desire to know what animals are doing. Dreaming piles things together for people. Possibly it also does for dogs, lions, and eels. Why dream if it does nothing for you? I have always been impressed by the oneness of the vertebrates.

I think of the philosopher Ludwig Wittgenstein, who famously said that if a lion could talk we wouldn't understand him. This is far from true. We might not understand everything he said, but some of us—the Ju/wasi, for instance—would certainly understand most of it. After all, every creature who lives in the natural world spends most of its time trying to get enough to eat. The lions and the Bushmen did so by hunting the same animals with many of the same techniques, the only important difference being the time of day when they did it. Animals need to understand other species, if only to prey on them or escape from them. The concept of commonality is far from wrong, and can be a powerful tool.

Some of my observations came about because a friend named Katy Payne discovered that elephants communicate with infrasound. During a visit to the elephant barns in the Washington Park Zoo in Portland, Oregon, she felt a strange sensation that I cannot describe, but it struck her that the elephants were causing it. She had been among the first to discover and record the songs of humpback whales, so she knew about sound waves, and she wondered if the elephants were making sounds she could not hear. She told me she was going to explore that question and asked if I would join her and Bill Langbauer, a graduate student, to do the research. I was delighted to join them.

We went to Portland, Katy with a recording device that captured very low frequencies. When she speeded up the recording, she could hear what the device had captured. From this she learned that the elephants were making extremely loud calls that none of us were aware of, even though the sound waves went right through our bodies. Elephants have been in the service of people for more than two thousand years, and all that time they've been making these calls. But Katy was the first to notice. Before this, no land mammal was known to make infrasound, so hers was among the most important biological discoveries of the twentieth century.

As for me, I gained some insight into an elephant named Tonga. He had been a circus elephant, but while his owner was riding him around the circus ring, he yanked her off the back of his neck and crushed her to death with his forehead. People said he was angry from having lost a fight with another elephant and he took it out on her.

After that he was transferred to the Portland zoo, where, understandably, he was considered dangerous. He was therefore alone in his pen, which had an outdoor area but was within reach of another pen containing another male elephant, the tip of whose trunk Tonga had managed to seize and bite off. One day as I was walking past his outdoor enclosure, he took exception to my presence. He glued his eyes on me as he tried in every way he could to climb over his elephant-proof wall and get at me. I could not have escaped from him. Not only could he outrun me, but he could also demolish almost any structure in which I might take refuge.

What I liked most about the elephant barns was being there at night, just me, Katy, Bill, and the elephants. In the semidark silence, we'd inhale their elephant odor and listen to their shuffling and breathing. Ears forward, body stiff, Tonga would glare at us. We kept out of his reach.

One night a three-legged rat came through a hole in the wall of Tonga's enclosure. I thought he'd kill the rat, but instead, ears loose, shoulders relaxed, he just looked down at her. She went right up to his feet, where a few morsels of his food had fallen. He blew a little air at her, which I thought might be a greeting. For about fifteen minutes she limped around his enclosure while he kept turning slowly and carefully, mindful of his feet so he didn't step on her. This way he kept her in view, as if he liked to look at her. Elephants, of course, are very social, but Tonga had no one, and surely he was lonely. He seemed to welcome her presence.

But he liked her more than she liked him. After collecting every morsel, she went back in the wall without looking at him. Tonga went over to the hole and blew a little air in behind her. *Remember me,* he might have said.

My next project included a study of zoo and circus tigers. I went to Illinois, to the Hawthorn Corporation, a facility where groups of tigers were trained for circus performances. As a child, all I ever wanted was to shape-change into a cat and I would have loved to be a tiger. This never happened, but from the tigers at the Hawthorn Corporation I learned how to sound like one. Later I went to the Brookfield Zoo and noticed two adolescent tigers lying on the grass of their enclosure, comatose with boredom. I said, "Aaaaaaaong!" The two youngsters leaped to their feet and looked all around, ears up, tails stiff, eyes wide, all excited. Where was that tiger? But they saw only me, whom they disregarded. So I said it again. This time they saw who did it and seemed disgusted. *Blast, it's one of them,* their manner said.

Elephants were also trained at the Hawthorn Corporation, and among them I saw an elephant who looked like Tonga. In fact, he *was* Tonga. But he was with some other elephants in an enclosure that consisted of no more than a few cables strung up to make a fence, nothing like the fortress that had contained him in Portland. He seemed relaxed, as calm as any other captive elephant might be under the circumstances, taking exception to no one, threatening no one. That evening when he was brought to his indoor enclosure, one of the elephant keepers, a woman, went right in with him. Tonga seemed fine with that. I told the keeper I'd met Tonga in Portland. She told me that as soon as he had company, his whole demeanor had changed. He pretty much did what was expected of him, and although people were cautious, no one was truly afraid of him.

I believe I'd observed a short part of an elephant's psychological history, and the tool that helped me was empathy. I know how it feels to be lonely—who doesn't? For that I was named Kothonjoro. Like some of us, Tonga dealt with emotional stress by blaming others. In Portland

I would watch his angry gray face, his restless, twitching movements, knowing he would kill me if he could and even that wouldn't help him. So it made me happy to know that he at last was happy. I thought of the three-legged rat in Portland and hoped she was doing as well.

The Hawthorn Corporation has long been under attack by animal rights activists, especially by PETA, for mistreatment of animals, but over a two-year period I visited many times, spent many months there, and saw nothing of the kind. The elephants were more or less okay, except that captivity and circus performances are never appropriate for elephants, but the tigers were in great shape—up and about in their big cages. All cats like to watch things, and in the two huge barns that housed them there was plenty to watch—meat arriving on a rolling table, the veterinarian making an inspection, other tigers going through a chute to the training ring, the trainers stopping by to greet their tigers and be greeted by them. Research has shown that circus tigers are healthier and happier than most zoo tigers because zoo tigers are all but anesthetized by boredom and circus tigers have plenty to watch and meaningful work.[1] They live longer too. I learned that the average age of tigers in most zoos was about nine, while circus tigers regularly lived into their late teens and some lived well into their twenties.

The atmosphere at the corporation was due largely to the head trainer. He came from Holland, and his name was Roelof de Vries. While there I would stay with him and his wife, Elke, and would spend my days watching him at work, because his ability to work with animals, his methods too, made me think of Francis of Assisi, the saint whom we honor on October 4 when we hope that God will bless the animals. The tigers would brighten when Roel came to get them, chuffing greetings and rubbing their faces on the cage as housecats rub us when we stroke them. While training the tigers, Roel carried only a pole with a pointed end and a wand with a string attached to it, the pole to deliver small rewards of meat to the tigers' mouths, the wand to flick the string under a tiger's chin as a cue to back up. Roel trained his tigers with praise and pleasures. They liked him.

At the Hawthorn Corporation, perhaps seventy or eighty tigers were caged in the barns, one to a cage, each cage with a shelf for the tiger to sleep on. Often the gates between some of the cages were open to let compatible tigers socialize. Also every day in fine weather the tigers could spend time outdoors. Normally the barns were noisy, with tigers moaning at each other (making the *aaaaaong* sound that I learned) or chuffing greetings as their keepers or trainers passed by. Usually a lot was happening—cages being cleaned, food being brought in, the floor being washed with a fire hose.

This was the routine, but I witnessed two exceptions. The first took place because circus acts were sometimes boarded at the Hawthorn Corporation, and one day a lion was brought in. He had been there before and didn't like it. While still in his cage in a trailer, he realized where he was and started roaring. Inside the barn, the tigers looked up and seemed anxious. The lion was then made to run down a passage between the rows of tiger cages, and he roared every step of the way. The tigers stopped moving, as if they hoped he wouldn't notice them. But their effort was useless. As soon as he was in his own cage he sprayed the tigers on either side with urine.

I was watching this with surprise and interest when my glasses went blank like a windshield when the car ahead splashes through a puddle. I felt warm and wet inside my clothes. He had sprayed me too. But who can blame him? Whenever possible, lions live with other lions and stand together in times of adversity. He was alone with dozens of enemies all around him, as he saw it. His only hope was to keep them intimidated, so while he was there he had a roaring session every fifteen or twenty minutes, making thirty or forty roars each time. During these sessions the tigers kept still but looked in his direction, their ears ringing. The lion left after a week or so, and when he did, the barn returned to normal.

The second exception took place one day when I entered the barn and was surprised by its perfect silence. The tiger in the corner cage had gotten to know me and would chuff a greeting, but that day she was up on her shelf, looking at something at the far end of the barn. I chuffed at her, but she paid no attention. The tigers in the next cages were also on their shelves, all tense, all in more or less the same position, all looking in the same direction, heads up and ears high.

Obviously they were looking at something important. I climbed a ladder to the top of the cages to see what it was. Ordinarily the tigers below would have reached for me (a wire netting prevented them from catching me), but they didn't come after me this time, so I climbed higher and I saw — what? The barn was almost a hundred feet long, every tiger was up on a shelf, and at the far end four men were standing in a doorway. Nothing more.

I knew three of the men — a trainer and two keepers. The tigers saw these men every day. It was the other man on whom they focused. Then, in a kind of gestalt, as often happens when I'm with animals I know, I got it. The fourth man was John Cuneo, the president of the Hawthorn Corporation.

I was right. That's who he was, although how I knew is hard to explain because I had never seen him before, not even a photo. How the tigers knew is even harder to explain, because Cuneo lived about thirty miles away and came to the barns only on rare occasions. Roel told me that he never interacted with the tigers so they had no experience with him. But their fate was in his hands, and evidently they knew it. Soon enough Cuneo turned and left, although the other men stayed. And when he was gone the tigers got down off their shelves and resumed their normal activities.

Often events with animals appear to be minor, as the event with Cuneo might seem — tigers got up on their shelves, they looked at some men, they got back down — but in fact such events can be revealing, especially about the animals' minds. At the time I had four parrots, among them an African grey parrot named Pilgrim. One day I was giving them grapes to eat, and as I'd hand each parrot a grape I'd say, "For you." When I got to Pilgrim, he said, "For me." That might at first seem insignificant, but I was shocked. Pilgrim had never been taught to speak. He had figured out for himself which pronoun to use by listening to people. What did it say about his thoughts? If nothing else, it said that he valued communication.

People aren't very good at cross-species messaging. Perhaps I could sound like a tiger, and I also knew what *aaaaong* meant, probably because tigers and people are not that far apart on the evolutionary tree. But 200 million years have passed since we shared an ancestor with birds. I can't deduce what a parrot's call means, nor can I reproduce it. I'm not proud to say this, but to me their calls are just different forms of screaming. Pilgrim was way ahead of me.

I then remembered the tigers and John Cuneo, and wondered if they acquired their awe of him from watching people, perhaps noticing respectful behavior and speech on the part of his employees on the rare occasions when he came to the barns. That's just a guess, and not a very good one, because the trainers and the keepers were also respectful of me. Perhaps tigers can read minds or have ESP. Animals are sometimes credited with this ability, but proof is lacking. Whatever the tigers perceived about Cuneo would have been subtle, but then, most animals are significantly better at observation than is our reductive species in its present state. But if observation is your major tool for gathering information, you'd better be good at it. The tigers were all of that.

If one watches animals often enough and long enough, one sees some unexpected things, especially from the cat family. Once in Namibia I came upon two lionesses who had killed a female wildebeest but were not eating. Instead, they were resting. The day was hot, and to bring down a wildebeest must have been tiring. After a very long time, one lioness got up, trudged over to the corpse, lay down beside it, and began to eat at the belly. The wildebeest had been about to give birth. When the lioness opened the belly the fetus fell forward. The lioness cleaned the caul from its face, then cut the umbilical cord and licked and nudged the fetus as if to start it breathing, just as she would if birthing her own cubs. But the fetal wildebeest was dead, which the lioness soon realized. So she ate it.

I'm sure her behavior was caused by hard-wiring, which I've always admired in cats, but I would not have expected anything like what that lioness did. Cats also have a prodigious amount of original, independent thought, which leads them to do other kinds of unexpected things, sometimes in response to practical situations as Cuneo's tigers were doing, but sometimes not.

I think of another lion, a male this time, whom I saw after Katy completed her study of the elephants in the Portland zoo and took her project, myself included, to Etosha Park in Namibia. There she studied the calls of wild elephants.

Several herds of elephants drank from a certain water source, usu-ally assembling at about the same time every evening, vocalizing as they came. Not far from the water, Katy and Bill built a high observation platform from which to observe and record them.

Late one afternoon, Katy and I were on the platform waiting for the elephants to show up when the lion in question came from the east and lay down near us on a rise of ground. Many animals, especially the large ones, don't bother to look up (which is why deer hunters use tree stands), so I think the lion didn't see us. But if he did, he wasn't inter-ested. Propped on his elbows with his head raised, he fixed his eyes on the western horizon. The sun was setting. Not long before it touched the horizon, he roared. A moment later, he roared again. Many times he did this, never taking his eyes off the western sky, roaring and waiting, roar-ing and waiting, until the sun went under. Evidently that's what he had come to do. When the last red bit of the sun disappeared, he got to his feet, turned around, and walked away to the east.

What had we seen? Mostly lions roar for the benefit of other lions, who answer. But that evening no one answered. Lions also roar at other species, as a pride of them once did in the Kalahari when we, with some of the Ju/wasi, camped at a place which the local lions owned. They came in a group — probably the entire pride — and they all roared together for a very long time, several lions taking up the roar when other lions ran out of breath, so the horrifying sound was continuous. Lions can't speak? Wittgenstein should have been there. And we can't understand them? They were doing what lions do to keep other lions off their land. They were saying the place was theirs and their group was so large and powerful that together they could make one continuous, deafening roar that lasted for half an hour, so we had better not think of moving in. We got the picture.

But that wasn't why the Etosha lion roared. So who was he, and why had he come alone to roar at the setting sun? He was mature, perhaps quite old. When he wandered off he went rather slowly, as if he had no immediate plans or special destination. He seemed lonely. It came to me that he did not belong to a pride, which would not have been unusual. Sooner or later, most older male lions are evicted from their prides by younger males. Thus wherever lions live, their population has aging, solitary males who live alone for the rest of their lives. And because they don't have much involvement with other lions they have plenty of time to think. The possibilities of what that lion might have been thinking are almost endless, and all are spine-chilling.

The lion wasn't the only animal who cared about the sun. When we lived in Cambridge, I saw something similar when a friend who owned two wolves came to visit us. The friend stayed in our house and the two wolves stayed in his van, which was parked in the street. Every morning before dawn the wolves would stand, heads together, in the van's east-facing window, where they would wait for the sun to rise. When its first red flames came into view, they would start to sing a song in two parts, which they would continue until the entire sun was above the horizon. Then they would stop. But they did this only if they actually saw the sun. If the sky was cloudy, they would not sing. They did this every morning, said their owner, singing if they saw the sun, not singing if they didn't. Why they did this is unknown, but again, the possibilities are spine-chilling.

It then became my great privilege to watch wild wolves on Baffin Island. I went there with four graduate students who, with Dr. Douglass Pimlott, director of environmental studies at the University of Toronto, had been studying the Baffin Island wolves for years. But by the time I went, Dr. Pimlott had handed the research over to his graduate students, and they were there to determine the size of the caribou population, so the wolves were left to me. As I think about them now, I realize that they were not the kind of wolves who would sing at a rising sun. That's the kind of thing a person might do if his basic needs were met and he had time to think expansively. The wolves of Baffin had too much to do and they lived in the moment, hunting most of the time, alert for every rustle of grass that might indicate a lemming. They slept when they weren't hunting.

We went to Frobisher Bay, now called Iqaluit, on a regular Air Canada flight, and there we boarded a military DC-3 of World War II vintage, bound for a DEW Line station farther north. The age of the plane was discouraging, as were the fumes rising from a dozen or so barrels of gasoline that were crowded around us, but before takeoff we were reassured by the pilot. Despite the fumes, he lit a cigarette, and dangling it from his lips because the plane was taking off and his hands were busy, he told us that any DC-3 that was going to crash had crashed already. A spark fell from the cigarette as he spoke.

Oh well. We got there. From the station we walked about seventy miles across the tundra to the place where the wolves were denning. We didn't bother to make camps on the way—we simply lay down and slept. This was in July so there was no night. The sky wasn't telling us what to do. We slept when we got tired.

Just as we arrived, two white wolves came trotting around a hill and saw us. One was an adult, who increased her pace and disappeared over a ridge between two distant hills, but the other was a juvenile, and he kept right on trotting as before, doing exactly what the Ju/wasi had told us do in the presence of a predator—don't run, just move away in a moderate manner at an oblique angle. The young wolf did this beautifully until he came near the nest of a jaeger, who repeatedly dove down and bit him. She tore out tufts of his fur, but rather than spoil his facade of unconcern, he pretended to know nothing about her until he was far enough from us to leap up and grab her tail. He pulled out a feather. The jaeger shrieked and flew higher and the young wolf ran away at full speed.

Later we heard a wolf howling. One of the graduate students said that the adult wolf who had seen us was calling the rest of her pack. I don't remember his words exactly, but I gathered that the wolf would communicate to the others that something bad was near the den so they all would have to move. No one knew how she did it, but that is exactly what happened. Later we heard all the wolves howling. They had gathered at the den they were about to leave. Why they were howling at that point wasn't clear, but wolves are like people in that they sometimes sing before taking important actions. For us, this might be going into battle or competing in a team sport. Perhaps it strengthens their unity.

My colleagues knew from past visits that these wolves had four dens. If things went wrong near one, the wolves could move to another. We soon went to look at the nearby den, but the wolves had gone already, taking the pups. The graduate students camped nearby because they had camped there on earlier visits and their task was to count caribou, not to watch the wolves. But one of them took time to show me the way to another den, several miles from the first. We found a fresh wolf scat near it, and although no wolf was in sight, the graduate student thought we were at the right place. The next day we set a date for me to rejoin the others, then he returned to their camp and I was alone.

I had a backpacker's tent and set it up. But I wasn't there for long before I thought I had a problem. Here's a letter I wrote to Steve (but had no way to mail it).

A big storm has blown up from Greenland which is where the weather comes from. I saw ice crystals around the sun and said uh-oh and decided to walk out. But then, since I'm not expected until August 4, I decided to stay. And then I found a little cave! Not a breath of wind in it, though it must be 50 mph outside. I made a little fireplace, put in a huge bed of heather, put in a good supply of heather for fuel, put all my food and things in nice little cracks in the rock. I am so nice and warm, so optimistic and happy. I could survive a winter storm.

Since at first we saw no wolves, I'm not sure why the graduate student was confident that we were at the right den. Maybe he was guessing, or maybe I was lucky, but the wolves were there, no question. After the grad student left, I scanned the surrounding hills with my binoculars, never doubting that I was in the right place, and after several hours I saw a wolf approaching. She trotted up the hill toward the den. Then all of a sudden seven little pups came bursting out and ran to her, crowding around her face and licking the corners of her mouth. She lowered her head and vomited up some partly chewed meat. They bolted it and begged for more. She sniffed each of them quickly, perhaps to learn how they were doing, and then she lay down on her side, loosened her thigh, and let them nurse. Evidently she was the mother.

I guessed that the pups were perhaps five weeks old. Their ears were still floppy and their fur was gray-brown, the color of the earth, unlike the adult wolves, white and conspicuous on the green summer tundra. Other wild canids are also earth-colored as infants. So are some domestic dogs, who change to the breed-appropriate color when they grow up. Earth color seems standard for puppies of the dog family.

The pups nursed hungrily but not for long. Soon enough their mom stood up and jumped to the top of a nearby boulder, where, out of reach of the pups, she lay down to sleep. The pups stood below, looking up at her, but when they accepted the fact that she was finished with them for the time being, they went back in the den. After many hours the mother wolf got up and went hunting again.

After a few more hours, a second wolf arrived. The pups must have been listening carefully, because again they came right out and swarmed around his mouth. He too vomited some food and fed them, and he too jumped up on the boulder to sleep where the pups couldn't reach him.

That's mostly what happened, again and again. Five grown wolves belonged to that pack, the two parents and three younger wolves, who were probably their young of the year before. For most of the time, four grown wolves would be out hunting and the fifth would be babysitting, even though asleep. Interestingly, no adult wolf was present when I arrived, but after they noticed my presence, they never again left the pups unattended.

At first I assumed that the wolves were hunting caribou, because wolves hunt large ungulates wherever they can. But to bring down the big ones takes the effort of a pack, and the Baffin Island wolves appeared to hunt individually. During my entire stay, I never saw more than one wolf at a time return from hunting, and the vomit piles were always fairly small. That left carrion, eggs, baby birds, Arctic hares, lemmings, perhaps Arctic foxes, and even dead fish as food items, because few other animals lived on Baffin Island.

Eventually it came to me that those particular wolves were not hunting caribou, or not during the denning season. However, their den was halfway between the coast and the caribou calving grounds. The caribou spent the winter near the coast and went upland to their calving grounds in spring, and these seasonal migrations took them right past the den. Female caribou, like females of some other ungulates, bear their calves all at the same time in the same place. Suddenly there are hundreds of calves. The number of the local predators remains the same, so the predators who live nearby can kill some of the calves but not all — not even a significant number. This could be called a good thing for both species, as most of the calves survive and the predators get to feast for a little while in spring when—hungry from the winter but required to raise pups—they have the greatest need of food. As for the wolves I was watching, when the caribou passed by the den in spring, the wolves would know where they were going and why, and for a short time they could hunt the calves. It would be wrong to say they had no interest in caribou.

I had a strong interest in caribou but seldom saw them. Sometimes I did, though, as I wrote in another unmailed letter to Steve.

Today a caribou appeared in the valley where my camp is. She must have seen me, she took an alarm position, i.e. with one hind leg stuck out, then came up to investigate me. Then she seemed to change her mind and headed up the valley. I thought I'd have another look at her so I crept up to a ridge overlooking the valley. She was gone. How could I lose a caribou in that vast landscape, I wondered. I turned to go back and saw her standing right behind me, as curious about me as I was about her.

I like to think about that. Probably I was the first human being she had ever seen. If the Kalahari showed what the world was like before the Neolithic, Baffin Island showed what the world was like before there were people.

Now and then the wolves would visit my cave, but only when I was sleeping. How did they know? That's hard to say, because their den, where they spent most of their time when not hunting, was about two hundred feet away and my cave was on the far side of my hill. But they never came to see me when I was awake. Here's another letter to Steve.

The wolves are lovelier than ever. Yesterday I was going up to my lookout post when a wolf coming along the stream saw me. I stopped dead but the wolf kept looking. She then proceeded to the den, taking the course of least visibility. When she got to her hill, her pups rushed at her. She regurgitated for them, then rested about an hour, then started back along her trail, sniffing very carefully and marking here and there. She squats and lifts one leg a little to do this, like female dogs do when they're in heat, and it means they're marking, not just peeing. I expected her to reappear on her old trail, but she did not, nor did she appear on any hillside. I figured I had lost her and as I was tired, I went back to my camp, forgetting to bring my head-net with me. [The head-net was for mosquitoes, which were frightful.] *What she had done was to creep up under the hillside and wait for me to leave, whereupon she investigated the place where I had been and ripped up my head-net. I found it later full of holes and white fur. But the wolves don't seem to mind me. I thought that after this they'd move the pups to another den, but they didn't. Still there today, white and beautiful as ever.*

Another time they found my only sweater, which I had carelessly left on my hill, and they tore it to shreds. That caused a problem. I was cold without it, so I had to devise a garment with my only towel.

The wolves' treatment of the head-net and sweater raised an interesting question: Why didn't they do the same to me? They hunted all the time, I was easy prey and also about the size of a young caribou (I weighed about 125 pounds), and my carcass could have saved them much labor. But needless to say, this never happened. I can't have seemed dangerous, because the only other people they might ever have seen were Dr. Pimlott and his students. My guess is that it never occurred to them to hunt me. Nobody knows why not. Dr. Pimlott and others studied wolf predation at great length, and if I remember rightly, they found only one instance of wolves attacking a person, an instance involving a man who, for whatever reason, disguised himself as a bear cub and rolled around in a field as if he were helpless and wounded. He was attacked by wolves, but whose fault was that?

Mostly the wolves were something like the Kalahari lions who didn't hunt the Bushmen. But those lions knew what people were and the wolves of Baffin Island didn't, because with the exception of Dr. Pimlott and his students, people had never lived inland on Baffin. Even so, not even the young, less experienced wolves hunted me, although all the grown wolves together were working very hard to feed the current litter. They could easily have hunted me if they wished. I had no way to defend myself, because unlike some people who venture into places owned by other species, I would not have dreamed of taking a weapon or harming those who lived there.

So perhaps I was something of an anthropologist after all. When you visit people of other cultures, you aren't supposed to hurt them. I was later to learn that while I was watching my wolves, one of the graduate students was trying to trap some other wolves, perhaps to tag them, but managed only to trap one wolf by a few of her toes, which she chewed off. The wolf had gone but her toes were still in the trap. How was she supposed to make long hunting forays without toes? An anthropologist would not do something like that.

Sometimes I hiked around the area to see where the wolves were going, following their trails that led from the den. One trail went past a lake. On one side of the lake the ground was boggy, but on the other side a big hill of bare rock formed a bank, and there the trail disappeared. I looked more closely and saw a little ledge on the rock, a few inches under the water. The wolves had chosen not to wade through the bog, but instead crossed the lake by walking on the firm footing of the ledge. And because the ledge was narrow, a trail was worn into the rock.

It took me a moment to understand what I was seeing. Worn into the rock? Wolves had done this, I felt sure, as the ledge was too narrow for caribou. Also the trail led back to the den, an unlikely choice for caribou. But wolves would use that trail mostly in summer, not only because the lake was frozen for the rest of the year, but also because in late summer the pups would be too big for the den and the wolves would move them to one of their camping places on the tundra. After that they would have no reason to visit the den, or perhaps even to use the trail, until the following spring.

How long it had taken for a few padded feet to wear a trail into a rock? Wolves came to Baffin Island so long ago that they had formed their own subspecies. I don't know how long that took, but it was long enough for a few wolves to wear a trail used only in summer, and not every day, in a rock that was under water.

This also said something about the den. If the trail had been used for a very long time, perhaps the den had been too. A good den is a prized commodity and can be used for generations, and the den I was watching was one of the best. A den must be deep in stable earth that won't collapse—a tunnel perhaps thirty inches or more in diameter and about fifteen feet long in the side of the hill with a room at the end which could be thirty cubic feet in size or even larger, big enough to hold several pups and their mother. All in all, to make a den, about a hundred cubic feet of earth must be moved at least twice, once to get the earth out of the hill and again to scatter it a bit, so no big pile develops to indicate the presence of a den or to collapse and fill up the entrance, trapping those inside. Because most wolves already have dens, new dens are often made by a newly mated pair hoping to start a pack of their own, so all this digging might be done by two wolves with their front paws. The mouth of a den doesn't look like much, but what's underground is an astonishing achievement.

The location is important. The den I watched was on the sunny side of a hill in a large basin, with more hills all around. Nothing could approach without being seen. The den was above a stream where the wolves could drink. The stream also served as a fence for the pups, who couldn't cross it. If they tried to follow an outgoing wolf, the wolf would cross the stream to scrape them off. Alone, they'd stand on the bank, tails drooping, watching their parent or older sibling grow small in the distance. When the departing wolf was out of sight, all the pups would trudge back to the den and go down the tunnel.

In short, the place was exceptional, a treasure. No wonder wolves use the same dens for generations, refreshing them by digging out more dirt from time to time. And those who used it must also have used the underwater trail worn into the rock. It's quite an experience to see very old things made by animals, but there they were, the trail, which may have been used for centuries, and the den, which, judging from a small amount of fresh dirt at its mouth, was not new — far from it — but was probably cleaned up a bit when the wolves moved in.

Most of the time I'd lie on my stomach on top of my hill and watch the wolves with binoculars. I think I was happier there than I had ever been before, or at least happy for a longer time. I felt joy, pleasure, serenity, and wonder, especially wonder, because the wolves were so much like us. Wolves became wolves at about the time that we became people. Their two-parent families are like ours, and they hunt in the daytime just as we do, for the same kinds of game that our ancestors hunted. Given a difficult climate and helpless young who must be kept warm, there are not many ways to live by hunting. Wolves and people made the same choices.

The choice, of course, is to leave the infants at home while the adults forage—just the opposite, say, of some of the ungulates whose infants stand up and follow them right after birth. Referring to the wolf/human practice, an anthropologist called it "the bird's nest arrangement" because, of course, many kinds of birds also forage from a nest, a home base where they leave their infants, just as hunter-gatherers forage from an encampment where the children and the old people stay.

As for the wolves, the babysitter was merely a guardian, not a playmate, as he would sleep on top of the boulder where the pups couldn't pester him. Many hours or even days later, another adult would come back from the field with food in her stomach. The pups would burst out of the den and rush up to her, and she would vomit the food to feed them. She would then become the babysitter, and the wolf she replaced would come down from the rock.

The two adults might greet each other briefly, but not always. I found this fascinating, as to me it showed their unity. The adults were in this together, committed to months of hard, skilled work, and they didn't need to prove anything to one another. Everybody knew where he or she stood in the hierarchy. Never once did a wolf show dominance or hostility toward another wolf, because the social order seemed acceptable to all of them. The five adults were as tight as a clenched fist.

Because of this, and because four of the wolves were always hunting individually, so that an incoming wolf would spend only a short time with the outgoing babysitter when they changed places, they were far apart most of the time and had little interaction. But the distance didn't seem to matter, because in their minds, I think, their pack was always together.

Now and then the wolf at the den might howl. A moment would pass, and then, from an enormous distance, would come the faintest possible howl—another wolf answering. For whatever reason, the wolf at the den had been thinking about the other wolf. Many years later, it was learned that a component in a wolf's howl serves as the name of another wolf. The wolf in the distance heard her name and answered. The only time I heard all the wolves howling together was on the day we arrived, when all of them needed to take action.

When a returning wolf arrived at the den, the babysitter would prepare himself. He would stretch, then walk around a bit, perhaps trying to decide where to go, or perhaps not quite ready for the difficult work that lay ahead. He might drink from the stream. Then he would cross the stream and choose a direction, trudging at first, as if he were reluctant to get started, then gathering himself and moving a bit faster until he broke into the businesslike, ground-covering jog of a wolf with a far destination. Soon he'd be out of sight. By then the wolf who had just come in would have fed the pups and gone to sleep high up on the boulder, and nothing would happen for hours.

I'd lie on top of the hill with my binoculars, waiting. Every twelve hours or so, three ravens would fly overhead. They always came from the west, which meant they were making a big circle. I say the west, even though when you are that far north, the only direction is south. But when I was looking at the den, I couldn't actually see the sun unless I turned my head slightly, and the ravens came from the left. At home, that would be west.

Every time the ravens passed, they'd look down at me carefully, sometimes circling for a better look, and for years after that I'd wonder if they remembered me. I liked to think of my image in the brain of a raven, somewhere in the Arctic sky. Ravens have good memories, and not many unusual things other than me were available to look at, so I was hopeful.

The perfect tundra stretched as far as the eye could see, and the wind blew so quietly I couldn't hear it, but I could feel it on my skin. The sun was always in the zenith, so it was always midmorning. If no wolf appeared for many hours, that was fascinating. The long absence of the wolves spoke of the hardship of hunting.

I especially remember the return of one wolf who had been hunting. She'd been successful. She lowered her head and vomited some chewed-up meat. The little crowd of pups bolted down the food and begged for more.

The wolf might have had more food in her stomach, but if she did, she was saving it for herself. However, I'd seen the mother wolf throw up twice for the pups, as if in response to their begging, and although the wolf in question wasn't the mother, I wondered if the begging might be softening her. She looked down at the pups for a moment, perhaps reconsidering. But after a long pause, she must have decided that she needed the nourishment herself, and she jumped up on the boulder. Discouraged, the pups went back in the den.

The adult was worn out. She fell fast asleep. I watched her. She slept for nine hours without moving. Then she sighed, settled her tongue, shifted her legs slightly, and went to back sleep, again for nine hours without moving.

All this time I watched her. At last another wolf came up to the den and fed the pups a little belch of something, perhaps a lemming or two. Most of the pups therefore got nothing, and they looked up at the newcomer, pleading. The newcomer didn't offer any more. The hungry pups cried. The sleeping wolf woke up, stood up, shook herself, jumped down off the rock, urinated, sniffed here and there for a moment, then trudged off slowly across the tundra to hunt and feed the pups again.

I had been watching her for somewhat more than eighteen hours, during which I came to understand her dedication to her task and what it cost her. The observation took a little patience, but the wait was worth it. I've forgotten what I did this morning, but I'll always remember her.[2]

The time came for me to rejoin the graduate students. I packed up my few possessions and studied my map. I had consulted it as we walked from the DEW Line station just to see if it matched what we were seeing and it seemed accurate enough, but when I unfolded it to figure out where I should go, I saw to my horror that at least in my area it wasn't accurate. I'd come there along an east-flowing stream—the stream that served as a fence for the pups—and I planned to start back the same way, by following that stream. But according to the map, the hill where my colleagues were camped was on a different river system. That was discouraging. I wasn't sure what to do. Worse yet, I distinctly remembered that up ahead the stream would fork. I had planned to follow one of the forks. The map didn't show a fork. How was I to find my colleagues' camp?

Baffin Island contains approximately 200,000 square miles. The only geological feature that might lead me to other people was the coastline. But I was very far from the coast, which at best was sparsely populated, and I would not know where to find a settlement if I got there. The map didn't show the coastline anyway. Meanwhile, the constant daylight I had so enjoyed was fading. Soon enough it would be evening for a while and then the Arctic night. No doubt my colleagues would eventually try to find me, but that would inconvenience them enormously—we were just acquaintances, not family or friends—and for them to find me, assuming that they'd try, I'd have to go back to my hill.

I might have panicked, but I didn't. I might have thought the map was right and I was wrong, because maps are always right and people are often mistaken. But, strangely, that wasn't what I thought. I'd lost the self-doubt and the nervousness that so affects humanity. And why was that? Because I'd been alone.

It's one thing to be alone in a town or city but quite another to be the only member of your species where the other large mammals are caribou and wolves. With the exception of my colleagues, wherever they were, I was the only person in 10,000 square miles. But I hadn't been alone. Perhaps I'd been nothing more than an observer, but my time with the wolves had given me so much peace that I trusted myself and my memory. I crumpled up the map and stuffed it in my pocket.

Then I followed the stream. I came to the fork which the map had omitted, saw some faraway hills, and crossed them as a wolf would cross, by the lowest pass between them, and kept on going until I walked into my colleagues' camp. A person is perfectly capable of doing such a thing, but the conscious mind must be clear to do it. Mostly our minds are jumbles of problems, obligations, time constraints, things other people said, and things we wish we'd said, but because I'd spent so much time in the quiet wind under the Arctic sky as one of the large mammals of the tundra, my mind had been purified of that.

Since then I've watched the animals who live in the woods near my house. In the devastating winter of 2008–2009 I fed the local whitetail deer and got to know them as individuals. I wrote a book about them, *The Hidden Life of Deer*. Then one morning in September I saw from my window a dark-colored lump in the field. It wasn't there the day before, so I went to look at it. To my sorrow, it was a dead whitetail doe, the mother of one of the groups I knew best. She was a very big deer, an adult with fawns when I first got to know her, so I believed she might have been at least six years old. Often enough, this doe with her older daughter and twin fawns would come to the field before sunrise and graze there together until broad daylight.

The field had recently been mowed, so the grass was short. We don't gather the hay — we leave it in the field — so dry grass was all around her, and her head, neck, and rump had been covered with some of it. I looked more closely and saw that something very sharp had made a clean, circular cut on her rump from which some meat was missing. I could find no other injuries except for a few long scratches on her shoulder. I would have liked to look at her throat, but I couldn't see it without moving her head and disturbing the grass that covered it, which I didn't want to do because I was thinking of calling a friend who knew an alleged expert in animal forensics and I didn't want to destroy evidence.

I was heartbroken about the doe, but the grass was interesting. After I finished my study of circus tigers I went to Utah, Idaho, and Colorado to study cougars and saw several deer who had been killed by cougars. All were covered with leaves or grass, just like my whitetail doe. A cougar does this because a deer is too big to eat all at once. The cougar hides the carcass as best he can and sometimes stays around to guard it.

The clean cut was also interesting. One cougar-killed deer in Idaho, although partly eaten and covered with leaves, also had a clean round cut in her skin, just like the doe in my field. As far as I know, the large members of the cat family are the only predators who hide a kill with leaves or grass or who — because of their virtually all-meat diet — have carnassial teeth sharp enough to make a clean, sheared cut in another animal's hide.

According to Fish and Game, cougars would be an endangered species if there were any in New Hampshire. It was said that if their presence were acknowledged, Fish and Game would have to protect them and didn't have the money. But our neighbors saw one; Sy Montgomery's husband, Howard Mansfield, saw one on the morning of his wedding day; Steve and I, driving home one day, saw one leap across the road; our son saw one near that road; a friend found a young one dead by the edge of a highway; and I saw one walk out of the woods not fifty feet from where the doe was lying. Four of these sightings took place in an area of about twenty square miles and could have been the same cougar. The only other wild cats in our vicinity are bobcats and, very rarely, Canada lynxes, but these are too small to kill a deer like her, as she weighed about two hundred pounds. Adult bobcats weigh between nine and forty pounds (with very few at the high end), and adult lynxes weigh between eighteen and twenty-four pounds. Adult cougars, in contrast, weigh between seventy and two hundred twenty pounds and one had been measured at three hundred pounds.

In some ways the scene was confusing. The corpse of the doe was in the open. I wish I had measured the distance to the nearest cover, but I didn't. A cougar tends to stalk a victim from cover, then make a lightning charge, but he also can flatten himself almost to invisibility, especially if he's in dry grass, because he's the same color. I thought the carcass was a bit far from cover, but maybe not, or maybe the cougar, if it was a cougar, sneaked a short way.

I found the dead doe at about eight-thirty in the morning. She was beginning to stiffen, so I guessed that she had probably been killed at first light. No doubt she had been grazing with her fawns and older daughter. What puzzled me was that while she lived, she was vigilant. I'd seen her grazing with her family dozens of time, and always she would look up every few seconds. Also she was lying partly on her belly with her legs somewhat sprawled, as if she had been jumped on. The other kills I'd seen were lying on their sides. Her daughters would have been with her, and I wondered if she died protecting them. If so, she might have faced the cougar.

Whitetail deer, especially the females, normally protect each other by flagging their white tails as they run away, the most conspicuous sign in all of nature. Then the other deer also bolt with their tails flagging. But on two occasions I've seen a large doe and her family encounter a coyote, and far from flagging and running, the doe raised her head and with her ears straight up like a rabbit's she marched stiffly toward the coyote as if she meant to kick the stuffing out of him. She would have done this with her front feet. On both occasions the coyote lowered his head, ears, and tail, and assuming an indifferent demeanor, he trotted away (but did not run) at an oblique angle, just as the young wolf on Baffin Island had done the day our group arrived, just as the Ju/wasi had told us to do in the presence of a predator. Possibly the doe didn't understand cougars. Possibly she'd never seen one before. Most of us have never seen one. So although she would not have mistaken him for a coyote, he might have seemed chase-able. I have some trouble with this theory, though. Virtually all mammals (except us) are good at recognizing the intentions of another mammal.

More easy to understand was why whoever killed her had eaten only a few bites and then covered her with grass. Cougars don't want to be seen, so he certainly wouldn't want to be out in the middle of a field with daylight coming. Perhaps he was in the woods somewhere, up in a tree, planning to eat later. I looked in all the nearby big trees but didn't see him. I also looked for tracks, but cougars are difficult to track except in soft snow, so I found none. That night I set up a game camera near the carcass, but all I got was a photo of a bear's nostrils, taken soon after dark when the bear came up to sniff the lens.

I think he didn't like its scent, which no doubt was my scent, because he dragged the carcass away from the camera. In the morning we found the carcass at a distance, ripped apart with much of the meat eaten. That was too bad, because the forensic expert hadn't seen it. After that, there was no use in him or anyone else looking at the throat because the bear had torn it up.

The bear was very large, unfortunately for the cougar, who at first might have hoped to eat after dark but had no chance of a meal if that bear was eating. The next day buzzards, mice, ants, and flies ate more of the carcass. By evening it was covered with maggots. That night the bear or the coyotes ate more. After the following night, even the head and the bones were gone. Someone must have carried what was left into the woods. Someone else, probably someone much smaller, had licked up all the dry blood and tiny scraps. Not a trace remained.

I worried about the fawns. Soon enough it would be winter. The fawns were born in the spring. They had never experienced winter. They wouldn't know the warmer microclimates or the best sources of winter food. Every winter deer die of cold and hunger. How were those fawns to survive with no one to guide them? Deer can be selfish, but their older sister wasn't. The next time I saw the fawns they were with her. She had spent the previous winter with her mother and from her had learned how to survive. She and her sisters stayed together, and all of them were healthy in the spring.

· · ·

I knew more deer than I knew cougars, despite my efforts to study cougars in Colorado, Utah, and Idaho. There I learned about them from their tracks and from sightings. By this method, the closest I came to knowing a cougar was by figuring out how a young male cougar happened to appear in a schoolyard in Boulder. He had been emigrating, as male cougars do when they grow up and their fathers chase them out of their territories. So he had come east and found a stream. He followed it upstream because the bushes on its banks gave him cover. But near the school the stream came out of a pipe, and the nearest cover he could find was by the schoolyard. There he took refuge. He was probably not hunting the children, as many supposed, and he was gone before the authorities could do anything about him.

I did come to know two cougars, however. One belonged to a wonderful woman named Lissa Gilmore. Lissa lived in Telluride, at the top of a hill with fields and forests stretching away as far as the eye could see. The cougar's name was Ruby. She had been with Lissa since infancy, but by the time I met her she was full-grown and huge—I'd say she was seven feet long from nose to tail and weighed over a hundred pounds. It was my enormous pleasure to be Lissa's guest for several days, which is how I came to know this cougar, and eventually I wrote the following about an afternoon I spent with her, taping all that went on.

Ruby is sitting with us in Lissa's living room, where, in a confined space, the cougar seems much larger and more daunting than she had seemed outdoors. Worse yet, she seems restless. She has found an odor on the rug. It is a drop of amniotic fluid from Lissa's pregnant cat, Yehti, who, it turns out, has been in labor all this time. However, at the moment in question no one knows this, as Yehti is holding back her kittens, surely because she is afraid of Ruby. Ruby does nothing to reassure her. Rather, she begins to rumble, then to spit. She is singing the murderous song of a cat's dark feelings, a contralto solo of envy and displeasure, which fills Lissa's house and finds its audience of one, little Yehti, crouched in hiding under a chair, quietly considering the seriousness of her situation.

Lissa and I keep right on talking, so involved are we with the relationship of guest and hostess that is developing between us. Prowling Ruby keeps up her disconcerting spits and growls. On my tape, I hear myself tell-

ing Lissa that I respect Ruby. Then Ruby turns and walks toward us, eyes front, as if she meant to walk between us when plunk — as if her rump, not her head, made the decision — her hip hits the floor beside us, gracefully followed by the rest of her body. She then twists on her back and shows us her furry white belly. I wonder how many breasts she has. As Ruby remains on her back, I ask if I can search for her nipples.

In attentive silence, Lissa and I then do just that, with Ruby lying very stiffly, her head raised, her paws bent at the wrists, her thighs spread, looking down at her belly uneasily while our hands roam like spiders through her fur. However, as Lissa quietly predicts, we find nothing. Maiden cougars have no sign of nipples or breasts. This is fascinating. I keep searching, but when Ruby's body stiffens, I stop fast. A housecat at that point might have seized my hand, clapped it to her mouth, and bitten it, and I don't want that treatment from Ruby, whose eyeteeth seem as long as my fingers and whose triangular carnassials are as massive as my folded thumb.

In the late afternoon, Ruby grows more restless. Soon she is jumping on and off the furniture, which she dwarfs. Next, she nervously paces to and from the window, growling and switching her tail. Judging from my voice on the tape, her agitation must have been making me nervous. I keep asking what Ruby is doing. Lissa's voice is very gentle and soothing. Soon a silence falls. Lissa has offered Ruby her arm, and Ruby, stretched at full length, starts to suck it. Her massive paws knead alternately, slowly, making bread. Ruby is like a kitten and has even aligned herself to Lissa by heading in to Lissa's side as a kitten aligns itself to the body of its mother.

In a low voice, Lissa asks if I'd like to let Ruby suck my arm. I whisper yes, I would. Lissa shows me how to take her place in front of Ruby, and I do. My arm slips under Ruby's mouth. Feeling the change, Ruby slowly opens her great, yellow eyes and looks up, but by now I am deeply moved by her tenderness and vulnerability, and I just wait, not speaking. In perfect silence, we all wait. There is no tension in the moment. Ruby again begins to suck. Then she purrs. The room fills with her purring.

Little Yehti creeps out from under the chair and leaves the room. She will later deliver two kittens on a rug behind the bathroom door. Ruby no longer minds that Yehti is having kittens. She lets her velvet eyelids shut. On the skin of my arm I feel the slow, gentle rasping of her rough tongue, which gradually turns as smooth and slick as a piece of raw liver. Has she

turned her tongue over so that I am feeling the underside? Has she col-
lapsed her papillae? I mention this to Lissa, who nods. She knows what
is happening, but not why. It doesn't matter. Ruby drowses, her black lips
and smooth tongue gently pressed against my arm. And that's all. We stay
a long time in the peace of Lissa's quiet room, not talking or whispering,
just relaxing, purring, dreaming, gently breathing, mildly aware of cloud
shadows, of the afternoon sun, of a light breeze from an open door, of being
alive there together.[3]

The next cougar I came to know—although not nearly as well as I knew Ruby—was a wild male cougar whom I saw in Utah. I had joined a wildlife biologist and some of his helpers who were studying cougars, and one day we came upon a cougar lying on the thick branch of a tree. The biologist and his helpers wondered what subspecies of cougar he was, and we stared at him until lunchtime, when everyone but me went back to the vehicle, ready to return to camp.

I didn't join them because while the cougar was watching the other people—his body tense, his ears half turned, the tip of his tail slowly flicking—I lay down on the ground and covered myself with dry leaves. He was preoccupied with the other people and wasn't looking in my direction, so he didn't notice. I thought that when he believed himself to be alone, he would come down from the tree, so I waited.

But when the other people left, he relaxed. He had no thought of leaving. Alone at last, or so he believed, he was perfectly happy on his branch. With eyes half shut, he dreamily enjoyed the sunshine. I knew the other people were getting hungry and might drive back to camp without me, so at last I reluctantly stood up.

The cougar was dumbfounded. He'd thought he was alone. Never before or since have I seen a more amazed expression on anyone's face. That's all that happened—he stayed where he was and I walked away. Maybe he was a *Puma concolor kaibabensis* or maybe he was something else, but that would be just our name for him and had nothing to do with his actual persona. Actually, he was someone unprepared for a huge surprise, so I treasure the memory of that moment.

15

WRITING

I F RESEARCH IS REWARDING, so is writing. I start before dawn, and
the next thing I know, it's dark. I wake up anxious to get back to work
because while I'm asleep, my mind keeps going and I'm anxious to write
it all down. My hope of seeing another cougar will never fade, so my desk
faces the field where I saw the first one and later found the doe's carcass.
As a deer looks up often when she's grazing, I look up often when I'm
writing, but I also keep typing, and if nothing interesting is in the field,
I go right back to my sentence without having lost my thought. It gives
me great serenity, to be able to write and watch the field at the same time.

I do other things too. I have always loved Peterborough, the town I
live in, where much of the work of the town is done by volunteers, so I
joined in by volunteering at the library, then served for many years on
various boards and committees, and wound up by being elected five times
to the Board of Selectmen, on which I still serve at the time of this writing. Why do I do it? Because Peterborough has been home to me since
I was five and I want to advance everything that's good about it, everything from open space and clean water to the success of the downtown
businesses, as these are the lifeblood of the town and give us our sense of
community. For this, I'm happy to take time out from writing.

But for every hour I've worked for the town, I've worked dozens of
hours on my writing, and during all that time, real life has eluded me. It
is almost as if I went to sleep in the 1980s and woke up in the next century
with gray hair and three or four grandchildren.

I've been told that working like that is an addiction, like the misuse of alcohol or drugs. There is a similarity, of course, in that full-time concentration on work removes you from your troubles. It also feels good. The difference is that if you work all the time you could become rich and famous, while if you drink or drug all the time you could find yourself under the proverbial bridge. So I'm not sure that anything is wrong with continuous writing except in the eyes of those who don't see it as work. An acquaintance, a psychiatrist, once told me rather snippily that she wished she had time to write, as if writing were some kind of recreation and only for people with leisure. I won't say I wasn't miffed. I wish I had time to psychoanalyze people, but I don't because my time is taken up by figuring out where the paragraphs go and composing topic sentences.

Now I am close to the end of my story, having described all my problems and nonverbal adventures. Yet ever since I began to write again after a hiatus, writing has been my life, as important to me as my family. So the next part of this book is about words, sentences, and paragraphs, and if you, the reader, are bored by such things, you can safely skip to page 260 if you like, to read the last two chapters. But when Freud said that marrying the right person and doing the right work were important, he was right, and in my case, given a good husband, writing is not only essential to me, it's who I am and always was. Without it, I'd be nothing. Why bother to write an autobiography if you omit what's most important to you, the very center of your life?

I have always admired Marcel Proust. His great opus, *A La Recherche du Temps Perdu*, has seven volumes, 14,000 pages, and 1.5 million words. And the whole thing came from his unconscious mind after he took a bite of a madeleine — a little muffin which he had dipped in tea. My writing too comes from my unconscious — not as prolifically as Proust's, of course, but it explains why real time disappears while I am working.

Thus my brain is like two people, one who's in view and does her best to keep things going and one who's hidden but keeps toiling and every so often coughs up a useful surprise. I'll never forget a surprise that came when I was reading Kipling's *The Jungle Book* to my youngest grandson. The book was read to me and my brother when we were children. Thirty years later I went to Baffin Island, where I watched the white wolves and noticed things about them that my scientist friends found unusual. I mentioned how hard wolves work, for instance. "No scientist would say that," one scientist friend told me. "They don't see animals in such terms."

I had no idea how I'd come to this conclusion except from the seeming reluctance of a wolf to get started on a hunt, as if she foresaw the hard job ahead of her, which of course she did. I was intrigued to think I'd seen what a scientist wouldn't. It's because I'm so smart, I decided.

Again, thirty years passed. I read *The Jungle Book* to my grandson, and lo and behold, in an opening scene in the first chapter a wolf returns to his den, worn out with hunting. I knew immediately why I'd surmised that the Baffin Island wolves worked hard — that was the first thing I ever heard about them.

The unconscious is filled with things like that — old images that come up unexpectedly and also new ideas that would never appear without its help. I got my all-time favorite sentence just by looking out the window, mindlessly zoning. Then suddenly I got this: *The Woman Ohun starts the char, out in water as deep as the sky and almost as far as the Camps of the Dead from our river.* Isn't that a nice sentence? Char are fish related to salmon, but to explain the rest would take forever, so never mind what it means. But did you notice the progression of vowel sounds and how the sentence moves in metered steps with a sense of reach in the middle and a sense of distance at the end? Tragically, a copy editor screwed it up when the book was first published so the effect was lost. But even so, it was a good sentence.

It is often worthwhile to trust your unconscious. I didn't at first, because when we lived in New York I was seeing a psychoanalyst. At the time, I was swamped with housework and a go-nowhere job that had nothing to do with writing, so I became the patient of a shrink in hopes of dealing with my angst and stress. The shrink was quite famous, even though I didn't know it then. He was called "the dean of American psychoanalysis." And he had power over me because he had probed my unconscious and found the self-doubts and inhibitions that were trying to hide there. Like a broken-legged deer who has asked a leopard for a physical evaluation, I accepted his power until the day I told him that William Shawn at *The New Yorker* wanted me to write about pastoralists in Uganda. The analyst never asked what that meant to me or how much it would do for my career. Instead, he told me not to go. I should stay home, he said, explore my unconscious, and finish my analysis.

I should not go to Uganda? I should relinquish this once-in-a-lifetime opportunity? Astonished, I asked him why. He didn't tell me why because back then, I believe, the ethics of confidentiality excluded the patient. I said, "Well, why can't I continue when I come back?" But he was adamant. If I ignored his instructions and went to Uganda, I could never go back to him as a patient.

I might have been a broken-legged deer at the beginning of all this, but at that point my legs felt fine. I told him I'd write to him from Uganda, and then I went home to pack.

Interestingly, this analyst had also written a book. Why didn't he see that I might want to do the same? The answer, I think, is that much as he might have known about the mind, he had no idea what the hidden part can do other than make trouble for its owner. To him, I think, the unconscious was like a mental colon, filled with matter to be cleaned out and flushed. To me, it's like a mental lung, to breathe things in and absorb for later use.

Then too, he didn't understand writing. His book was offered as an "elementary text," but the word *elementary* was false advertising. The book is unreadable — hundreds of pages of psycho-speak in twisted sentences going on forever with no thought that someone might be trying to figure out what they meant. Too bad he's dead. He could have learned about clarity from the next section.

I compare my unconscious to the swamp near our house. Beavers made it by damming a stream, so it has large areas of open water, dark and smooth, perfectly still. You stand there and wait. The swamp is quiet. But suddenly a bubble comes to the surface and gently pops. What caused it? That's hard to say. Swamp gas, probably, from something down at the bottom. But there's no need to understand it. Whatever is down there is far from stable, and sooner or later, another bubble will come.

Those who find fault with this book might use the image against me, believing that a swamp is an unpleasant place. Perhaps I should have likened my brain to a salt marsh or a wetland, as these conjure slightly better images. But in reality, swamps are places of fascination and wonder, filled with life, filled with more species per square meter than, say, upland forests, let alone the much-touted mountaintops. I love my real-life swamp with its otter and beavers, with the great blue heron who hunts there, with the jelly masses of frogs' eggs and salamander eggs that appear there in the spring. You can see the dark eyes of the tadpoles inside the jelly. So many lives, so much happening. It encourages me to imagine something like that going on undetected in my brain.

Interestingly, the effect is canceled by antidepressants. I took some once for a week or two, and my mood leveled out quite noticeably — without the highs, to be sure, but at least without the lows — but I couldn't write anything. I'd sit at my desk for a while without results, then go off and do something else. That wasn't good, so I threw away the pills, waited a day or two, and sure enough, that mysterious swamp in my head began to bubble again. I started writing, and out came the last few chapters of the book I'd been working on before I got depressed. The inability to work is more depressing than anything else, so I never again took antidepressants.

If the back brain is where it all comes from, the front brain must organize the material, and for this one needs rules. The first rule I came up with for this memoir was not to follow a timeline. Everyone's life story has enough events to require 1.5 million words and fill seven volumes like Proust's lengthy novel, but my life story would be tedious, even to me, if presented sequentially — plodding along like the ant who carried out a grain of wheat, followed by another ant, and so forth. Better to organize by subject matter, picking out whatever seems interesting, then connecting the subjects by a theme or two in which events can be shoved as they arise. So I have not put the events in order, confident that no one will care.

An autobiography should be truthful, or as truthful as possible, although a friend once said, "Why ruin a good story with truth?" But, at least in my case, actual events have been more impressive than anything I might imagine, so sticking to the facts was easy. My memory isn't perfect, though. If readers should find discrepancies between my chapters on the

Kalahari and my mother's book, *The !Kung of Nyae Nyae,* they should go with my mother's version. My mom had an awesome capacity for accuracy. In that respect, if not in all respects, the apple fell some distance from the tree.

An autobiography should say what the author wants to say, so the advice of others should be ignored. My mother's fans, for instance, thought I should write about her, my father's fans thought I should write about him, and my brother's fans thought I should devote at least a chapter to his accomplishments. But I had enough trouble getting my own life sorted out. Nor did I take the advice of a friend in the publishing industry who thought I should include my "sexual development," as he put it. Why did he think so? Because sex and violence sell books.

I'm sure that's true. But as far as I know, while romantic encounters are sometimes found in the memoirs of women, they're not often found in the memoirs of men. When my friend Judy Sullivan wrote *Mama Doesn't Live Here Anymore* — a fiery autobiography that boosted the women's movement — she was told by her editor, who was in a wheelchair, that she must include her sexual adventures. Judy didn't want to. The editor kept insisting until Judy slammed her fist against the wall, threatened to push him in his wheelchair down the stairs, and shouted, "There'll be no fucking in my fucking book!" That goes for me too. But there is a little violence. I hope it's enough.

Finally, an autobiography should not be an opportunity for revenge, however tempting. Grievances can be important, but to wheel them out can present the writer as a spiteful person, not a generous, forgiving person, and besides, clinging to grievances corrodes the psyche. Everybody has grievances and I've dealt with a few, but I'd rather be a sunbeam than a pail of dirty water so I've buried the rest.

My second set of rules concerns the writing itself, and Rule One starts with words. These can be weak, as in "Have a nice day," or they can have enormous power. I'll always remember a man in a short-sleeved shirt with his forearms on a table when I said, "You don't need to shift gears if you leave it in second and ride the clutch." I would never do that, of course. I merely spoke the words, but when I did, the hair on his forearms rose.

I try to use words that spring from Anglo-Saxon rather than Latin because Latinate words can be offish and can impart remoteness. Anglo-Saxon words have more power and also are closer to the earth. They make people happy, or most of them do. We use them to talk with, and resort to the four-letter ones when all else fails. On the other hand, Latinate words are helpful, so it's good to have them handy. Some require strings of Anglo-Saxon words to replace.

One good thing about Latinate words is that they can stupefy. You might not want to stupefy your readers, but what if you did? You could use a word such as *encomium*. One day I told an intellectual gentleman that I liked something he'd done, and he asked, "What prompts your encomium?"

Wow! But I had no idea what he meant. I've learned it means *praise*, but why use *praise* when you can floor everybody with *encomium?* I'd be afraid to use it myself, but I think it's spectacular, especially with an old-fashioned word like *prompts* in the sentence.

If words can stupefy, they can also enthrall. One night my little grandson, Jasper, looked up at the sky and said he saw a waxing gibbous moon. Wow again! My jaw dropped. The kid had just started first grade, so his informed observation surprised me. But the words *waxing* and *gibbous* are also surprising if you think about them, because both are almost exclusively moon words. You once could "wax lyrical" about something, but nobody says that anymore, and you could wax a floor, but that wax is different. The *waxes* all come from the Indo-European *aug-*, from which we also get *August,* but around 1066 the word went different ways and collected different meanings. As for the word *gibbous,* except on extremely rare occasions it now has one use only, to describe the moon when it's less than full but more than half full. And this, to the best of my knowledge, makes it the most specific adjective in English.

All three of the moon words thrill me. *Waxing* sounds like something getting bigger. The sound of the *x* makes it strong. *Waning* sounds like something getting smaller. That long *a* is like a cry from the soul, lost and disappearing. And *gibbous* is perhaps the best word I know. It comes from the Latin *gibbus,* which meant *hump,* and to some extent *gibbous* still means *hump,* but nobody uses it that way now, so the unpoetic past of *gibbous* is forgotten. Today the word is mysterious and exciting and the moon has it all to itself.

Perhaps the most exciting thing about words is the sound of them when they are put together; hence the inner ear should never be ignored. Take *A La Recherche du Temps Perdu,* for instance — di di di DAH, di DAH DAH DAH. It's strong. Beethoven's Fifth Symphony begins with di di di DAH. Also, in Morse Code those beats are *V for Victory.* The mind's ear finds something thrilling about them.

Now look at one of the English translations, *Remembrance of Things Past,* di DAH di di DAH DAH. It's nothing special. No great composer would use that rhythm. Another translation, *In Search of Lost Time,* is not much better. But if the first word, *In,* were omitted, it would be DAH di DAH DAH, another famous rhythm, as in *Merry Christmas, Happy New Year, As the Crow Flies, Back to Square One, Live and Let Live, Submachine Gun,* and many other significant phrases. But rhythm isn't everything. That title needs the *In.*

Words that stir the inner ear open the lower layers of the mind where our emotions hide. But to do this, a word or phrase must come as a surprise, as poets know. For example, the poet Stephen Spender when referring to people who were no longer living wrote, "Born of the sun, they traveled a short while towards the sun, and left the vivid air signed with their honor." The phrase *Born of the sun,* as far as I know, is unique in literature, but the image conjured by *traveled a short while towards the sun* is even more surprising. *Vivid air* is also splendid, even though the word *vivid* is somewhat dangerous and no longer in much use. These phrases come from Spender's poem "I Think Continually of Those Who Were Truly Great," which in itself is a knockout title (and is also the first line of the poem) because the businesslike, overlong, unpoetic word *continually* is in the middle of it. Imagine having thought of that! It makes me think of Spender when I think of those who were truly great.

The surprise element applies throughout the verbal spectrum. I think of the third verse of "I Know You Rider." The music is familiar country blues, but it's the words that make this song.

Wish I was a headlight on a northbound train
Wish I was a headlight on a northbound train
I'd shine my light through the cold Colorado rain.

There's nothing rational about wishing you were a headlight. The image connects because the line scans beautifully and also resonates. It doesn't hurt to have a train in there, though. By now the train image is deep in our culture.

Incidentally, I know it's sometimes *cool Colorado rain*, but *cold* is better. Also some versions of the song say *California rain*, but the versions with *Colorado* are better because the word *California* sounds upbeat and festive, and the long *o* sounds in *Colorado* make it lonely and far away. That's good because the message of the song is about distance and departure. As for what resonance can do, consider the fact that the above verse has just twenty-seven words — nine of them repeated — which are vastly more evocative than the hundred and fifty words that follow in my effort to discuss it.

Meter and vowel-sound progressions can make or break a manuscript. We tend to associate such sound effects with overwritten descriptions of landscapes and storms at sea, but that's our mistake. Some of my favorite prose was written by George V. Higgins in his novel *The Friends of Eddie Coyle*. Higgins presents all kinds of information mostly with dialogue, but more quickly and with more punch and color than any other writer I know. Placing his book spine down on the table and letting it fall open revealed the following sentences, which, like all the others, scan like a dream and are as far from overwritten as it is possible to be.

> *"I got my fucking insurance bill,"* the bearded man said. *"Then I went out for a ride and I had to fill the goddamned thing, and it cost me nine bucks worth of superpremium, and I said the hell with it. Goddamn car was eating me blind."*
> *"Went like a bird with a flame up its ass, though,"* Jackie Brown said.[1]

There's a breathless, cantering effect in the words spoken by the bearded man, a discouraged sigh (*was eating*) in the sentence about the goddamn car, and a blast at the end — *blind*. Then comes Jackie Brown's observation, which just sends me. Forceful, repeated rhythm in the words spoken by Jackie, all with muted vowel sounds except for the *a* in *flame,* which jumps up at you, then the famous DAH di DAH DAH rhythm at the end. Perfection.

I try with everything that's in me to write sentences that scan like that. And speaking of rewards, my favorite came from the poet Maxine Kumin, to whom I had sent a copy of my book *The Old Way* and who found a poem therein. She said, "On page 122 you wrote a poem and I have given it a title and lineated it." And she did. Only when I saw it, I thought she had written the poem based on information from *The Old Way.* So I looked on page 122 to find the information. But, oh my god, the poem was there. It just wasn't lineated.[1] Maxine found it, so I gave it to her.

Specific meanings are the heart and treasure of language, so choosing the right word is essential. Everyone has an opinion about usage and can hardly wait to air it, and I am no exception, thus it has been my great privilege to serve on the usage panel of the *American Heritage Dictionary.* I'm well aware that English is somewhat fluid, its forward motion determined not by linguists but by all who speak it, and I'm also aware that the dictionary is not the voice of God but will alter its definitions as the language changes. However, I do love words as we know them now, and want us to cling to their present meanings as long as we can. So I was glad, for instance, to be asked about *disinterested,* as in *he is disinterested in solving the problem.* No, no, no! He is *uninterested.* A disinterested person has no involvement with the problem. I was equally glad to answer a question about Los Angeles being *no less unique* than New York, and for the opportunity to say that as far as I'm concerned, *unique* is still an absolute. You can add more words, of course—unique in this way, unique in that way—but that's a different sentence.

Yet we must accept the fact that meanings shift. The language police

---

1. What does *lineated* mean? It means putting down words
   In lines like this
   As poets do
   For poems.

have much to say about that, but I don't necessarily. Nouns such as *contact* that became verbs long ago don't worry me one bit, although I'm not sure I'd use them. *Friend* became a verb very recently, but it's also okay as far as I'm concerned because, at least for now, it's exclusive to Internet communications, which being so new and widespread will develop their own vocabulary.

The decline of certain words is troublesome, however. For instance, *incredulous* seems to be replacing *incredible*, at least among television newscasters, one of whom, when referring to floods and extensive wind damage, said that Hurricane Irene was incredulous. But who knows? Perhaps even the hurricane could not believe what it was doing. A similar problem has appeared with *nauseous*, which is no longer used exclusively for things such as spoiled food that cause vomiting, but is also used for those who eat the food and feel like vomiting or, in other words, are *nauseated*. It hurts me, though. I'm always saddened when perfectly nice people say they feel nauseous. "You're not nauseous, you're delightful," I want to tell them. But I'm not a member of the language police, and that word is already in transition.

A few words, such as *majority*, have slipped so far that they're poisoned. For some reason, *a majority of the water* sounds even worse than *somewhat unique*. Of course, *majority* fits with something that has a number, like *a majority of the voters*, as long as we're speaking of more than half of the voters, but these days you sound illiterate if you use *majority* for any reason. The exception would be for idioms already set in cement—*majority leader* and *majority rule*, for instance. As for me, I'm now afraid of the word *majority* and find that *most of* does the trick.

Some things have more than one noun associated with them, thus choice is involved, as in *meadow* and *field*. I've learned to look for implications, because as far as I'm concerned, a meadow is a field. But *meadow* conjures people wandering around and smelling flowers. You never hear of a corn meadow or a cotton meadow. In New Hampshire we have fields, and if cows are grazing in them they are pastures.

Sad to say, in my case, word choice isn't always inspired by a word's implications. I had a problem with the term *mountain lion*, which is what I would normally call these cats, but for my sixth book, in which I used the name maybe five thousand times, I got tired of typing all those letters and thought it would be easier to type *puma*. But after that, I became disillusioned with the word *puma*. It seemed fanciful. So in this memoir I call them *cougars*. They're also called *painters* and *catamounts*, but those names are countrified. I'm countrified myself, but I wouldn't want readers to see that.

On rare occasions, there may be no right word. I had a problem with *slime*, for instance, because *slime* is totally negative. One might as well say *goo* or *mucus*, because there is no pleasing alternative. I noticed this behind the exhibits of the Boston Aquarium where I met an octopus pup named Octavia. (The language police wouldn't like this. You don't *meet* an animal — you *see* it, because *meet* implies involvement by both parties, and *see* implies that you, as the highly evolved human individual, are viewing some dumb beast.) The young creature put one of her eight arms toward me and I stroked its outer surface. It was soft, and also — what?

I refuse to say it was slimy but can find no other word to describe it. Thus I'm left with no choice but to describe the inner surface of the arm, the surface with the suckers. These were small, strong, and prickly, and although Octavia was in the water, her suckers seemed almost dry as they fastened her arm to my fingers. My heart went out to this amazing little creature, with her intelligence, her awareness, and her clearly conscious mind. My friend Sy Montgomery, who was with me that day, was doing research for a book about octopuses, which was why we were at the aquarium. I knew she would find the right words for the thick, soft, slippery feeling of the waterproof substance on their skins.

My Rule Two involves usage based on ideology, and the most significant involves animals. For instance, there's the question of what animals do. If it's anything like what people do, such as *wonder*, I'm not afraid to say so, but plenty of people believe that it's just plain wrong. To attribute any human action to an animal, or worse yet, to actually recognize such an action in an animal, makes these people angry, as if the writer challenges their top position on the evolutionary pole. Rule Two says two things: (1) Ignore Those People, and (2) There Is No Evolutionary Pole.

The same people use the pronoun *it* for an animal. Not me, though. Rule Two says that animals must be *he* or *she* but never *it* except in special cases. In real life, all animals have gender. People are more inclined to acknowledge gender in their pets, but not even a maggot is an *it*, and to refer to any animal in that manner is an affectation, an ignorant stab at science-speak, a pathetic attempt at political correctness. Imagine if we spoke of people in this manner. "My friend wanted to cross the river so it took off its shoes and it waded across."[2] I unfailingly use *he* and *she* for animals, also *who* and *whom*, never *which* or *that*, and speaking of the passions inflamed by words, I'm infuriated by people who find this improper. Who do they think they are? High and mighty humans getting *he* or *she* and *who* or *whom* while everything else gets the same pronoun as dirt? I'd like to shake those people. An editor may sometimes disapprove, but I'm firm about it.

Much as I love resonance, clarity is probably more important. Thus paying attention to what one is actually saying cannot be overstressed. One morning on the local TV news a newscaster reported that a man had been arrested for groping a woman inappropriately. Was there an appropriate way to grope her? Such mistakes are easy enough to make, but I hope I never make them.

I've also learned not to start a sentence with a dependent clause, or not often, because the reader shouldn't have to wait to learn what the sentence is about. Then too, if the reader ignores the punctuation, a clause beginning a sentence can be confusing, as in one of my own sentences: *Now it was gone so I walked. In the form of a falcon, Marmot slowly circled me a little while.* Here again, never mind what it means, but just please note that the above is two sentences with a period between them. One reader didn't notice the period so he took this to be *I walked in the form of a falcon* and he sneered at me because falcons don't walk, or not far. Since then, I've wished that the phrase about the falcon was at the end of the sentence. Not that I was wrong, and not that the sentence is unacceptable, but the book in which it appears was published fourteen years ago at the time of this writing, and the unfair criticism still burns.

I warn myself against passive voice. This is standard for the military, as in *the battle was won* or *the mission was canceled* rather than *the enemy won the battle* or *the high command canceled the mission*, thus hiding what actually took place. Passive voice is dry, and the only reason to write anything, in my view, is to provide full disclosure with as much emotion as can be squeezed from the material. Scientists also like passive voice, but might want to reconsider doing so. Too often when writing scientific papers they use sentences like this: "Relatedness among individuals has been suggested as a potential factor in individual associations between aggregating squirrels."[3] Alas, the science that inspired this was riveting. The squirrels were also riveting. Readers would be on the edge of their chairs if the paper were written in a more lively manner.

I warn myself against expletive sentences. These start with an empty word such as *this* or *there* followed by some form of *to be,* as in *There is something limp about these sentences,* so these too can be boring. When I was in college, the writing teachers spoke against expletive sentences but I didn't listen, and while still in their classrooms, I started my first book with one: *There is a vast sweep of dry bush desert* etc. Gosh. Every book I've written has them—a bad habit but one that's hard to break because of the ease with which *It is* or *There is* can launch a sentence. From there you can throw in whatever you like without worrying too much about how you say it. Here a word processor can be helpful—you can quickly search through thousands of words for *it is* or *there is* and fix it. But I didn't do that so this book is probably riddled with them.

I try to go easy on modifiers. These suggest self-doubt on the part of the writer. Usually I find too many modifiers in my early drafts—mostly adjectives, but adverbs can also be overdone—and often enough, a point is better made without them. An unmodified word is stark, just standing there looking at you with nothing dangling around it. So if a word doesn't seem strong enough, rather than try to intensify it, I look for another word. *Very* is one of the worst modifiers (I was tempted to say *one of the very worst modifiers,* but I controlled myself.) I'm more careful of the word *so* as an intensifier, as in *The air was so clear.* Never do that. Not if that's all there is to the sentence.

Clarity raises the question of double nouns. A few examples could be *moose festival, coffee table, horse whisperer, water park,* or *stone wall.* Editors once hated all but the most common of them (*coffee table, stone wall*), and would make a writer revise entire sentences to get rid of them. But I like them. A copy editor removed so many from my first book that I was forced to point out that she was the *copy editor* for a *book publisher.* Today they're more acceptable, but they can be confusing, and triple nouns are worse. Once while listening to National Public Radio I became confused by three nouns in a row of "NPR News Quiz." Was the quiz about news? No, it was about all kinds of things and NPR News asked the questions. The word *news* thus belonged to *NPR*, not to *quiz.* It's not clear what else the quiz could be called, though, despite the problem.

Clarity also raises the question of word placement, especially pronoun placement. My grandson told the following joke. "Question: how can you drop an egg on the sidewalk without cracking it? Answer: sidewalks are hard to crack." The joke is very important even if not very funny because it points out that a pronoun refers to the noun that precedes it, which a writer should never forget.

Then what about the pronoun *they?* It's plural, of course, so can it be joined to a singular subject? The language police wouldn't like it, and I try not to do it myself, but I believe that if someone wants to do it, they should. The clarity is not interrupted, and without it they'd have to write "he or she," which is awkward, especially if often repeated, and makes the reader say with a sigh, "Oh please," or "How persnickety."

One cannot achieve clarity without thoughtful punctuation. Commas are the most controversial punctuations, and should be used sparingly. But they should be used. At one point they fell out of fashion and the with-it writers did away with them, which I think was inconsiderate. The reader's mind runs out of breath as it struggles through a long unpunctuated sentence. Perhaps those writers had second thoughts, or their editors did, because nowadays one sees more commas.

Where commas belong can be confusing, at least for me. Consider the following sentence: *They screamed at him to get back in the safari van but, with his headphones on, he didn't hear the warning.* To my way of thinking, the *but* belongs with the main message. The part about the headphones is just an observation. If the comma is after the *but,* the sentence could almost mean that they screamed at him to put his headphones on before he got back in the van. However, not every usage pundit would agree. They insist that the comma should come after the *but.* By showing me passages from books about style, grammar, and good usage, the copy editor of this book proved it to me, causing me to rewrite this section, which at first was a series of bitter remarks about copy editors who, in my other books, had moved my commas. Now it is a humble admission of error. But even now, in my mind, comma placement has the aura of a religious belief. Thus I'm like a confused pagan in some jungle village and the copy editor is like the missionary who is trying to save me. She is so impressive that I struggle to convert, and if all the commas in this book are correctly placed it's because she fixed a number of them.

I also have strong feelings about semicolons. To me, either a sentence ends or it doesn't; a semicolon begs the question. At first this book had only three semicolons, two of which are nearby because I was thinking about them and the third because my spell and grammar check insisted. Normally I use that device just for spelling because it's mindless when it comes to anything else — for instance, it thought that my sentence *nor could I shape-change into an animal* should be *nor could me shape-change into an animal,* so I pity the people who depend on such devices — but on that one occasion with the semicolon I hesitated for a long time, then decided that for once the device could be right and used a semicolon there despite my darkest doubts. The book now has twenty-nine semicolons thanks to my benefactor, the copy editor, and of course it's much better.

Finally, I try to be careful with symbols such as hyphens and dash marks — although I'm fond of hyphens and dash marks — but they make the writer's thoughts seem jumpy so it's best not to overdo them.

Rule Four has two parts, and the first involves style and uniformity. *We went swimming and sailing* is better than *we went swimming and sailed.* Another nice trick when listing words or phrases is to start with the shortest and end with the longest while preserving the uniformity. Take this sentence, for instance: *One was Antarctica, another was southern Tasmania, and another was the western third of southern Africa.* Originally this sentence was *One was Antarctica, another was southern Tasmania, and a third was the western third.* . . . Uh-oh, too many *third*s and the second is more important. Better to change the first even though that makes too many *another*s. On the bright side, though, having two sets of *southern-another* seems intentional, put there to give mass to the sentence. If I were grading the sentence I'd give it a B for effort, but perhaps I'm too soft on myself.

The second part of Rule Four involves originality. If a phrase or sentence seems familiar, Don't Use It. Not everyone believes this — one writer took passages from my book *The Hidden Life of Dogs* and published them as his own in *The New Yorker*, and an anthropology professor used passages from my book *Warrior Herdsmen* and published them as his own in *Natural History*. Of course that's outright plagiarism and honest people wouldn't do it. So here I'm thinking of overly common phrases. I'd avoid *in any way, shape, or form*, for instance, and I try to be careful of sunrises and pounding surf or anything else that's inspirational, because such things have been described since the dawn of literature. The basic tenet of Rule Four Part Two is Don't Be Trite.

A sidebar of this rule is that tiny events are almost never trite. They're also economical. I'm thinking of the elephant, Tonga, who blew a little air at the three-legged rat. If I'd blinked, I would have missed it, but it seemed to say something about Tonga's feelings for the rat, and it's as original as all hell because nothing like it has ever been mentioned elsewhere. For that I thank Tonga.

Rule Five says Never Be Coy. I would not, for instance, use *rather* before a verb, as in *I rather think it's bad to do that*, because I freaking well know it's bad to do that — the *rather* is arch and nauseating and a majority of my favorite readers would be incredulous if they saw it. Rule Five says Speak Up.

This doesn't mean I can't use hidden themes, though. I happen to love hidden themes — not that all readers detect them, but what can I do? There's something pedantic about a theme stated outright rather than sneaked in quietly. One theme in this book is the mention of Gaia as a personification of the natural world, for which I have a reverential, almost religious feeling. Here I say that outright, but in parts of this book it's veiled because a fact can be less compelling than a feeling. I've used the Gaia theme in other books too, but a blogger took exception. He didn't pick up on the hidden theme, and assumed from my mention of Gaia that I belonged to a cult.

Which brings me to a peripheral issue—how much should one fear one's readers? The answer, I think, is some but not much. Readers can be scary, but most of their issues come out of left field so you cannot foresee them. In a review of my book *The Old Way*, the anthropologist Mel Konner found fault because I neglected to say that Bushmen were "fully human." I can't imagine what else they could be, which is why I didn't say so. As for the blogger, he might have found the Gaia theme unfamiliar, hence the misunderstanding, as some readers do better with well-processed, predigested themes. That doesn't mean a writer should use them, though. The blogger can fly at the moon. So can Mel, for that matter.

Of all the rules of writing by which I try to govern myself, Rule Six is the most important, and it's Revise, Revise, Revise. Revision is essential for writing, or it certainly is for most people, although I wonder about Proust. How long would it take just to handwrite 1.5 million words with a pencil, let alone revise them? But everyone else revises, or they should.

The most compelling advice about revision was told to me by a friend who had heard it from someone else, so I don't know who offered it. But it's this: Look at your manuscript, then find your best sentence and delete it. You won't want to do this, but until you can, your revisions will be struggles because you will twist and turn to save a good sentence. This will consume your time and create complications. So my rule is to revise and keep revising, tossing whatever doesn't fit, no matter how hard I worked to produce it or how good it looks. Revise draft after draft and then revise the galleys.

I revise all the time, even when away from my desk. Revisions erupt in my head especially when I'm driving. I keep a notebook and a pencil in the car and pull off the road to write them. Once the book is in print it's too late, and if you've missed something, you'll be sorry. Nothing is worse than opening a copy of your newly published book only to see something you wish you hadn't said. But sadly, this happens to me all too often. My finished manuscripts bear no resemblance to the early drafts, but even when I read the printed version I still want to make changes. A good way to avoid this (not that I always keep my own rules) is to set a finished manuscript aside for a few weeks, then reread it. That way, mistakes you have internalized will jump out at you and you can fix them.

The importance of revision cannot be overstated, but revision can be overdone. Often enough, after I've finished a section, I think of something else that could be in it, but sometimes the addition makes the section cumbersome so I try to be strong and not include it. But I can't always resist. For instance, I very much wanted to add a piece about my father's sense of humor and his proposed will. He said he planned to leave his money to a pilot who would fly his embalmed body in its coffin around and around the world, stopping in every country at every point of interest and sending postcards to all his friends and relatives saying "Wish you were here." Dad had enough money to keep this going for years, but of course it was a joke and of course he didn't do it. I loved the idea, though, but couldn't find a good place for the story, so I put it here.

Sometimes I revise too much. I once wrote a very funny paragraph about some Namibian villagers who had been exposed by missionaries to the Bible story known as "The Woman in the Well." In the story, Jesus sees a woman getting water from a well. He's never met her before, but somehow he knows she's been married several times and by then is living with a man to whom she isn't married, so he confronts her.

The villagers were shocked. Was Jesus a sorcerer, to have supernatural knowledge? And why was he so interested in the love life of a stranger? He was trying to score, the villagers decided. That was gall, even for a sorcerer.

Unexpected interpretations can be funny, and my account of the story was hilarious. Then I began to tweak it, then revised it completely, and ended up with a mess that was obviously meant to amuse but that my editor disdainfully crossed out, saying it wasn't at all funny. By then the better draft was gone and could not be resurrected, and I still anguish over it because I'm not exaggerating when I say how funny it was. I'd try it again here but it's one of those heartbreaking memories that one somehow can't revisit.

So I try to be careful. But even when I'm doing more good than harm, I still fuss for weeks over revisions. Should this comma be here? No. Take it out. Now it's worse. Put it back. The whole sentence is bad. Fix it. Get rid of those hyphens and dash marks and for God's sake check the spelling. Dang! There goes the spell and grammar check. The place where the Bushmen lived was Nyae Nyae. This stupid gadget wants to make it Nyae. If I could see that grammar check, I'd kick it.

Word use, sentence structure, punctuation, and revision are accomplished with the conscious mind doing its best to make the right decisions. But for forward motion, one needs the unconscious, and when I can activate mine, I'm in business. Once I get my head filled with good subject matter, I'm carried to the place I'm writing about, and get to live there every day from five-thirty in the morning until eight o'clock at night. It's heaven.

I've liked the settings of all the books I've written, but the place I liked best was the site of my caveman novels, *Reindeer Moon* and *The Animal Wife*. These take place 20,000 years ago on the Siberian tundra or steppe. Why there, and not somewhere more familiar? Because I loved the African savannah and the Baffin Island tundra. They're the same thing, more or less, except that the savannah is warmer.

The reason for this is that many plants and animals occur in clines. Some of these ran north from Africa to the edges of the glaciers, and thanks to Bergmann's law, which says that the more massive you are, the less surface you have to release heat from your body, many southern mammals such as elephants and lions had large-sized relatives adapted for the cold. I liked to think of the animals I'd seen on the savannah living on the steppe — mammoths and cave lions, for instance, to say nothing of cave hyenas, woolly rhinos, tarpans (the northern relative of zebras), and many others. The difference was mainly in the two-toed ungulates, because the deer family dominated the steppe and the antelope family dominated the savannah. Bears were the only animals important to my novels who had no African counterpart. But bears were in Siberia just as they are today, and they're also in the woods near my house and come up to raid my bird feeder — a different kind of bears, to be sure, but bears nevertheless. I liked to think of revisiting all the animals who so greatly enriched my life.

Some readers complained because my Paleolithic ecosystem included both lions and tigers and these cats don't coexist. And so they don't, or not today.[2] But they did during the Paleolithic, tigers ranging throughout Asia and cave lions ranging almost everywhere except Australia. There's no point in being striped like sunlight shining through the trees if you don't live in a forest, and no point in being the color of dry grass if you don't live on a plain, but since my novel had both ecosystems, I could include both kinds of big cat.

There aren't many ways to live by hunting and gathering, so the people in these novels were partly modeled on the Ju/wasi. What I learned from the Ju/wasi that helped me here was how it feels to be part of the natural world and why survival depends on keeping everyone together and cooperative.

But that isn't exactly culture, so the culture of my Paleolithic hunter-gatherers was drawn from my imagination, as were their tools and clothing. Except for their lodges, which are made with mammoth bones and tusks as were some real Paleolithic lodges, I didn't try to replicate an actual culture, because to do so was off the point. All that an archaeologist can find are the material leavings. What the Upper Paleolithic felt like is forgotten. So I thought if I could get the environment right, the life of the people would follow.

Where to put this? I thought that 50° north latitude by 50° east longitude would be easy to remember, but these coordinates were near Lake Baikal, which was too big for my story. So I made the lake smaller. The fictional people who lived on its shores called it Woman Lake after their goddess, the fictional Woman Ohun. But those people were peripheral to the story. The main characters lived about eighty miles northeast of the lake in a mammoth-bone lodge near the top of a terraced valley through which flowed the Char, a fictional river that rose in fictional mountains something like my Wapack Range but much higher and longer. In summer, those people camped by the Grass River, about two days' walk northwest of the Char, not in lodges but in grass shelters something like those of the Ju/wasi.

An important lineage of my fictional people comes from the Fire River, which flows west from Woman Lake. This lineage gave rise to

---

2. Except in the Gir Forest in India. But that's a relict community of Asiatic lions.

shamans, the most important of whom was a woman named Sali. By the time my first novel begins, Sali has already died in childbirth, along with her baby, some said at the hands of her husband, since the child she bore wasn't his. But unlike most departed spirits, Sali didn't go to the Camps of the Dead, whose fires you see in the west while the sun is setting. Instead, she became a tigress and stayed among the living. The people would see her near their camps or following a river, sometimes as a woman carrying a baby, sometimes as a tigress with a cub in her mouth. Sali had a sister named Hama. Hama had two daughters, Lapwing and Yoi. Lapwing had two daughters, Yanan and Meri, and Yanan tells her story in *Reindeer Moon.*

At a book signing for *Reindeer Moon,* a woman in the audience asked if the novel was autobiographical. Excuse me? Yanan lived in a lodge made of mammoth bones and became a spirit who turned into a wolf, a mammoth, a cave lion, and a red deer. Does that sound autobiographical? However, since Yanan narrates the book, it's written in the first-person singular, which could have caused confusion, and the narrator's description of sex with a kinsman (not a close one) could be what raised the question.

Needless to say, in real life I never lived in a mammoth-bone lodge; nor can I shape-change into an animal, much as I might like to. I've never had sex with a kinsman either. But the question got me thinking. If the book wasn't autobiographical at first, it was by the time it was finished.

Or some of it was. For instance, after Yanan became a spirit, a shaman asked for her help in hunting reindeer. To do this she became a wolf, and in my imagination, I did too. The wind lifted my fur, and on the wind I caught the faint odor of an ungulate. I headed off in that direction, and on the way heard other wolves howling. I didn't want to meet them and I worried. It felt risky, to be a wolf alone on the land of wolves who didn't know me.

When Yanan became a mammoth, so did I. My nostrils filled with the scent of the elephant barns in Portland. I was a mammoth for a long time, and wanted to join a herd of other mammoths who at first didn't welcome me. But in time they did and I spent the winter with them.

And once, Yanan became a lioness, asked by the shaman to drive a pride of lions from a cave that the people wanted to occupy. So I became a lioness, but as it turned out, I didn't dare confront the pride. Two male spirits, also in lion form, came with me to help, but when they caught the scent of all the lionesses they changed their minds, evicted the resident male lion, killed some of the cubs, and took possession of the pride and also the cave. This wasn't what the shaman wanted. I didn't know quite what to do about that, but I knew the pride would see me as an intruder so I ran away.

Yanan never became a tiger, and neither did I. But I hope to in a third Paleolithic novel which I plan to start when this book is finished. It will be narrated by Yanan's younger sister, Meri.

The shape-changing will be different in this third novel. In *Reindeer Moon*, Yanan's spirit becomes an animal who wasn't there before. Yanan would find herself standing on four feet with pointed ears, a long tail, and a fur coat, but without a past. She would be like a dog, say, suddenly transforming into a person and finding himself on Main Street without an address or a Social Security number. He'd have to cope as best he could, which is what Yanan did.

But Meri will become a powerful shaman like her great-aunt Sali, and while she is in trance, her spirit will enter the bodies of animals. There, she will learn everything about them, from the taste of their last meal to their relationships with other animals, if any. Meri will visit the body of a certain tigress whose hunting grounds are next to those where Sali hunts when she is a tigress. Then in my mind I too will be that tigress, hunting red deer and trying not to trespass on Sali.

Sali will appear in this novel for the first time, but as a spirit. In the earlier novels she was known only by the stories people told about her. It will also be the first time a tiger appears in any significant manner. Mostly in the earlier novels you just hear them roaring or see their footprints in the snow.

Ever since I finished *The Animal Wife*, the second of those novels, I've looked forward to writing the third. For most of the day I'll live once again on the Paleolithic steppe. It won't be my last book, or I hope it won't, but everything I've always cared about will be in it, from the pristine Kalahari and the windswept Arctic tundra to the wolves and caribou, also known as reindeer, that I watched on Baffin Island, the lions I knew in the Kalahari, the elephants I knew in Etosha and in Portland, the bears and deer I know in New Hampshire, and the tigers I knew at the Hawthorn Corporation, except that in the novel these will be large Siberian tigers like the one my gran and I would visit in the Museum of Comparative Zoology. I believe it will bring me full circle.

16

A MILLION YEARS WITH YOU

WHEN I LOOK at the Wapack Range, I think of my father. One day when I was in my forties, I sat with him in the kitchen in New Hampshire, looking out the window at the autumn leaves. He was in his eighties, and had always been fascinated by trees. That morning in the kitchen, he wondered aloud if the shift in weight of all the leaves in the Northern Hemisphere, up in the trees for half the year, down on the ground for the other half, could influence the speed of the earth's rotation.

The Wapack Range was thick with trees whose leaves would soon be falling. That was a lot of leaves, just in that one place. Many tons of them would be, on average, about thirty feet closer to the earth's center of gravity. Wouldn't a worldwide shift of so much weight make a difference to the planet, changing, however slightly, the length of nights and days? My dad mentioned a law of physics which I now know is called the conservation of angular momentum and is the effect a skater achieves when she brings in her arms to spin more quickly. This would persist in any similar situation, no matter how imperceptible the increased speed might be.

That day in the kitchen, we spoke of the time when the Northern Hemisphere was tropical, when the leaves would not have fallen all at once. We wondered what the world was like all those millions of years ago. Would the days have gone by a bit more slowly, at least while the Southern Hemisphere was tipped toward the sun? We wished we could go back in time to see what those hills looked like then. We spoke of climbing the hills together. That took us back through time, if not far enough, so I reminded my dad of walking through the juniper when he told me to stop whining. To please him, I had promised to do so, and I meant to keep that promise. I couldn't always do it, but I tried.

So I thanked him for the fact that some people thought I was tough. One such person was Sy Montgomery, who in the dedication of her book about snow leopards, *Ghost of the Mountain,* wrote the following: "To Elizabeth Marshall Thomas, strong as a snow leopard, tough as Genghis Khan." The book was published after my father's death, but I wish he could have seen it. This comment was because of him, and I know he would have liked it. But perhaps he didn't need more proof of what I'd learned from him, because that day in the kitchen, thinking of the hills and their antiquity, he spoke the most beautiful words I ever heard. "I'd like to spend a million years with you," he said.

I might be marginally as tough as Genghis Khan, but not all the time. I was moved so deeply that my eyes filled with tears, and I still cry when I think of what he said. I would have liked to spend a million years with him, but because his health was failing we both knew we might not have much longer together.

And we didn't. When he was ninety-one, he was taken by ambulance to the Mount Auburn Hospital in Cambridge. It was Election Day, and at that moment I was near our home in Virginia, standing in front of a polling place, holding a political sign for Jimmy Carter. Suddenly Steve and Stephanie drove up to tell me that my dad was in critical condition in the hospital. I dropped the sign, got in the car, and Steve rushed us to the airport, where Stephanie and I clawed our way onto the next plane to Boston. After a nightmarish struggle to get her and her wheelchair out of the plane and both of us into a taxi, we joined my mother at my father's bedside. He wasn't conscious. We held his hands. News of the election blared from a television in another room. But in my father's room, we sat in silence while his life slipped from him quietly and slowly, like the life of a tree.

After that, his phrase became my lodestar of love and also of sadness. Unlike a million years with him, the forty-odd years we'd spent together didn't seem enough. But that day in the kitchen, he had added a few words that made everything right. After all, it was he who first told me that our bodies contain molecules that could have been in dinosaurs, and that after we die, those molecules would go to other life forms. So after he said he'd like to live a million years with me, he added, "Who knows? Maybe we've done that already." That seemed altogether likely, and I expect the process will continue. The thought gives me great peace.

When I look at my flourishing climbing rose which is at least seventy years old, or at a certain maple tree beside our house, I think of my mother. She planted the rose, so the associated memory is of her wearing stylish, wide-legged slacks and digging a hole with a trowel. But the maple tree conjures the memory of her with three elephants. It springs from a big party we gave to celebrate the publication of an important book by the wildlife biologist Richard Estes, *The Behavior Guide to African Mammals.*

In honor of the subject matter, I arranged for three elephants to be at the party. Actually, they were Asian elephants, not African elephants, but they were the best I could manage. Their arrival was spectacular. The guests could not believe their eyes when they saw elephants passing by a window in New Hampshire, and everyone, including my mother, went outside to meet them. One of the guests took photos, most of which show a big crowd of us milling around together, all excited and talking. But one photo shows my mother way off to the side, alone, with the elephants standing calmly beside her. They are reaching the tips of their trunks toward her. Knowing nothing of the photographer, my mother is offering them twigs with leaves. These enormous creatures could have pushed her down and taken all the leaves they wanted. Instead, they are accepting them carefully.

For her one hundredth birthday, also in Peterborough, we gave an even bigger party. My mom was much loved, so people came from all over the United States and also from other countries. This time I arranged for there to be a lion and a tiger. The tiger was a big teenager who jerked his handler around like a dog on a leash, but the lion was an infant. Several little girls were at that party and couldn't get enough of the baby lion, whom they carried around like a doll, grabbing him from one another.

This upset him. Whenever the girls would put him down he'd try his best to toddle away from them.

Then someone handed him to my mother. He was tense and exhausted as she reached out for him — fur bristling, eyes darting, tiny teeth bared — but she cradled him gently. He looked up at her, sighed with relief, and at once fell fast asleep.

His was a normal reaction to my mother. As has been said, she took care of every animal and every person who came into her life. No one was too young or too old, too rich or too poor, too famous or too obscure, for her to treat any differently than she treated the little lion. Multiple children were named for her — a Ju/wa girl was named Norna (the !Kung language doesn't have an *l*), an Ambo girl was named Lorna Hameva, my mother's first cousin once removed was named Lorna Grant, and the daughter of one of my mom's admirers, a scientist from Holland, was named Norna, perhaps because of the Ju/wa connection.

I used to think my mom was too obliging. Nobody hesitated to phone her while she was trying to write *The !Kung of Nyae Nyae,* or to drop in for a cup of coffee and a chat. In the evenings, groups of people would drop in for a drink, in which case the conversation would go on so long that she would cook dinner for them. Despite her endless phone calls and streams of visitors, she managed to publish a series of papers in the anthropological journal *Africa,* but it took her twenty years to finish *The !Kung of Nyae Nyae* for the Harvard University Press. The only time I ever heard of her getting really angry was because of this. My dad also thought she was too obliging and once suggested that she hire someone else to write her book. He was trying to be helpful, but she was enraged. I didn't see this, but a friend of ours was there and well remembers that to his surprise, she uncharacteristically exploded. So I'm glad it wasn't me who made that suggestion, because during those years I also criticized her for being too available. This didn't mean I didn't phone or visit her myself whenever I felt like it, but she was my mom, not those other people's.

Her friends would compare us. Sympathetically, they'd say she was a hard act to follow. But I didn't think so. I'd read F. Fraser Darling's *A Herd of Red Deer,* and from it learned about female leadership. Darling points out that male leadership involves authority and domination, but female leadership does not, or not often, and not among red deer. Their large herds are composed of females and young and are led by a mature hind, whose entire attention, while the herd is on the move, is focused on getting everybody to the next place safely.

I saw such a herd in Scotland on the Isle of Mull, stronghold of the McLean clan. My mom was a McLean, her very Scottish family came from the Isle of Mull, and we had gone there to see its castle. The man who lived in the castle was head of the clan and was known as the McLean. (He was so taken with my mom that he too came to visit her in Cambridge.)

On that island I saw two hinds protecting their herd, whose members, no doubt, were their younger relatives. They'd be on a hill, about to cross a valley from which they couldn't see very far, so the first hind would lead the herd across the valley and up the next hill while the second hind stayed in place and kept watch. When the first hind reached the top of the hill, she'd wait until all the deer, including the second hind, caught up to her. Thus there was never a time when one of the hinds couldn't see approaching danger. Darling compares their behavior to that of a teacher taking children across a street. The teacher is in charge, of course, but she isn't trying to be the alpha female and she isn't dominating the children. She is using her authority, to be sure, but in a concerned manner and only to protect them.

When I was in my early twenties, I had an interesting experience that spoke of my mother's protection. I was staying at her house, which, as has been said, was near Harvard's Peabody Museum, and one afternoon I was in the basement of the museum working on something related to the Kalahari, but I can't remember what. I lost track of time, so I didn't realize that the museum was closing until the lights went out. I found myself in pitch darkness, and at first I was shocked. Then I was frightened, very frightened. As far as I was concerned, the museum was full of terrors, which began with the stuffed tiger that I'd seen with my gran but had advanced to a collection of mummified human corpses which I knew were in large drawers in the basement. I'd seen them too.

I wasn't safe. I wasn't at all safe. The darkness was absolute, but somehow I groped my way toward the door. It was locked. I thought my hair would turn white and I'd gibber streams of nonsense. I groped my way toward the stairs, and suddenly heard slow, heavy footsteps. A mummy had climbed out of its box and was coming for me. I groped my way up the stairs and into the hallway, where I found the front door. It was unlocked. I burst out into the night and ran all the way to my parents' house.

My mom was standing on the front steps, her head forward, her feet slightly apart, her arms slightly away from her sides, looking in my direction as if she'd just heard an explosion. I ran up to her. She said she had suddenly become terrified for me. She suddenly knew that something horrible was happening to me. And she had come outdoors to look for me.

Well, that's all that happened. I wasn't, of course, in any danger, and the footsteps would have been those of the janitor who was closing the building. But from the experience, my mom and I learned that there is after all such a thing as extrasensory perception. And I seemed to have learned something from majoring in English — the idea of gibbering came from "The Rime of the Ancient Mariner," by Samuel Taylor Coleridge. I must have been forced to read it, and some of it must have stuck.

But the event also says something about my mom's attunement, which was profound. I think of the red deer in Scotland. The leader didn't need to look to know that her herd had caught up to her. When all were present, she just plunged forward.

The attunement enabled my mother's leadership. When I was fifteen, I remember, I was about to go out. My mom was near the front door, and she looked at me. "You're so pretty," she said. "And that sweater looks nice on you. If you brushed your hair the effect would be perfect." Isn't that better than "You're a mess. Can't you even brush your hair?" which would have sent me right out the door. Instead, I brightened. *Wow! I'm pretty and I have a nice sweater!* And I ran upstairs for a hairbrush.

I strongly felt that she was our most important link to the Ju/wasi, as she was always with them, making cocoa for them in the evenings, never pressing them for information, admiring their children, giving gifts, remembering everybody's name and everything they told her. She even found favor among anthropologists, although these are an aggressive lot, especially toward people like us who dared to work in their field without graduate degrees in their subject. But when my mom published her find-ings despite her lack of academic credentials, very few of them attacked her. The anthropologist Alan Barnard described her as "one of the most sensitive, meticulous, and unpretentious ethnographers of all time."[1]

On second thought, maybe she was a hard act to follow.

When she was in her nineties, she left her house in Cambridge, where she had lived for more than seventy years, and came to live in our house in New Hampshire in an apartment we had made for her.

She settled in with us comfortably. I was able to find some superior caregivers to help her. A day did not pass without my mom saying how glad she was to be with me. We were glad too—all of us. One of our dogs, a Belgian shepherd named Misty, immediately adopted her, as did two of our cats, all of them seeing her as a welcome refuge from the three higher-ranking dogs and four higher-ranking cats, who favored me and Steve. One of the cats once caught a mouse, whom I rescued on behalf of my mother. Thinking she might like to keep him for a while, I put him in a cage with an exercise wheel and put the cage on her table. But all this did was enthrall the cat, who watched the mouse with burning eyes, then tried to push the cage off the table, perhaps expecting it to burst open and release the captive. Quietly, my mom asked the cat not to do that. The cat looked at her, then jumped off the table and walked away. I'm not sure why this happened, but it seemed almost miraculous. One wouldn't expect a cat to be so sensitive to a human request, or, for that matter, so obliging.

All in all, my mom's apartment was an interesting place. One of her caregivers, whose name at the time was Susan Culver but later became Susan Campbell, had three dogs whom she brought with her to work. By this time my mom was using a wheelchair, so Susan's dogs would sit on the couch and Misty would sit in the armchair. In the evenings Susan and I with our seven dogs would go for a walk in the woods. We'd assemble in my mom's apartment, where she'd enjoy watching all of us get ready, then she'd watch us cross the field as the sun was setting. When we came back, she would want to hear what we'd seen—such as a barn owl that flew over us—or what the dogs had done. In the daytime they would have run everywhere, but at night in the woods with bears and coyotes afoot, they stayed right with us, close together like soldiers on patrol. My dog Ruby, a little German shepherd, would be out in front as the scout, and Susan's dog Betty, a big part-basset, would bring up the rear as the commanding officer. Betty was not the tallest dog, but she was the most massive. As such, she was Dog One.

Over time my mom's confusion deepened. She wanted to sleep. One snowy morning in mid-January I got a call from her doctor's officious assistant, who informed me in no uncertain terms that the doctor wanted to see her so she must come to his office that afternoon.

Oh really? I said she was a hundred and four years old and fragile. I said it was snowing. I said there was no easy way for her to get from a car into that doctor's office, and even if she did, the office was freezing and my mother couldn't sit up in a chair for the half-hour or so that the doctor always kept her waiting. In short, I said, she wasn't going anywhere. If the doctor wanted to see her, he could get his ass to our house. I'd have an icy room ready where he could wait for half an hour. And I slammed down the phone.

Then I looked at it thinking, *You know, she never would have done that. She would have found a way to communicate her message without losing her temper or saying* ass. Obviously I had not achieved her social graces. But maybe I didn't really need them. Guess who came trotting up our walkway that same afternoon.

I have no idea why the doctor wanted to see her. I suspect he was wondering how close she was to death. He never did tell us what he'd learned from his visit, but at least he never bothered her again. She had been accepted by hospice, and the hospice nurses took care of her. They knew what she needed, and if the doctor didn't want to renew her prescriptions without an office visit, they'd bully him until he did.

By spring my mom was eating very little. We made custards and other high-calorie dishes and fed them to her with a spoon. In June I began sleeping on the floor of her bedroom in case I was needed during the night.

I didn't think of her dying—I'd spent too much time with her Christian Scientist mother to have a negative thought like that. I knew she didn't want to think about death either, despite the hospice nurses, who seemed to feel that all dying people are anxious to discuss their deaths and are prevented from doing so by the fears of others. I think I persuaded the nurses not to discuss the subject unless my mother brought it up, but I couldn't be there all the time.

So I suspect that some of them privately asked a few probing questions in case she wanted to discuss her death but felt shy about doing so. Also, without asking me or my mom, one of her caretakers gave her last rites. The caretaker obviously meant well, but my mom didn't need or want last rites. If she didn't want to think about dying, why should she have to? If she wanted to talk about it, nothing was stopping her. I thought she should take the lead on that issue, and that others should mind their own business. That's one reason I slept on the floor.

One afternoon in July, my brother and his fifth wife came for a rare visit. My brother had written a lengthy poem entitled "Lorna Jean" (her name), which he read to her aloud. He was a filmmaker of international reputation, but no one told him that a poem doesn't need to rhyme, and if it does, it goes better if the rhymes aren't forced and are spread around a bit. But that his poem was a dreadful jingle didn't matter. It's the thought that counts. Our mom was asleep and barely woke up when they came in, so I doubt that she understood the poem, but if she did, she would not have been critical. She liked just about everything my brother and I did, or she seemed to. And even if she didn't take in all of the poem, she would have heard my brother's voice. She would have been glad that he was with her.

When my brother finished reading, he and his wife stood up to leave. I asked them to stay at least for dinner because our mom might not live much longer and my brother's presence would comfort her. But owing to some differences involving my mother, the fifth wife didn't like me, so they refused to stay. As I walked them to the door, I begged them to change their minds. But they had come so my brother could read his poem and that had been accomplished. They left.

I went back to my mother's room to sit beside her and hold her hand. She knew I was there — now and then I'd feel faint pressure from her fingers. The windows were open to the warm night air. On the Wapack Range, we heard coyotes calling.

. . .

I didn't sleep on the floor that night. Our son, Ramsay, was in Yosemite, where he and Heather would be married the next day. Steve was with them, and if my mother had been well I would have been there too, but under the circumstances, that was out of the question. However, I wanted to talk to them, which meant going to another room.

So one of my mother's companions slept in her room. I went by several times to see how she was doing and found her quietly asleep, so I took a nap on my own bed upstairs. Before I fell asleep I heard the coyotes again.

Toward morning, the companion called me to come quickly. My mother had taken two deep, shuddering breaths. I hurried downstairs to be with her. She seemed to be asleep. I held her hand. Now and then she took a shallow breath — a whisper, really. I didn't try to take her pulse because I didn't want some curious probe to be our last contact. So I just stayed there quietly, holding her hand as the sky turned gray and then pink with the sunrise. The coyotes called again and again. May they do that for me when I am dying.

Within the next few hours a medic had pronounced her dead — as if we didn't know that. The hospice nurses had taken her medications — as if we might sell them on the street. *Hey, kid, you want some eye drops?* And the undertaker's assistants had taken her body, wrapped in a sheet.

It was too late to postpone the wedding, as most of the guests were already assembled. I called my son, my daughter, and Sy to tell them what had happened, and told them I would try to get to the wedding. Sy came and drove me to the airport, where I got a flight to Reno. My daughter and her husband met me there and drove me to Yosemite. So I attended my son's wedding after all, dressed in black.

Sy wrote an obituary for my mother which she read on National Public Radio. She told of a time in the Kalahari Desert in the dry season when my mom was washing her face in a basin. Suddenly she was surrounded by a swarm of African bees, who were attracted by the water. Instantly the sides of the basin were covered with bees and more were coming, trying to shove their way to the water, pushing and crowding so that many were falling in. My mother was coated with bees, but she wasn't frightened—she quickly rescued the bees in the water and floated pieces of wood in the basin so that every bee had somewhere to stand and could drink her fill. When they were gone, no bee had drowned and none had stung her.

The name of the wife of a Bushman god was Mother of Bees. Perhaps she was something like my mother.

❦

17

80

Except for one's genes, one is more or less the sum of one's experiences, so for someone like me who is not particularly reflective, it can be instructive to write a memoir. At first a focus on one's past yields the adventures and the scary stories, but a closer look shows that tiny events, especially those from the deep past, were those that shaped one's persona. A few hikes through the juniper on the Wapack Range when I was six or seven had as much influence on me, say, as two years of college, and more influence than anything I did after I was forty. The insight I got from this was that I'm glad my lifetime took place when it did. Much of my childhood was during World War II, when my brother and I and the kids from the neighboring farm would roam the woods looking for German spies. Rumor held that they were out there, and—never doubting that the Third Reich needed to know what was going on in our woods—we considered it our patriotic duty to find the spies and report them to the authorities. Thus our early years were different from those of many children today with the cell phones and the social networks, to say nothing of the drugs and the addictive pharmaceuticals. We smoked a few cigarettes behind the barn, but nothing more.

Then too, even as late as the 1950s, large parts of the world were still unexplored. It was my enormous privilege to go to one of those places. It was also beneficial to go at a time when we could penetrate a part of the African interior in trucks, a very different experience, and safer too, than that of the Paleo Indians crossing the Bering Strait on foot or the Vikings rowing themselves across the North Atlantic to Newfoundland.

But in some ways the world has since become more dangerous, not that it wasn't always dangerous. The dangers change with time and apply to different people.

It's common enough to look back at one's early years and think that times were better then — just about everybody does it. My mom remembered that when she was young, a distinguished old gentleman said that civilization is finished. That was in the 1920s and he was thinking of the 1800s. But in many ways it's true. Certainly our planet is in worse shape than it was when I was born, but it's not as bad as it's going to get unless we take better care of it. My maternal lineage, which is to say me, my mom, and her mother, did not favor negative thoughts, so I've learned to put a positive spin on everything and therefore believe that no matter what we do to our planet, Gaia will make something out of it, even if it's just more bacteria. As for my lifetime, it's true that it's almost over, but it took place during a reasonably good historic interval. Yet if the planet was in better shape in the 1930s, I was too, so aging seems worth consideration.

I turned eighty in 2011. It felt kind of strange, but I wasn't sure why until I read a brilliant article in *The New Yorker* by the poet Donald Hall. The title is "Out the Window."[1] From his window, Hall sees the land in New Hampshire that was farmed by his family. That spoke to me because from my window I see the same thing. Hall sees the cow barn built by his grandfather in 1865. I see the hay barn built by my father in 1938. Such sights are evocative.

Before I read Hall's article, though, the view from my window seldom evoked the deep past. Often enough, my window evoked the cougar mentioned earlier, whom I saw in our field, also the possible cougar who, more recently, had killed the whitetail doe. Cougars were one of my most persistent visions, even though New Hampshire Fish and Game insisted that they didn't live in our state. I wanted to see them again.

I never have, but to expect to see a cougar was to live in the moment, which seemed a good way to deal with aging. Or so I thought. Yet I was merely dodging the issue, which I realized after reading Hall's article. He saw aging more deeply, his article caused me to think more deeply, and my thoughts caused me to look less often at the field where a cougar might appear and more often at the Wapack Range. I'd think of the age of the granite, and of the glaciers that shaped the granite. I'd think of climbing those hills with my dad. I'd think of the years that have passed since we did that. During those years, tall trees grew where once there was juniper. I grew up, did some interesting things, and grew old.

On my eightieth birthday we had a little party. Ramsay and his family came to dinner. We had spaghetti, a salad, and a little store-bought cake with birthday candles shaped like an 8 and a 1. We would have used candles shaped like an 8 and a 0, but the store had run out of 0 candles. Ramsay took a photo of me lighting a cigarette from the 8 candle. I wanted to use it as the author photo for this book, but my family wouldn't hear of it because they so disapproved of my smoking. But everyone must die of something, so smoking was another response to aging, a privilege for those of us who don't have much life left to lose. "This woman can do what she wants and you can't," says the cigarette to younger people.

At my stage in life, almost everybody is a younger person. When I read "Out the Window," I remembered how I felt when almost everyone was older than me, and later when only half the people were older than me. Then came the time when I was older than them, which is why I was smitten by the article. Hall too was older than them, but unlike me, he had thought about aging, and I took him very seriously because he and I were similar. Both of us were writers, both of us had gone to the same college at the same time, both of us wound up in New Hampshire on land once owned by our respective families, both of us remembered our grandparents with much affection, and both of us had always respected old people, with my own respect strongly reinforced by the value placed on all elders by the Bushmen and on some elders by the Dodoth.

But deep in my heart I was bothered by aging. Although I'd always liked old faces and didn't mind having one, although I'd looked forward to gaining the wisdom which I believed great age would bring, I hadn't been as confident as I'd thought. I'd worried about turning thirty, for instance. When I was twenty-five or twenty-six, thirty seemed like death's door. I spent the middle 1960s in Nigeria and came home to hear hippies crying "Don't trust anyone over thirty!" I was then thirty-five, and already people were excluding me. That bothered me too.

Concerns about aging didn't stop there, though. To prepare myself for turning fifty, I began saying I was fifty when I was forty-eight. Thus when it happened, I was used to the idea. I did the same at seventy-eight to prepare for turning eighty, but by then was somewhat disillusioned with aging because the promise of wisdom had failed me. After all that time, the only wisdom I had to offer was that if you want a long marriage, you must marry young and wait. Still, that's a step up from my youthful reasoning — I married Steve because he had a sense of humor and a motorcycle.

My joints get stiff if I don't keep moving, and when I got glaucoma I had to remember to put drops in my eyes, not just when I happened to think of it but every single night. I was glad enough to do it because I'd learned of a woman who went blind because she didn't, and yes, it controlled the glaucoma, but I wasn't ready for any of that.

Why couldn't I look squarely at aging? Revelation came from Donald Hall. "However alert we are," he wrote, "however much we think we know what will happen, antiquity remains an unknown, unanticipated galaxy." Our antiquity is "alien," he continues, "and old people are a separate form of life."

Why hadn't I seen this? Didn't I know I'd be called a senior citizen? Didn't that remove me from the normal citizens? And what about the so-called compliment, "She's eighty years young"? The only thing that's young at eighty is a giant sequoia or a baobab tree. Do we ever hear the phrase "She's twenty years young"? No, because there's nothing wrong with being twenty. We are indeed a separate form of life, but I hadn't faced that squarely.

I thought about my heart. It had beaten continuously, day and night, year after year, with never a rest since I was a fetus. That seemed like a lot. So did the number eighty. Some people said I didn't look eighty. The remarks were well meant, I guess, but those who made them had a mindset. The number eighty set me apart, but until they knew the number, they hadn't seen me as apart. They seemed surprised that someone whom they thought was one of them was not. Some people said I should retire. Retire from what? As long as my eyesight lasts and I can move my fingers, I won't need to retire. But at eighty it's time to retire, people said, which I took to mean "You don't belong in our workforce." Hall describes a chilling experience after eating a meal, when a nice man meaning only to be kind "wags his finger, smiles a grotesque smile, and raises his voice to ask, 'Did we have a nice din-din?'" That's the perfect storm of alienation. Nothing so bad has happened to me, but I'm three years younger than Hall and I know it's in my future.

It can seem, as Hall suggests, that we aliens don't exist. He describes a family occasion when his grandchild's college roommate pulled up a chair and sat right in front of him, cutting him off from the gathering. To the roommate, Hall wasn't there. I knew about nonexistence from observing my daughter's when, for instance, the person behind the ticket counter at an airline would talk to me instead of to her although it was she who was trying to buy the ticket. She and her wheelchair weren't there. Standing on my feet with my face the proper distance from the floor, I was a person.

Then too, I'd experienced mild nonexistence for myself. For instance, when I was in my late fifties I took a stop-smoking class. Several other older women also took the class, but we couldn't open our mouths without the male instructor interrupting us and talking to other people. I asked him to stop doing that, and for a few minutes he was more careful. But because he hadn't realized what he was doing, and because we were old women who didn't matter anyway, he was soon interrupting us again.

One night I went to a crowded local bar where people were dancing to live music. I went because I happened to know two of the musicians, and didn't plan to stay long because I didn't like to leave my husband alone. I knew quite a few people in the bar, and one of them, a smiling young woman, asked me how I was doing in such a wild crowd. The average age of the crowd was probably forty and people were dancing in an orderly manner, so I didn't think the crowd seemed all that wild. But I understood her message. What was an old woman like me doing in a bar with live music and dancing? Such things happen often enough. The above are just two examples. However, such things can be shrugged off, as I learned from my daughter.

But not forever. One autumn night soon after I turned eighty, Willie J. Laws, a Texas-blues musician, was playing guitar in the barn that Ramsay and his friend Doug Frankenberger had made into a recording studio. With a drummer and a bass player, Willie J. was recording a song called "Too Much Blues" or maybe "Too Much Blues for Me." Also present was a group of Willie J.'s fans, there to observe the recording.

I was overwhelmed by the quality of the music. The big door on the front of the barn was shut, but I opened a side door to look in. The musicians kept playing with their backs to me, but the fans heard the door and turned to look. As if a wind had opened it, they saw no one. Like a dry leaf, the old woman standing there was nothing.

It was my barn, and for a moment I wanted to focus them. "Record *this*, motherfuckers!" would have done it. But instead, I sat on a rock near the barn to listen and wondered if I really needed my existence. Either way, I could hear the music. And perhaps nonexistence was helpful. The musicians played parts of the music over and over. It wasn't a performance. Would they want a stranger listening?

But these thoughts were veneer. As has been said, all my life I've tried to ferret a silver lining from each and every cloud, and even as I wondered if I needed existence, somewhere inside I knew that things had changed for me.

Not long before that, I'd had a different experience. Because of my age, I sometimes forget things, and one moonlit night I forgot to bring in the bird feeder. When I looked out our kitchen window, I saw a large black bear bending down the pole of the bird feeder as I would bend a paperclip. I was awed by his strength, because the pole was a leftover pipe that Doug and Ramsay had used to renovate the barn. The bear crushed the feeder with his teeth and ate the seeds. Then he looked at the house. Then he came toward the house. Then he came to the window and started to climb in.

He wasn't aggressive — his facial expression was calm and pleasant — but our kitchen is small and my husband can't move quickly. A bear inside would not be good. I had a boat horn handy for just such an occasion, so I blew it at the bear. He looked at me.

While I sat outside the barn, listening to the music, I thought of that bear. Unlike the fans of Willie J., he saw me. No only did he see me, he looked right into my eyes. As far as he was concerned, I was very much there. He also knew what I was saying with the boat horn. He turned and walked gracefully into the woods.

After thinking about the bear, and how his eyes were brown like mine, I thought about the barn. The inside was changed but the outside wasn't. The wood was gray and weathered. I thought of the hay we put in it. We'd mow the tall grass in the fields and let it dry, then we'd rake it into windrows with a hay rake pulled by an ex-racehorse named Blue, then we'd pile it on a haywagon pulled by two huge workhorses named Bucky and Don, then we'd unload it in the barn with pitchforks. There were rules about the pitchforks. We must never leave them lying with the points up. Our gentle mom, whose idea of punishment was to send us to our rooms, said she'd beat us if we got stuck with a pitchfork.

Hall wrote the following about his barn: "Over eighty years, it has changed from a working barn to a barn for looking at." My barn had changed from a hay barn to a barn for recording music. I had not yet read "Out the Window," but the change in my barn stirred yet another thought in my elderly brain. Ramsay and Doug were musicians themselves, and while doing the renovation they listened to classical music loud enough to be heard over the drilling and hammering. About a week before they finished their work and about three weeks before they recorded Willie J., I had gone to the barn to see how the work was going. That day they were listening to Bach's Orchestral Suites. The big barn door was wide open, and admiring the music, I went inside, where I saw two hummingbirds flying around the ceiling.

I had seen no hummingbirds for weeks, as it was late in the year and those who lived near me had migrated. I assumed that these two were also migrating but had come from farther north. In the barn, they were wasting the calories they would need on their journey. I assumed that their instincts were telling them to escape by going upward, and that they couldn't find the open door, and I was worried.

Doug and Ramsay had noticed them too, so we tried to guide them out. We couldn't. We tied nets to long poles and tried to catch them.

Again we couldn't. I put two large pieces of red cloth just outside the open door, knowing that hummingbirds like the color red, and yes, they flew down to look at the cloth but then flew back up to circle the ceiling. I put a red hummingbird feeder full of hummingbird sugar water next to the door. They looked at that too, and flew back to the ceiling.

Time passed. Nothing changed. Now and then they would fly out the door without our help, but they soon flew right back in. We grew more worried, and I called a friend, a well-known bird expert, who told me to put something red by the door. But I'd tried that already, so I called the Audubon Society. They too suggested something red. I called New Hampshire's department of nongame wildlife and also a local conservation center, but they had no better suggestions.

As the afternoon wore on our anxiety mounted, because by then the hummingbirds were tired. Sometimes they'd perch for a while on a beam, but then they would continue flying. Late in the afternoon, Doug and Ramsay finished their work and turned off the music. Instantly the hummingbirds flew out the door and up to the sky to continue their migration.

Obviously we'd seen something important, but what? I called some of the experts whom I had consulted, but they had no explanation. Then it came to us that the first few times the birds flew out the door, Doug had been changing the disks in the CD player so there was no music. It thus seemed clear that the music had captured them, but how? I fervently hoped that no one would stupidly suggest that they liked Bach. That wouldn't help. Doug knew about wavelengths and the physics of music and thought that the answer might lie in there somewhere, but so far, whatever happened is Gaia's secret. Maybe someone could fathom it, but maybe not. Gaia doesn't care if we fathom it.

When Willie J.'s music ended, I got up and left, just as the hummingbirds had done. In my case, though, no mystery was involved. I was old and tired and it was past my bedtime. Even so, walking home alone in the dark, considering my nonexistence and the fact that things had changed for me, I passed the place where I'd found the grass-covered corpse of the whitetail doe. Cougars might not exist for Fish and Game, but they did for me and they did for the doe — she'd been killed only a few days earlier. I might not exist for the people in the barn, but I'd exist for a cougar, so I walked a little faster and now and then I looked over my shoulder.

A few months later I read "Out the Window" and everything came together. The article dealt with the subject of aging, but when I read it, I remembered that a bird flying around inside a house is an omen of death. The belief was common in rural New England when my dad built the barn. And yes, down in some deep part of my mind, deaths were waiting to surface — the passing of those who made the hay, me in decline and nonexistent, and the hummingbirds who were at risk. They had wasted a day's worth of calories. Even if they hadn't, their journey would be difficult and dangerous. If they lived to reach their destination, that would be important.

If they came back in spring to raise their young, that would be more important. Ever since I was a child, hummingbirds have appeared in the spring. They know where I hang the hummingbird feeder, and if it isn't there and filled, they fly over to look in my office window. Those who keep coming are doing what hummingbirds have always done, just as they are meant to do. Birds descended from dinosaurs and dinosaurs also migrated. It's a time-honored tradition. The wings of hummingbirds when they hover make our symbol of infinity.

As has been said, while wandering down the road of life, it helps to look for something more meaningful than oneself, and I've never had to look far to find it, from the stars when I look up to the soil when I look down, where the microorganisms live that keep everything going. Our planet will be here until the sun burns out, and life forms will be on it — maybe not big ones like cougars and deer, but little ones will, like waterbears. We hominids aged when we lived in the trees and we're still doing it. If I seemed nonexistent to some, who cared? Certainly not Gaia.

"Out the window," Hall writes, "I watch a white landscape that turns pale green, dark green, yellow and red, brown under bare branches, until snow falls again." Yes, Gaia has been doing that kind of thing for 4.5 billion years and we are part of it. Aging is part of it. If the young see the old as alien, well, perhaps that too is part of it, at least in our culture, and if they're lucky enough to live as long as we have, they too will be alien someday. By then my scattered ashes will be part of it. I'll have entered the trees at the edge of our field. I'll have entered the grass at the roots of the trees. A deer or two will eat the grass and maybe a cougar will eat the deer, because despite what Fish and Game may think, there are cougars in New Hampshire. What a nice interlude that would be, to spend time as part of a cougar.

NOTES

Prologue: Gaia

1. Lynn Margulis and Karlene V. Schwartz, *Five Kingdoms: An Illustrated Guide to the Phyla of Life on Earth*, 2nd ed. (New York: W. H. Freeman, 1988), pp. 228–229.

5. The Ju/wasi

1. Elizabeth Marshall Thomas, *The Old Way: A Story of the First People* (New York: Farrar, Straus & Giroux, 2006), pp. 272–273.
2. Lorna Marshall, *The !Kung of Nyae Nyae* (Cambridge, MA: Harvard University Press, 1976), p. 112.

8. Uganda

1. In *Warrior Herdsmen*, the book I later wrote about the Dodoth, I changed everyone's name because in the book I sometimes discussed cattle. A tax was levied on the number of a person's cattle and some of the men had told the tax collector that they had fewer cattle than they really had. I didn't want to reveal anyone's secrets inadvertently. But that was long ago, and here I use real names.
2. This adventure appears in a slightly different form in Peter H. Kahn, Jr., and Patricia H. Hasbach, eds., *The Rediscovery of the Wild* (Cambridge, MA: MIT Press, 2013).

11. Warrior

1. Thomas, *The Old Way*, pp. 198, 199.

14. Research

1. Personal communication from Dr. Ronald L. Tilson, biological director of the Minnesota Zoo and senior editor of *Tigers of the World*, 2nd ed. (New York: Academic Press, 2010).

2. The observation of the sleeping wolf appears in slightly altered form in Peter H. Kahn, Jr., and Patricia H. Hasbach, eds., *The Rediscovery of the Wild* (Cambridge, MA: MIT Press, 2013).

3. Elizabeth Marshall Thomas, *Tribe of Tiger: Cats and Their Culture* (New York: Simon & Schuster. 1994), pp. 231–233. The text has been slightly altered.

15. Writing

1. George V. Higgins, *The Friends of Eddie Coyle* (New York: Ballantine, 1981), p. 23.

2. Courtesy of Peter H. Kahn, who also sees the problem of calling an animal *it*.

3. Katherine K. Thorington and Peter D. Weigl, "Role of Kinship in the Formation of Southern Flying Squirrel Winter Aggregations," *Journal of Mammalogy* 92, no. 1 (February 2011): 180.

16. A Million Years with You

1. Alan Barnard, review of *The !Kung of Nyae Nyae* by Lorna Marshall, *Africa: Journal of the International Institute* 48, no. 4 (1978): 411.

17. 80

1. Donald Hall, "Out the Window," *The New Yorker*, January 23, 2012, pp. 40–43.

ACKNOWLEDGMENTS

Passages from this book have appeared in other books and articles I have written, most especially in *The Harmless People* (New York: Knopf, 1959), *Warrior Herdsmen* (New York: Knopf, 1965), *Tribe of Tiger: Cats and Their Culture* (New York: Simon & Schuster, 1994), *The Old Way: A Story of the First People* (New York: Farrar, Straus & Giroux, 2006), and *The Rediscovery of the Wild*, edited by Peter H. Kahn, Jr. and Patricia H. Hasbach (Cambridge, MA.: MIT Press, 2013).

Acknowledgments for a memoir are quite a challenge. My friends Sy Montgomery and Peter Schweitzer, also my husband, Steve, my daughter, Stephanie, and my son, Ramsay, have helped immeasurably in the writing of this book. Not only did they provide much of the material, but they also read chapters for me, and I am grateful. Naomi Chase also read chapters for me, and I am grateful to her. The inaccuracies (which I hope are few) would be mine, however.

I am exceptionally grateful to those who helped this book be published — Ike Williams and Hope Denekamp of the Kneerim, Williams, and Bloom Literary Agency; the book's gifted editor, Bruce Nichols; and the wonderfully accomplished copy editor, Liz Duvall. Liz saved me from misplaced commas and also such things as mistakes in addition and in the spelling of people's names. Not all publishing houses have copy editors these days. One of my other books could have used one — in the published version I refer to a mountain in Namibia as the Drakensberg. The Drakensberg is in South Africa. The mountain in Namibia is the

Brandenberg. I considered changing my name and moving to another community.

For helpful advice on many occasions, I am grateful to my friend Anna Martin. Beyond that, with the exception of Idi Amin, Mel Konner, and that stupid psychoanalyst who told me not to go to Uganda, I am grateful to everyone I've written about herein.

Life is a collection of indebtedness, and during a life as long as mine, one becomes indebted to countless people — friends, relatives, in-laws, neighbors, employers, coworkers, employees, service providers, class-mates, teachers, students — a group that in my case would include the people among whom I did fieldwork or tried to, also those who did the anthropological and wildlife research from which the fieldwork bene-fited, and to name them all would not be possible. That doesn't lessen my debt.

I am equally indebted to those who are not people — the elephants in the Portland zoo and Namibia, the lions in Namibia, the leopard in Uganda, the bobcat who comes to the edge of our field, to say nothing of the cougar who did the same thing, probably to the consternation of the bobcat. I'm grateful to the bears in our woods, who leave messages for other bears by scratching the trees, also to the wild turkeys and to the whitetail deer, and, of course, to the wolves and the ravens of Baffin Island.

But I'm especially grateful to my dogs and cats, all of them, and to the older daughter of the whitetail doe who was killed by a cougar. Thanks to her, three deer live near the edge of our field, not just one.

I am continually filled with gratitude for these nonpeople, especially at night. One of our dogs finds our bed crowded so she sleeps on her own bed beside me, but the other dog sleeps between me and my husband. For some reason she sleeps on her back. Three of the cats also sleep with us, two curled up against us and one curled up against the dog. If a cat thinks we are awake he purrs, slightly more loudly as he inhales, slightly more softly as he exhales. Sometimes after a soft purr there's silence. The cat has dozed off.

Shortly before sunrise the dog who sleeps on her back wakes up. She descends the little staircase we built so she can get on and off the bed (she has a touch of arthritis) and she barks, but just once. *Yap*. She means that dog breakfast-time has come. I get up in the dark. The cats do too. The dog whose bed is on the floor gets up. We walk down the dark hall to the kitchen and start our day together. I couldn't ask for more.